MYSTERIES *of the* JAGUAR SHAMANS *of the Northwest Amazon*

MYSTERIES *of the*

JAGUAR SHAMANS

of the Northwest Amazon

Robin M. Wright | Foreword by Michael J. Harner

UNIVERSITY OF NEBRASKA PRESS | LINCOLN AND LONDON

© 2013 by the Board of Regents
of the University of Nebraska
All rights reserved
Manufactured in the United
States of America

Library of Congress
Cataloging-in-Publication Data
Wright, Robin, 1950–
Mysteries of the jaguar shamans of the
northwest Amazon / Robin M. Wright;
foreword by Michael J. Harner.
pages. cm
Includes bibliographical references
and index.
ISBN 978-0-8032-4394-1 (cloth: alk.
paper) ISBN 978-0-8032-9523-0 (paper:
alk. paper) 1. da Silva, Mandu. 2.
Baniwa Indians—Biography. 3. Shamans—Brazil—Biography. 4. Baniwa
Indians—Religion. 5. Baniwa phi-
losophy. 6. Baniwa Indians—Rites and
ceremonies. I. Title.
F2520.1.B35D3 2013
299'.8839—dc23   2013001790

Set in Sabon Next by
Laura Wellington.
Designed by Nathan Putens.

Contents

Illustrations

Foreword | Michael J. Harner

Since the seventies, Robin Wright has immersed himself in the study of the shamanic practices of the Baniwa of Northwest Amazonia. In this book—much of which is seen through the eyes of the elder jaguar shaman and "wise man" or prophet of his people, Manuel "Mandu" da Silva—the ancient ways of the Baniwa shamans come to life, not only for scholars but in a way that will be familiar to anyone who has practiced contemporary shamanism.

Dr. Wright is my kind of anthropologist. In this writing his scholarship is meticulous, and as a scientist he maintains an attitude of objective inquiry, yet he probes beneath the surface of the shamanic practices described, observed, and experienced to see what is actually happening. He does not merely study and record the spiritual practices of a people, but recognizes that their shamanic traditions, centuries old, have persisted precisely because they have worked for the people. The shamans' knowledge is valued and treated with the respect it deserves.

What emerges from *Mysteries of the Jaguar Shamans of the Northwest Amazon* is an intimate and fascinating portrait of the spiritual heart of a people. The story begins with a look at Mandu's shamanic training and apprenticeship through a rare telling in the shaman's own words. It continues with the trials he faced and the successes he achieved during a lifetime of work as a healer and as a carrier of, and an advocate for, his people's traditional ways, which he recognizes are essential to the cultural survival of his people.

The remaining chapters encompass an entire shamanic tradition, including the problem of sorcery in the villages and Mandu's lifelong struggle against it; missionization and other challenges to the continuity of shamanic traditions; the interrelatedness of Baniwa cosmology, ecology, and shamanic knowledge and power; and the significant role of the ancestors, as revealed and preserved in the memories of the elders, chants, living myths, and a landscape of sacred places and petroglyphs.

The last chapter is devoted to describing the continuing efforts of Mandu, now in his late eighties, and his daughter Ercilia and son Alberto, to revitalize, "valorize" as they term it, Baniwa traditions and preserve them for future generations. Dr. Wright has played an important role in seeking support for the revitalization project through public and private sources. In 2009, he contacted the Foundation for Shamanic Studies, which raised funds to build a village longhouse and help launch the Baniwa shamanic renaissance. The longhouse was intended as a place for the community to gather for cultural events and where traditional ways could be practiced and taught. The longhouse now serves as the House of Shamans' Knowledge and Power, Malikai Dapana, a school for a next generation of shamans. Mandu has several new apprentices seeking to learn the ancient mysteries of their jaguar shaman ancestors. Much more remains to be accomplished.

With *Mysteries of the Jaguar Shamans of the Northwest Amazon*, Dr. Wright makes a significant contribution to the understanding of the shamanic practices of the indigenous peoples of the region. But more than that, he has assured that the decades of spiritual knowledge and practices of Mandu da Silva, jaguar shaman and wise man of his people, will not be lost and will be available for the generations to come.

Acknowledgments

To the most important of my teachers, Manuel "Mandu" da Silva, Hohodene jaguar shaman, his wife, Flora, and all of their family, *phiume nukitchienape*, more thanks than I can express, *matchia hape*. A ceramic vessel for beer, an ancient stone ax head, and shamanic knowledge and power are some of the lasting gifts and living memories I have received from Mandu and his family.

José Cornelio, jaguar shaman and paternal uncle of Mandu, taught me some of his extraordinarily detailed and extensive knowledge of shamans' power, with the invaluable assistance of his stepson, José Felipe, during my first field research in Uapui village in the 1970s. Today José Felipe has become an important pajé (shaman) of Uapui, carrying on his stepfather's and uncle's teachings and practice.

Mandu's wife, Flora, and their daughters, Anninha and Ercilia, are well versed in shamanic knowledge, chanting for initiation rites, and herbal remedies.

José Garcia, jaguar shaman and one of the last savants or wise men (*sábios*) among the Hohodene Baniwa, was another great teacher who, besides sharing some of the jaguar shamans' wisdom, healed my leg. But he left this world too early, before he had attained the greatness of his father, the sábio named Kudui.

I also had the good fortune to learn from Ricardo Fontes of Ukuki village and Marco of Santarém village, both highly respected "owners" of chants and dance masters. Their explanations and teachings of the Kuwai story only became clear many years after they too had left this world.

Ercilia de Lima da Silva, daughter of Mandu, was my research assistant in the field in 2009 and 2010, and she did an outstanding service by taping, filming, transcribing, and translating interviews with her father. If there now exists an extensive collection of taped and filmed material on Baniwa shamans of the Aiary River, it is due in large part to the collaboration of father and daughter in this project.

Isaias Pereira Fontes, *kuekato*, a young Hohodene man from Ukuki, also my research assistant, filmed and taped various dance festivals (including the initiation rite) and interviews with his uncle Laureano, son of Ricardo, and shaman grandfather Augusto. For many years, Isaias has shown a strong interest in documenting the traditions of his ancestors, and he holds great promise for producing something of lasting value for his people.

I wish to thank many other teachers and explainers of stories: Laureano Fontes (one of the few true *mandero*, dance leaders), João Fontes, and Augusto Fontes—all from Ukuki village and the same local descent group, known throughout the region for their knowledge and practice of traditional forms of shamanic healing and dance festivals.

Ercilia's brother, Alberto de Lima da Silva, conceived the idea of constructing a longhouse in his village of Uapui (or, in the Baniwa language, Hipana), where the revitalization of the old dance festivals and the transmission of shamanic knowledge could continue "with dignity." His idea was that "if no one does anything now, then the memory of ancient traditions of the pajés and of Kwaipan will die." With his family's support, the House was built and inaugurated in 2009.

Special thanks to Dr. Michael Harner, world recognized scholar and teacher of shamans and president of the Foundation for Shamanic Studies in California, and to Susan Mokelke, the Foundation's executive director, for their support in turning the project for constructing the House of Shamans' Knowledge and Power into a reality and for honoring Mandu da Silva with its Living Treasures award in 2009.

I must thank Dr. Omar González Ñáñez, *el poeta*, with whom I have long exchanged information and publications regarding the Arawak-speaking peoples and their religious traditions and to whom I am grateful for permission to publish a jaguar shaman's drawing of Kuwai-ka Wamundana, and Santiago Obispo, of Puerto Ayacucho, Venezuela, who provided contacts with researchers on the upper Guainia River.

Very special thanks to Dr. Elizabeth Reichel, who read early versions of this book and provided incentive with enormously helpful suggestions and many thoughtful criticisms. It was in no small part because of her strong interest and encouragement that the most difficult part of organizing this book was accomplished. Likewise, my colleague Manuel Vasquez, Department of Religion, University of Florida, made valuable suggestions and criticisms early on that I deeply appreciate.

Thanks to Carlos Xavier Leal, doctoral student at the Museu Nacional, UFRJ, in Brazil, for allowing access to his dissertation on the petroglyphs of the upper Içana and for the fruitful exchange of ideas on the meanings of the Kuwai story. Thanks also to my advisees who had important roles in completing this project: Marcio Meira, formerly president of the National Indian Foundation (FUNAI) in Brazil, was instrumental in the inauguration of the Malikai Dapana in 2009/10.

Dr. Maria Luiza Garnelo Pereira, with Fiocruz Amazonia, has published several excellent analyses on the health situation of the Upper Rio Negro, especially of the Baniwa on the Içana River. I thank her for her friendship, support, and insights into the ever-shifting political dynamics of contact in the Northwest Amazon. She graciously made available her notes, reports, and experiences of more than twenty years of fieldwork in the region. Yara Costa's M.A. research on dance festivals and music provided the first systematic ethnography of dance choreography of the Aiary River Baniwa.

A very special thanks and *abraços fortes* to my son, Michael, for his fine illustrations. Michael filmed the inauguration of the House of Shamans' Knowledge and Power. He designed folders for both the Malikai Dapana and the House of Adorning that can be seen on my URL (www.robinmwright.com). He has been an outstanding companion during field trips to the Upper Rio Negro since 1998; we were instructed together in some of the mysteries of the Baniwa cosmos. I thank my wife and daughter for their unbounded patience and understanding throughout the whole ordeal of producing this and other books.

I extend my gratitude to Bron Taylor for his wisdom, good company, good counsel, and friendship. The inspiration of his 2010 book, *Dark Green Religion: Nature Spirituality and the Planetary Future*, and his encouragement to me appear in numerous ways in this book.

Finally, to the many South Americanist colleagues, especially of the SALSA (Society for the Anthropology of Lowland South America), who, in one way or another, over many years of exchanging ideas and participating in conferences together, were influential to this book: Renato Athias, Dominique Buchillet, Janet Chernela, Carlos Fausto, Mike Heckenberger, Jonathan Hill, Jean Jackson, Wolfgang Kapfhammer, George and Laura Mentore, Eduardo Neves, Augusto Oyuela-Caycedo, Joanna Overing, Fernando Santos-Granero, Lawrence Sullivan, Tod Swanson, Terrence Turner, Aparecida Vilaça, E. Viveiros de Castro, Neil Whitehead, Johannes Wilbert, and Eglee Zent.

To fellow Arawak scholars Fernando Santos-Granero, who evaluated the manuscript for the University of Nebraska Press, Neil Whitehead, in memorium, for his unfailing support, and Jonathan Hill, who generously provided many useful comments on pieces of the book all along the way, and to the anonymous peer reviewers, many thanks for your perceptive comments. Whatever errors that appear in this book are my own.

MYSTERIES *of the* JAGUAR SHAMANS *of the Northwest Amazon*

Introduction

This book explores the meanings of shamanic knowledge and power among the Baniwa, an Arawak-speaking indigenous people of the Northwest Amazon in Brazil, with whom I have worked since 1976. It focuses on the only living jaguar shaman among the Baniwa, Mandu da Silva of the village of Uapui, Aiary River, who has been a shaman for more than sixty-four years. The idea to write his biography came from his daughter, Ercilia, and Mandu gladly obliged. His narrative is the only one on record of a shaman who is today considered by many Baniwa to be a "wise man" (*sábio* in Portuguese; *kanhenkedali* in Baniwa), or what is referred to in the anthropology of religion as a prophet. By "prophet," I mean men and women believed to have the power to communicate constantly with the principal divinities, who advise them of things to come and of the attitude people should take in relation to those forthcoming events. Prophets are recognized by the culture as having the sole legitimate power to announce future events and warn of any imminent dangers.

The Baniwa people are well known in the literature for their history of engagement in religious movements of this nature (Wright and Hill 1986; Hill and Wright 1988; Wright 1998, 2005). Since the mid-nineteenth century, indigenous prophetic leaders have emerged in an almost continuous sequence among both Arawak-speaking peoples and Tukanoan-speaking peoples of the Northwest Amazon, on the borders of Brazil, Venezuela, and Colombia. On the history of these traditions, see my doctoral thesis, 1981; book, 2005; and numerous articles, 1983, 1992c, 2002a; also Hugh-Jones 1981, 1996).

Mandu's story is unique in that it reveals the struggles that a still-living jaguar shaman and sábio has faced during a lifetime dedicated to healing and counseling the people of the Northwest Amazon region. Like his predecessors, Mandu has demonstrated deep concerns for the future of Baniwa traditions. He has traveled long distances to warn the indigenous peoples of the dangers in losing their traditions, and he is a religious virtuoso in the sense of accumulating the powers and knowledge of healer shaman, priestly chanter, and dance leader. He has been an important political leader of the community of Uapui for decades, and above all he is internationally recognized for his important work on behalf of the continuity of indigenous religious traditions.

His prophetic message is perhaps best exemplified in *The Warnings of Mandu* (2008). This Venezuelan film shows what has happened to indigenous communities of the upper Guainia River who have lost their shamanic traditions or whose shamans were manipulated by nonindigenous political interests. The result has been, in Mandu's words, "domination by the enemy," a catastrophic situation foretold in the sacred stories shared by many Arawak-speaking peoples of the region.

ETHNOGRAPHY OF THE BANIWA AND OTHER NORTHERN ARAWAK-SPEAKING PEOPLES

The Baniwa, Kuripako, and Wakuenai are three northern Arawak-speaking peoples living on the borders of Brazil, Colombia, and Venezuela. In Brazil, it is estimated that there are over 100 villages of Baniwa and Kuripako, with a total population of 4,000; in Colombia, their population is approximately 6,000, predominantly Kuripako; and in Venezuela, the Baniwa and Wakuenai

Map 1. Northern Arawak-speaking peoples in the Northwest Amazon.

(an ethnonym for the Kuripako) together have a population of approximately 1,200.

All of the societies in this region are patrilineal and patrilocal. The Baniwa say that they have three main phratries: the Hohodene of the Aiary River, the Walipere-dakenai of the lower Aiary and most of the middle to lower Içana River, and the Dzauinai on the middle Içana (between the villages of Jui uitera and the hill of Tunui Falls). Beyond the ring of these central groups, there are several small sibs, fragments of other phratries, living in villages further up the Içana.

Each of the principal phratries consists of five to ten sibs, ranked according to a birth order of primordial ancestral siblings who emerged from the earth at the beginning of time in several places, the most important of which is called Hipana, where the universe began for the Baniwa and for many other northern Arawak-speaking peoples.

Hipana is a place of great potency, since many world-changing events took place there. The child of the sun was born there. It is considered to be the World Center. The boulders, the powerful flow of water through the narrow passage of the rapids, and the lake below are a place where the first ancestors emerged.

Among the Hohodene, the phratry with whom I did most of my fieldwork, there are five sibs ranked in order of agnatic siblings and ceremonial roles: the first-born is the maku or servant sib, grandparents of the Hohodene; the second-born is the chiefly sib, elder brothers of the Hohodene; the third-born is the warrior sib, the Hohodene themselves; and the two others are younger brother sibs without any clearly defined ceremonial attributes. This ethno-model of phratric creation, however, is one version of a story that varies with almost every narrator. There is no strong consensus on overall sib order in the hierarchy (similarly, among Kuripako in Colombia; see Journet 1995). There is a consensus that the Hohodene, the Walipere-dakenai, and the Dzauinai are the three most important phratries of the Baniwa in the Içana/Aiary River basin. Each of these phratries has its own emergence place (the Walipere-dakenai at Enukwa rapids immediately below Hipana).

The Hohodene mentioned the names of the Aini-dakenai (Wasp-grandchildren) and the Hipatanene ("children of the foam of the waterfalls") among the lower-ranking sibs of their phratry. The Walipere-dakenai (Pleiades grandchildren or descendants of the Pleiades) listed upwards of nine sibs in their phratry, with themselves at the head of the constellation Walipere (Pleiades) and the others arranged according to the order of stars in the constellation.

All along the Içana River, from the headwaters down to the Tunui Rapids, the villages are predominantly evangelical Christians, as are most villages of the lower Aiary. Evangelical Christianity was

1. Aerial view of Uapui (Hipana) falls, the origin of the universe. (Photo by M. C. Wright, 2010.)

introduced in the 1950s and quickly became a mass conversion movement. It is believed that 80 percent of the Baniwa villagers today are *crente*, or believers, baptized faithful to the Church. This may be so, considering the introduction of other Protestant churches in the region, such as the Presbyterians and the Baptists, in recent years.

In the early years of the conversion movement, there was bitter fighting between the crentes and the traditionals, the latter consisting mainly of the upper Aiary River villages, especially the two communities of Uapui Rapids and Ukuki Rapids. Uapui is the village built on the banks of the Aiary at the location of Hipana Rapids (which has another name, Kupipani, "house of the cipó Kupi"). Ukuki was built in the late 1970s at the rapids of the same name (Kuliriana, in Baniwa) on the Uaraná tributary of the upper Aiary.

For a long time Uapui was a village of shamans—five when I lived there in the 1970s. Today shamanism is practically focused only there. The Ukuki community nevertheless has been a solidly traditional community in keeping the dance festivals and sacred ceremonies of initiation. In 2008, on their own initiative, they constructed a new longhouse, called House of Adorning, which was basically intended to be a ritual dance house, not a living space. The following year, at Uapui, the community was awarded funds from the Foundation for Shamanic Studies, which enabled Mandu's son and daughter to construct Malikai Dapana (Shamans' House of Power and Knowledge).

"A NEXUS OF RELIGIOUS POWER AND KNOWLEDGE"

The chapters of this book are grouped around five main themes, each of which is part of an entire shamanic tradition. They are (1) a biography of the jaguar shaman Mandu, religious savant and political leader; (2) the problem of sorcery in the communities and other challenges to the continuity of indigenous religious traditions; (3) the interrelations among indigenous cosmology, ecology, and metaphysics of shamanic knowledge and power; (4) the interrelations of sacred geography, petroglyphs, and a body of living mythic traditions; and (5) the viability of transmission and revitalization of shamanic traditions now and for future generations.

The principal Baniwa specialists in shamanic and ceremonial knowledge and power possess distinct attributes and functions, summarized in Table 1. This will serve as a guide throughout this book. Each of the four specialists is said to "own" (keep or hold) or "be a master of" a specific kind of knowledge accompanied by certain powers. The term *malikai* was consistently translated by Mandu as "the pajé's [shaman's] knowledge *and* power," meaning that the pajé's art does not consist of simply knowing (*ianheke*), but rather it is knowledge that has creative or protective power inherent to it. One can know a myth, but unless one knows the orations or chants that go along with the story, then one has not yet exercised the power of the knowledge imparted in the myth.

When taken as a whole, the different shamanic and ritual "specializations" in "power and knowledge" can be seen to complement each other, forming what I shall call a nexus of (religious) power and knowledge in Baniwa society. The idea of a "nexus" refers to the interrelationship among these bodies of knowledge and power. Each supports or complements the other whether as an oppositional, confrontational type of relation (pajé vs. assault sorcerer), complementary relation as between the pajé healer and priestly chanter (both having to do with the health, well-being, and reproduction of society), or the ritual knowledge and power of ceremonial dancing, which is essential to the production of harmonious conviviality, the way to well-being and happiness, insofar as it celebrates the ties of reciprocity among communities of the same or affinal phratries.

The four principal owners of power and knowledge are

1 the *pajés* (a *lingua geral*, the old trade language of the region, term for shaman, *maliri* in Baniwa) who heal and protect their communities, the highest grade of which is the true pajé or jaguar shaman. In this book I shall use the word *pajé* with greater frequency than the word *shaman*, except for the term *dzaui malinyai*, "jaguar shaman–spirit–others" referring to powerful shamanic spirits of the "Other World."

2 the sorcerers who attack to destroy a victim or an entire family (*manhene iminali*, poison owner; *hiwiathi iminali*, owners of assault sorcery chants). These are also called *mantís*, a lingua geral term for assault sorcerers, and *dañeros*, a Spanish term for the same thing. From the sorcerers' point of view, their actions are justified as redressing what they perceive to be an imbalance of power or a personal loss that they attribute to sorcery sent by pajés or other sorcerers.

3 priestly chanters who "own" highly specialized chants called
   kalidzamai, performed during the all-important rites of passage in which they protect those undergoing life transitions
   from all potentially harmful places, spirits, and animals in the
   world.

4 the dance leaders (*mandero*) who lead the dance lines with the
   correct patterns for each type of dance, upholding the collective, aesthetic virtues of beauty, symmetry, and form. While the
   dance leaders have been treated in the literature as owners of a
   kind of secular knowledge, the term used for their knowledge
   is *manderokai*, the suffix *-kai* referring to the power they have
   to make the dances effective instruments of sociality.[1]

TABLE I. Religious specialists of northern Arawakan Baniwa

Jaguar Shamans (*Maliri, Dzaui Malinyai*)
Training: 10 years; involves fasting, abstinence, seclusion, taking psy-
   choactives, constant learning from master; experience of "death"
   and "rebirth," dismemberment and reshaping of inner self; "marriage" to auxiliary bird-spirits; advanced knowledge to kill; warrior
   ethos
Calling: sometimes a serious sickness, dream experience, or recom-
   mendation from parents; desire to learn; male or female
*Powers (*malikai*):* soul-flight; direct experience of spirits and deities in
   all levels of cosmos; transformation into jaguar spirit (predator and
   protector functions) and numerous other animal avatars; acquires
   "body" of jaguar-spirit; jaguar-tooth necklace; curing of sickness;
   weather control; guides souls of deceased to Other World houses;
   world-making and healing; hierarchies of power
Attributes: human-animal-spirit; multiple perspectives; double vision;

sounds thunder; sends soul at will; singing brings Other World into being; considered distinct from sorcerer; rattle is "body and soul" of shaman; numerous "shirts" (subjectivities); "mirrors" allow total, global vision

Characteristics: hunter of souls; master of fire (tobacco); cosmic warrior; cosmic traveler; mediator with deities; master of light (crystals); clairvoyance; diviner

Institutions: schools of instruction of apprentices by master shamans, beginning and advanced levels

---

Sorcerers (*Manhene Iminali*)

Training: informal learning from elder; continued practice until she/ he "owns" knowledge to kill; often part of a faction that seeks to undermine dominant village family or leadership

Calling: often sentiment of retribution due to loss; envy, jealousy, anger, self-exile, desire to destroy those more successful and powerful; in extreme cases the sorcerer sees no end to desire to kill; only thinks of killing

Powers: master of plant and numerous other kinds of poisons and antidotes; seeks to provoke disorder, does harm, sends sickness; de-structures persons, "families," or whole villages; sends soul to transform into predatory animals; physical and spiritual transformation into primordial sorcerer or spirit of deceased

Attributes: extreme secrecy, nocturnal attacks, shape-shifting; killing at a distance; attacks by soul-flight with bone containing poison; may be a member of kin-group or affinal group

Characteristics: serial-killing; victims are elderly, children, young women, successful hunters, successful leaders; increase in attacks during times of social, political, economic change

Institutions: mythically charged geographical locations, or "places of poison"

Prophets (*"Sábios," Kanhenkedali, Savants*):

Calling: already a jaguar shaman and priestly chanter; surviving lethal sickness or extraordinary dream experience or intense trance experience of deceased and/or divinity; often has lived in several ethnic contexts; the Baniwa "await" the appearance of "wise men/women" as protectors, guides, councilors

Powers: clairvoyance; sees future events; battles sorcerers; reveals locations of "poison"; interprets signs of times; extraordinary knowledge of cosmos; converses at will with principal deity and deceased kin; extraordinary power to heal; seeks to build community harmony; dance-leader; powers surpass that of the Whites' military/learned men

Attributes: immortality of soul; return of soul after death to tomb; speaks many languages; prescience; constant communication with divinity

Characteristics: ultra-moral message; anti-sorcery, reformer of society; associated by followers with important deity; considered by following to be immortal; outstanding charisma and translator (resonance with his/her message and what people want to hear); protects community; upholds traditions

Institutions: leader of movements which may become institutionalized ritual forms ("Dance of the Cross," evangelicalism).

Priestly Chanters (*Kalidzamai*):

Training: varies, but no more nor less than jaguar shamans

Calling: considered as elder's responsibility (men or women know)

Powers: a form of shamanic power, *malikai,* especially "Thought" journeys (*Kuwai ianhiakakawa*) in rites of initiation for males and females; protective shamanism with pepper and salt, making food safe for individuals, or families in transition (post-birth, male and female initiation, shaman apprentices, post-mortem); control of ancestral powers to reproduce society; managing the ancestral places and ancestral beings throughout known world, preventing them from harming the living; promotes growth of children; chanting over garden for growth and abundance

Attributes: master of canonical knowledge (litanies of names and places chanted in correct order, from beginning to end); lesser chants or whispered formulae (*iwapakaithe*) for innumerable tasks; using tobacco, remedies, words spoken in closed fist transferred with smoke to materia medica

Characteristics: performs either individually (post-birth, post-mortem) or in groups of 2–4 (initiation, end of shamans' apprenticeship); instruments: sacred ceramic bowl containing pepper and/or salt, cigar

Institutions: no visible connection to institutions or network of chant specialists throughout region; difficulties of learning have reduced numbers

---

Dance-Leaders (*Mandero Iminali*): usually elderly men and women who know the songs, the numerous types of dances of the *Pudali* (festivals of exchange) each with appropriate songs, dance instruments, and dance patterns. There are 24 distinct dances (Costa, 2007: 50) for the *Pudali*. The sacred rites of the *Kwaipan* (rites of initiation) are the domain of the shaman and the *kalidzamai* who are often one and the same person

Training: village elders and/or leaders learn the traditional dances, appropriate adornments, body painting, and dance calendar from previous village leader, traditional chief

*Powers (*manderokai*):* The *Pudali* are occasions of exchange, socializing, celebration of plenty, arranging marriages, much harmonious conviviality, Pakamaratakan (ritual partners) Songs. The pleasure of socializing and dancing together, with great quantities of lightly fermented beverages (*padzuwaro*) circulating, and the collective sentiment of happiness in the festivals produce harmonious conviviality; dance-leaders enforce the rules of gender separation at times of initiation

Characteristics: Mandero wears a distinctive *acangatara*, headdress of white heron feathers, with a long tail down the back, a woven and decorated apron, and the ankle rattles that establish the dance rhythm

Attributes: Mandero explains to community the correct dance patterns, starts the dance line in proper rhythm, increases the momentum, establishes the order of dancers and their instruments, leads the forward and backward movements around the offerings (like contracting and expanding circles as though to increase the offering), guards the dance instruments and feather headdresses, and redistributes them at correct time to dance

Institutions: Pudali have been undergoing a revival for at least a decade in four communities of the Aiary River. These same communities have never ceased celebrating the initiation rites, *Kwaipan*, the most sacred of all rites.

KNOWLEDGE, HIERARCHY, AND AGE

Each form of knowledge and power is acquired at a certain phase of the life cycle: a young adult, male or female, may begin training to become a healer and may either complete the full ten years required to become a "real pajé" or interrupt training at the end of the first major stage and remain a "half-pajé" with limited powers to cure.

Only the senior elderly men and women of the "grandparent" generation can learn the *kalidzamai* chants, which require great stamina (force, *kedzako*), memory, exact knowledge of places in the world, and the poetic spirit names (*naakuna*) of all living beings. There is also less chance that these very elderly specialists are embroiled in any of the struggles that involve shamans and sorcerers, which would detract from the great responsibility and the strenuous spiritual work involved in the transmission of culture through their chanting.

Dance leaders acquire their knowledge from within their own consanguineal kinship groups. As for sorcery, anyone can learn the practice or be an accomplice to a sorcerer, even young children, but the true sorcerers are those whose intentions have become so dominated by the desire to kill as to use poison against everyone whom she or he considers an "enemy." As Mandu stated, "Their only thought is to kill" (*manhene kada lima*).

The jaguar shaman is a high-level pajé whose power is considered to have been directly transmitted over a long genealogical line from the original creative powers of the universe, especially the deity Dzuliferi, the ancient shaman deity. The jaguar shaman is a "true pajé," considered to "know everything about the world," and is said to be able to attain a place "next to" the place of the creator deity, Nhiãperikuli. She or he is the only native healer who is believed to be capable of curing victims of assault sorcery by poisoning.

The *sábios* (wise men or women, *kanhenkedali tapame*) are religious leaders who provide moral guidance to their followers, who include peoples of different ethnic groups spread out over a large geographical area in the Northwest Amazon on three sides of the international borders; who maintain constant communication with the creator deities; and who perform cures or feats that are considered to be extraordinary or miraculous. The sábios combine most of the above named functions into one integrated knowledge and power. Yet, rather than keeping that power centralized in their person, they use their wisdom to protect and benefit the people of their community. In that sense, they are guardians of multiple communities located throughout a wide geographical area and of multiple linguistic groups, demonstrating qualities that are characteristic of the deities Nhiãperikuli and Dzuliferi (the creator deity and the primal shaman, respectively).

The ethnohistories of the Baniwa of the Içana and Aiary and, to a certain extent, the upper Rio Negro or Guainia amply testify to the importance of a tradition of wise men and women. These prophetic movements have been (1) regionally based, including indigenous and *caboclo* (*mestiço*) peoples of several language groups; (2) continuous from at least the mid-nineteenth century; (3) recalled in oral histories as struggles of the wise men and women against sorcery; (4) most definitely connected to the evangelical movement in the 1950s and 1960s, which is understood today by evangelical converts as having been instigated by the North American missionary Sophie Muller, who was attributed powers that only a powerful shaman could have to overcome sorcery (Boyer 1999); and (5) most definitely are grounded in the child of the sun, Kuwai, traditions (Wright 2005).

There is no historical evidence to argue that any of these wise people were of a "horizontal" or "vertical" type of shamanism, as has been discussed for the Tukanoan-speaking peoples (Hugh-Jones 1996; Viveiros de Castro in Chaumeil 2003: 38). The stories the Baniwa tell about these extraordinary people confirm that they were jaguar shamans, dance leaders, and chanters who were particularly concerned with the problem of sorcery, encouraging their followers to live in harmony, free of sorcery, and who utilized their formidable powers of prescience to benefit the people. They have been strongly against using secular political power for their own ends.

SENSE OF MYSTERIES

According to Baniwa traditions, sickness and sorcery were introduced into This World at the end of the first initiation ceremony by the great spirit "owner of sickness," Kuwai, about whom a significant part of this book is dedicated. The "mysteries of the jaguar shamans" revolve around this world-creating being, who is the "child of the sun father," Nhiãperikuli, the Baniwa creator deity, and the first woman, Amaru. There are numerous other mysteries in the sense of "hidden things"—the Unknown in Baniwa cosmology, sacred rites and narrative, and above all, shamanic practices. None, however, commands the secrecy and the force that the Kuwai traditions did and in some places still do.

How then do the jaguar shamans teach and transmit these mysteries to apprentices among a larger community of northern Arawak-speaking peoples? How do they make known the Other World of spirits and deities which they must experience directly in order to realize a cure? In our exploration of the features, qualities, and dimensions of the Other World, we shall consider shamans' songs, exegeses of sacred narratives, healing practices, and protective actions against sorcerers.

The knowledge and power of the shamans today ultimately derives from the primordial owners, the great spirits and deities who brought everything in This World into being. Anyone can learn the stories about them; they are considered "good to hear" and reflect upon. The powers they explain, however, are the basis of chants, songs, and prayers. These can be learned and transmitted only by people who are properly instructed in their use. To speak the words of an oration, chant, or prayer can be beneficial in healing, providing food, and making gardens grow well. They are protective in warding off potential dangers or attacks by sorcerers or spirits. By the same token, they are believed to be extremely dangerous in harming or even killing a person. In all these senses, malikai knowledge and power should be learned and used with great caution. One of the problems that the Baniwa face today is that, with the extreme reduction of their true pajés, the sorcerers' power to harm can become uncontrolled.

The greatest challenge in doing ethnography for this kind of book was in empathizing with the pajé's perspective, particularly when their heart-souls (*ikaale*) are said to be journeying in the Other World (Apakwa Hekwapi). This requires close attention to specific linguistic forms and the poetry of the shamans' songs, which can be understood as constitutive of their soul-flight and their encounters with the great spirits and deities of the Other World. Like Kuwai, the jaguar shamans can assume multiple shapes and forms in their journeys to the Other World. The pajé's body and soul become totally "other" (a jaguar shaman spirit, not human), and they acquire the resources uniquely capable of combating sorcery and sickness-giving spirits.

In order to cure the sick, the pajé's soul must visit the "netherworld of the dead" (Hill 1993). Actually, for the Baniwa jaguar shamans, their souls should visit all of the five "Houses of the Souls of the Dead" pertaining to the principal phratries of the Baniwa. But this is just the beginning of their search; from there, their souls travel "upstream" to various places in the Other World of the sky, where different deities are said to have their houses. The voyage we try to reconstruct in chapter 2 is based on curing sessions taped and translated over many years with the help of shamans' apprentices.

DEALING WITH SORCERY

Chapters 1, 2, and 3 concern the apprenticeship of the jaguar shaman Mandu da Silva and his struggles against the actions of several sorcerers in the village of Uapui, Aiary River. Pajés and mantís are opposing forces at either end of a gradient that separates good people (*matchiaperi*) from the wicked (*maatchipem*). To understand the struggles between them, it is vital that we take into account the motives behind the sorcerers' actions. To what extent have external influences on Baniwa society resulted in disruption and increases in assault sorcery attacks?

One of the principal objectives of the historical prophets, wise men and women, has been to control sorcery-by-poisoning, by transforming the negativity that permeates villages where sorcery has become dominant into harmonious conviviality. The prophets' powers are considered to be greater than the jaguar shamans' because they are practically the living voices of the deities and maintain an open line of communication with the creator. Chapter 2 presents material about the historical prophet Uetsu, who, like Mandu, battled much of his life against sorcerers (see also Wright 2004a). It is instructive to compare their campaigns to control sorcery and at the same time defend sacred traditions.

THE BEGINNING OF SORCERY

For the Baniwa, assault sorcery has existed since the beginning of the Universe. When the creator deity sought a better condition than the existing static and sterile condition of eternal Daylight, he ultimately let Night out of a small basket in which it was contained, forcing the sun to fall outside the sky vault of This World. Night covered the world, then miniature, in darkness. By bringing Night into existence, the creator deity made two distinct and equal states of living reality: Day (for work) and Night (for rest). This was good. The light of the Day divided time and space with the Darkness of the Night. Time was set into cyclical motion, two equal states of being.

It was a long, dark night, however, that brought "sadness" with it, for each being had to go its own separate way to find a place to sleep. During the first long night, sorcery came into being. The first woman, the creator's wife, began throwing "poisonous ants" (tocandira) in the direction of the tree where the creator was keeping vigil. The creator transformed each of these ants into harmless insects. When the Dawn appeared, Happiness returned, for a new Universe and a new Day had begun (day and universe are the same word, *hekwapi*). Day and Night, Light and Dark, Happiness and Sadness, Life and Death—all of these came into being with the knowledge and powers of pajés and sorcerers. The Story of Night is one of the first stories of creation.

The existence of the sorcerers is one of the all-time dilemmas for the Baniwa. The sorcerers' powers are necessary to keep in check social, political, and economic inequalities. In a society that highly values a relatively egalitarian ethos, anyone who accumulates power and knowledge becomes vulnerable to the "leveling mechanism" that assault sorcery represents (Whitehead & Wright 2004; Garnelo 2003).

Sorcery can come to dominate a practitioner's body and soul, with dramatic consequences for the entire village, placing its very survival in danger. The sorcerer becomes a "serial killer" — or at least the whole village believes this to be so. Such has been the history of numerous villages in the past, which the Baniwa recall and outside published sources have recorded (Koch-Grünberg 1967 [1909]; Wright 1998).

As Mandu stated in the film *Las Advertencias de Mandú* (*The Warnings of Mandú*) aired on Venezuelan national television several years ago, "If the sorcerers triumph, then chaos will prevail; for then the people and, with them, their traditional indigenous culture will be exterminated [producing a void that leaves the indigenous area open to] "the expansion or domination by the white people" (my translation).

The film, winner of the Venezuelan Ministry of Culture's Yulimar Reyes National Documentary Competition, has had positive repercussions on cultural revitalization and the historical memory of the native peoples of the town of Maroa, on the Rio Guainia, in Venezuela. Above all, the film called on communities who had left their ancestors' ways of life behind, to attempt to revitalize them, denouncing the nonindigenous politicians who were using powerful shamans to support their political campaigns.

Fluctuations in the incidence of sorcery can be linked to interventions by peoples seen as "outsiders" (sorcerers, white people) in Baniwa communities. These outsiders have produced situations of unequal distribution of power and knowledge, thereby creating tensions and conflicts that are propitious grounds for sorcery accusations and social transformations.

In the mid-twentieth century, for example, the Baniwa and Kuripako hoped to eliminate the "problem of sorcery" by converting en masse to fundamentalist evangelicalism (see Boyer 1999; Saake 1959–60a; Wright 1998, 2005) introduced by the North American missionary Sophie Muller. Today, however, the evangelicals speak of an increase in assault sorcery in their communities despite their having abandoned all, or most, of their most sacred ancestral traditions. Evangelicalism failed to provide an adequate, alternate solution for the continued existence of sorcery in the world, one not based on the sacred narratives which the evangelicals condemned. The Baniwa evangelicals had definitively abandoned the sacred ceremonies, along with the practice of the jaguar shamans, the only specialists who could cure cases of poison. The age-old mystery of how the universe came to be the way it is today is for the evangelicals no longer a secret.

Nevertheless, they continue to explain death as the result of unknown enemy sorcerers, even from within the same community. This is a stark demonstration that, in giving up shamanic practices, they created a vacuum that has been extremely difficult to overcome. Shamans are the only specialists who are trained to "see" (recognize) who the sorcerers are in a community and to combat them on a cosmological level.

Since the 1980s, NGO health programs have encouraged the evangelicals to train indigenous health agents and to plant medicinal gardens near their homes. Western biomedical practice and workshops, based on an entirely distinct logic, could not provide a convincing explanation either for what the Baniwa had for centuries understood as sorcery by poisoning or even attacks by forest spirits. These require the pajés' soul journeys to cure or knowing highly specialized chants, which implies a knowledge of the cosmos, the spirits and deities who dwell in it, their powers, and how to enlist their help in the healing of the sick.

As one young shaman perceptively observed, the indigenous peoples have sicknesses that Western biomedicine cannot even diagnose. For that reason, abandoning shamanism, as the crentes did, was a grave error. By contrast, pajés recognize Western biomedicine as complementing their own practice in the sense of treating ailments that are believed to be transmitted by or sent by the white people; also, modern medicine utilizes instruments such as X-ray technology that is similar to the pajés' power to "see" inside the body of the patient to locate the source of the sickness. However, Western biomedicine can interfere with shamanic treatment, for example, by altering the body (orthoplasty) in some way, making shamanic treatment more difficult.

COSMOLOGY AND ECOLOGY

To have a better understanding of the dynamics of sorcery and shamanic practices, we are led to cosmologies and their ecological foundations. Thus chapters 3 and 4 present the universe through an ecological metaphor. Animals, birds, and celestial bodies of major importance in the Baniwa cosmos are placed by pajé interlocutors in their correct positions on an enormous cosmic Tree at the center of the universe, Hipana, that is, the vertical axis of the cosmos. Through this metaphor, we can better understand the pajés' visions of the cosmos, the nature of existence, and their visions of the sources of good and evil in the world. The origin of the pajé's powers is intimately connected to the food cycles of the cosmos; at the same time that humanity received all food resources, the pajés received their powers to mediate between worlds. The pajés have a vital role in guarding the food resources in This World.

On the horizontal plane, the entire Northwest Amazon region

is populated by the memories of what the deities and primordial beings did and where they walked and inscribed images on the stones, known as petroglyphs. Through the chants sung during rites of passage, the sacred sites, and the memories of the elders, the entire region has a long tradition that connects present-day descendants to their ancestors. This "mythscape" is, in its totality, an open book of Baniwa cosmic history, an ever-present reminder of how This World came to be. More than that, the ecology is sacred in that the stones themselves are said to be the dwelling places of both spirits and deities, houses of the souls of the dead, of animals, of fruits and other food resources. There are at least five major sacred sites in this mythscape that can be seen to represent the endpoints of the entire Baniwa universe on the horizontal plane.

The Kuwai traditions are the equivalent of the popularly known Yurupary cults. The word *Yurupary* refers to a Tupian demiurge of the forest, but was introduced to the Northwest Amazon region possibly in the mid-nineteenth century, when Capuchin missionaries began to work on the Uaupés River south of the Içana and Aiary. The missionaries used the term in the sense of a demon of the forest, while the Tupian thunder god Tupã was used as a *lingua franca* term for God, reducing the multiple names for deity of the more than twenty ethnic groups to one exogenous deity which, for the indigenous peoples of the Northwest Amazon, had little or no relation to their deities. The name Tupã stuck, however, representing the colonial missionary God up until very recently when the different ethnic groups began publishing their sacred stories with the correct names of their deities.

The Yurupary tradition became the object of persecution by the missionaries from the late nineteenth century until recently. Again on the Uaupés River, Franciscan missionaries defiled sacred masks, which were believed to be the forest demon whose actual name was Kue for the Tariana Indians (Arawak-speaking), the equivalent of the Baniwa Kuwai. For the Baniwa, Kuwai refers to the sacred ancestral flutes and trumpets which are believed to be the body of the original Kuwai, the great spirit child of the sun, owner of sickness, also known as Wamundana, whom the pajés see in their soul journeys to the Other World.

The sacred flutes and trumpets have always been central to Baniwa notions of spirituality, cultural transmission, health and sickness, shamanic practice, and ecology, as they are for most other northern Arawak-speaking and eastern Tukanoan-speaking societies of the Northwest Amazon.[2] The sacred stories and rituals of Kuwai are intimately connected with shamanism and ceremonial traditions (healing, sorcery, initiation chants, and ritual dances), seasonal fertility, ecological cycles, and the souls of the first ancestors.

According to Reichel-Dolmatoff, it is very likely that the "Kuwai traditions" are Arawak in origin and that the ancient northern Arawak-speaking peoples (such as the Maipure) had a strong influence on similar traditions among the Tukanoan-speaking peoples of the Uaupés River and its tributaries to the south of the Baniwa (Reichel-Dolmatoff 1996).

In fact, the Kuwai traditions form a vast "mythscape" of "sacred sites" and "sacred geography" in Baniwa territory, discussed in chapter 5. These sites include petroglyphs, waterfalls, caves, hills, and numerous other landscape features, where significant events told in the sacred story of Kuwai took place. The chants sung at initiation rites re-create this mythscape in minute detail, encoding multiple layers of meaning all of which refer to the world-opening, all-encompassing, transformational spirit who is the child of the sun father and the first woman.

The spatial extensiveness and the temporal depth of the "Kuwai Religion," as these traditions have been called (Vidal 1987), connect living peoples' identities to their ancestral lands. To the Baniwa/Kuripako/Wakuenai who continue to believe in these traditions, the petroglyphs are evidence that their ancestors really were there, and that events in the stories really did take place. The ancestors left these memories for their descendants (*walimanai*) to learn from and live by. The greatest loss imaginable will come when the younger generation no longer knows the meanings of these traditions, which is already a sad fact in many communities.

Chapters 6 to 8 present a complete version of the sacred story of Kuwai, and discuss its intimate relationship to jaguar shamanism. My discussion of the story in three chapters coincides with the major episodes: the birth of Kuwai, the first initiation rites, and the struggle for ownership of the sacred flutes and trumpets, Kuwai's body.

The story unveils a "worldview," in the Diltheyan sense of the term, one which is grounded in an ideally balanced relation with the natural world. Jaguar shamans have a particularly deep understanding of this tradition, since it is to Kuwai that their souls must travel in order to realize a cure. Through the pajés' exegesis on Kuwai, and all things related to this figure, we can appreciate the mysteries of this paradoxically creative and destructive spirit.

The terms that Victor Turner used several decades ago of liminality and "semantic multivocality" (1995 [1969]), are particularly appropriate for understanding how layers of meanings, which may seem paradoxical to us, are integrated into the same being of Kuwai. Kuwai's multiplicity of forms and complexity of meanings all are part of the knowledge and power (malikai) of the pajés as well as of all peoples who have been initiated.

Kuwai is an extraordinary being, the child of the creator deity Nhiãperikuli with the first woman, Amaru. Nhiãperikuli wanted a child that was the product of his shamanic thought (ianheke) and that was the reproduction of his "heart-soul," the most lasting element of a person's being. By shamanic means, Nhiãperikuli brings into being a child of his heart-soul. Kuwai was a very strange creature: his body was full of holes that emitted the sounds and melodies of numerous animal parts of his being. This mixture of so many animal parts into one was exceedingly dangerous to humanity, forcing Nhiãperikuli to banish the child to the sky world.

This brief description is sufficient for now to understand that the story of Kuwai is about the transmission of shamanic knowledge and power. All of Kuwai's body is directly related to shamanism and growth. The growth of young children into adults and the apprenticeship of shamans require the materialization of the mysterious cosmic power of transformative change which Kuwai embodies and which is represented by the sacred ancestral flutes and trumpets.

Kuwai is growth: of the world, of the initiates, which he transforms through the power of his music. Yet as a protean type of spirit, it was too dangerous to allow him to stay in This World. Upon learning all his knowledge, at the end of the first initiation ceremony, his father pushed him into an enormous fire. He never died, though, for his spirit continues to live in the Other World. In our interpretation, we show how the "death" of Kuwai meant the incorporation of all his knowledge of the spirit world and its power as well into society. From his body came all of the forms of sorcery and sickness-giving spirits, such as the *Yoopinai*. From his body also came the first tree from which the sacred flutes and trumpets, which are his body, were made. With it, the men would reproduce future generations.

A TRADITION IN THE BALANCE

The Baniwa say that traditionally, there was at least one pajé, and often several, in each of their villages. Due to the evangelical crusades and their destruction of shamanism in the 1960s and 1970s, the number of pajés did not surpass much more than a dozen when I began my field research in 1976. As time passed, the elder "true pajés" died without having transmitted their power and knowledge on to their direct descendants who did not want to learn the traditions or were away from their homes; thus the situation became even more critical.

In 2009, among all Baniwa/Kuripako in Brazil at least, there were only two "true pajés" who had advanced knowledge, one of whom, Mandu da Silva, is a jaguar shaman and a priestly chanter. Many followers of Mandu also consider him to be a "wise man" or prophet. There are several "half-shamans" in Uapui village who have acquired the basics of the practice but do not yet have "advanced knowledge."

As a result of a project initiated by the adults of the village of Uapui to revitalize jaguar shamans, apprentices recently began instruction. There are perhaps five pajés and six apprentices on the Aiary River today, which is an area known for always having defended the traditions (from forced acculturation by the missions).

When Mandu da Silva passes on to the Other World, an entire corpus of living knowledge about the universe, the spirits, the plants, old shamans, and so much more will no longer be making worlds as when he was alive. This book, then, attests to the importance of his knowledge and powers for the Baniwa themselves and for others, providing a dual view from an anthropological interpretation and indigenous insight on how jaguar shamans compare with the other main forms of religious knowledge and power in Baniwa culture—except for evangelical Christianity (which is being researched by very competent fieldworkers amongst the Baniwa and Kuripako of the middle and upper Içana River).

Whether the new "House of Shamans' Knowledge and Power," Malikai Dapana as it is called, built in Uapui in 2009, will have continuity is a question discussed in the final chapter of this book. The idea came from the young leaders, especially the schoolteachers, but the House will surely be utilized for holding large festivals, such as those that Mandu describes in his autobiography.

Since 1976, and especially over the past several years, my relationship with Mandu has been much like that of master and apprentice, except that I have been unable to follow up with his suggestion to complete the first stages of apprenticeship, which involve a month of seclusion, ingesting numerous kinds of "medicine" (*-tápe*), and constant inhaling of the psychoactive snuff called *pariká*.

Pariká is a crystalline powder made from the blood-red exudates of the inner bark of *Virola theidora* and *Anandenanthera peregrina* trees found in the Northwest Amazon region. Its active chemical principle is DMT (dymethyltriptamine). The more experienced pajés sometimes use a mixture of pariká and another hallucinogen known as *caapi* (*Banisteriopsis caapi*). The only way to become a "true pajé" with advanced knowledge of jaguar shamans, Mandu said, is to endure prolonged fasting and the constant use of pariká until one's vision is transformed and one "sees the way the pajés see and feel the way they feel in the Other World."

In 1976–77 I studied with Mandu's uncle, who also was a well-known pajé and chief of Uapui village for over a generation. José Garcia, the son of the "wise man"/jaguar shaman Guilherme Garcia, about whom Mandu speaks often in his biographical narrative, also taught me a little of what he knew; even that "little," however, was enormously instructive. Another pajé, Edu, introduced me to pariká in 1977. I have observed innumerable curing sessions and have been a patient in one cure.

The research for this book began in 1997 and became more intensive over the past three years through weekly telephone conversations with Mandu and his daughter Ercilia, who translated and wrote down her father's knowledge of shamanic powers. She was as interested as I to know her father's life and his struggles, and she became an avid student, taping as he sang, filming as a group of shamans made pariká, and filming a curing rite.

The material on cosmology and sacred stories has been researched for thirty-five years and most intensively during the production of *Wisdom of Our Ancestors* (*Waferinaipe Ianheke*, 1999), a book in Portuguese with a great many of the sacred stories of creation, as well as minor stories of forest spirits and even texts of shamanic experiences in apprenticeship. During the years 2000–2002, while collaborating in a research project on public health questions among the Baniwa, I interviewed Mandu in depth about his knowledge of assault sorcery. Above all, over the past two years, Mandu and his daughter have been most interested in recording his extensive knowledge as the first part of the project of the Malikai Dapana.

Part 1

Shamans, Chanters, Sorcerers, and Prophets

1

"You Are Going to Save Many Lives"

THE LIFE STORY OF MANDU DA SILVA,
HOHODENE JAGUAR SHAMAN

Coauthored by Manuel da Silva and Ercilia da Silva

Mandu da Silva is the only living jaguar shaman among the Baniwa/
Kuripako population of the Northwest Amazon. In the 1970s and
1980s, he was chief of the village of Uapui on the Aiary River.
Mandu's story is extraordinary in many ways. It bears similarities
to the life narratives of the powerful jaguar shamans and prophets
of the mid-nineteenth century and early twentieth. Those narratives obviously differ from Mandu's because they were told in the
third person and were composed by their kin after the shamans'
deaths. Mandu's life narrative constructs his own living historical
identity. Inevitably the appropriate models of shamanic identities
shape and are shaped by Mandu's particular experiences.

No ethnographer of the Northwest Amazon has written extensively about the life of one shaman (except perhaps Arhem for the
Tukanoan-speaking Makuna people in Colombia, 1998). More often
in the literature we find rather generalized statements about the
shamans of a people and their healing practices. How they learn,
from whom, and at what points in their training they learned
specific kinds of knowledge are important questions because they
reveal that there are defined stages of acquiring knowledge and

power, that networks of pajés exist (some of them are quite likely very ancient) covering a vast geographic area extending into Venezuela, up to the Piaroa people, and that "schools" are formed when a group of apprentices come together to learn from a master pajé.

Each pajé has a specialization; for example, one pajé knows well how to cure sickness resulting from spirit darts [*walama]* or forest spirits [*awakarunanai, yoopinai*], two of the most important sources of sickness and pain from which people constantly suffer. A few pajés know how to deal with cases of assault sorcery using plant or leaf poison [*manhene*]. The pajés to the far north, among the Piaroa and Wanhiwa (Guahibo) peoples, are said to be skilled in killing at a distance. If one wants to learn that practice, one has to seek their instruction. Mandu, for example, needed that knowledge and power to protect himself and his family from attacks by other pajés. Now he can transmit it to his apprentices if necessary.

Mandu recounts how he formed longtime connections with important shamans of Venezuela, through whom he obtained great spiritual power located in certain sacred places. Later in his life, he would return to those places and, with the fame that he had earned as chief of Uapui, he offered counsel to communities in the Venezuelan Guainia River region that were rapidly losing their cultural traditions. Ultimately he and his children and grandchildren have undertaken a project to "valorize" shamans' knowledge through the construction of a longhouse in Uapui where shamanic and cultural events can take place.

Prophets have appeared since the mid-nineteenth century. The first of these not only thwarted the Venezuelan military's attempts to destroy him but also introduced a new religious practice, called the "Song of the Cross," which spread throughout the Northwest Amazon region (Wright 1992c). The jaguar shamans today incorporate the teachings from this historical tradition.

According to Baniwa belief, the death of prophets is foreordained. The time comes for their lives to end in This World when "Dio"/ Dzuliferi no longer "advises them" of imminent enemy attacks. Thus their enemies (frequently sorcerers from within Baniwa society) may act against them when their spiritual defenses are down. The prophets' explicit goal is to make their followers get rid of sorcery and to create a harmonious regime of sociality. Like Mandu, their struggles against the sorcerers have proved disastrous to their families, but at the time of this writing, Mandu, now in his nineties, has survived and the sorcerers have been banished from his village.

Mandu's daughter taped and translated her father's story from Baniwa to Portuguese. I then translated it into English, and we worked together to clarify specific areas of the narrative.

Three questions emerge from this biography:

What events does Mandu select as being of the greatest importance to his career as a pajé?
How was his apprenticeship structured in relation to the kinds of knowledge and power he acquired?
What changes in his personal life especially marked his memories?

In chapter 2, I develop essentially an in-depth ethnography of shamanic apprenticeship based on Mandu's and other shamans' exegeses. Since my experience in apprenticeship did not include the kinds of transformation of self that a pajé normally undergoes, I rely heavily on the language pajés use to talk about their soul-flights and encounters with what are, to the reader, totally unfamiliar beings and places "out there" in the "Other World" in the sky where the principal shamanic beings are found. Through the images created in their songs, their actions captured by photos, and analytic syntheses, I hope to bring the reader closer to the experiential level of shamanic knowledge and power.

In chapter 3, the narrative continues with Mandu's struggles against a particular sorcerer and his cohorts in the community of Uapui. By introducing this conflict, the narrative is obliged to discuss as extensively as possible the sorcerer's knowledge and powers. Nothing discussed there indicates any conflicts that may now be occurring in Mandu's village.

Mandu da Silva's Life Story: From Apprentice to Jaguar Shaman
(Translated and organized with Ercilia de Lima da Silva, Mandu's daughter)

CHILDHOOD IN THE GREAT MALOCA OF UAPUI

"My grandfather's name was Kaaparo, and he was a great pajé. My father's name was Seraphim, and he was Baniwa. My mother, Nazaria Trindade, was of the Wanano people from Caruru Rapids on the Uaupés River. I was born in Uapui Cachoeira, which in Baniwa is called Kupipani. I grew up in the longhouse of Uapui.

"The longhouse was beautiful, all painted with designs, called *diakhe*. My childhood with my parents was a very happy one with my three brothers Mário, Lourenço, and Gabriel. Lourenço and Gabriel have already passed on to another life. Now I have only one brother, Mário.

"At that time, still in the longhouse of Uapui, men and women did not use clothes like they do today. Men used a piece of cloth tied around the waist, covering in front and back. Women used a small skirt tied at the waist. At that time, there was no malice, like men staring at the women or women staring at the men. That was the custom. At the time, men, women, and children in Uapui, the longhouse, were painted red and black all the time. It was the custom.

"When I was 12 years old [around 1931, Ercilia calculates], my father and uncle organized a great festival of initiation (Kwaipan, when they blessed the food and taught the initiates about the world), and they showed the sacred flutes to us for the first time. There were more than twenty-two boys between 12 and 17, the age when their fathers or grandfathers pass on their knowledge. This was an unforgettable ceremony for me, and I remember it even today. This ceremony is very important for the Hohodene and Walipere-dakenai. Every boy must go through this ceremony.

"The longhouse served as a living space for the whole village. There were no separate houses like there are today. A longhouse was only one huge space. There were no separate rooms and kitchens for each family. We all lived together. The custom was that every morning everyone would come together to eat manioc porridge before going out to work.

"I participated many times in the traditional dance festivals in the longhouse. Uapui was the longhouse that received the most visits from people of other tribes. They would advise the chief that on such and such a day there would be a festival, and then they would prepare and fix up the longhouse. The people who would hold festivals there were from various tribes such as the Wanano, Cubeo, and Dessano.

"My childhood was full of good times and happiness. I was very thin and all painted up in red and black. I was educated by my father and uncles, and I learned the stories of Uapui. Our family always had a pajé. My grandfather Kaaparo was a great and respected pajé, a famous pajé. Unfortunately he died too young to pass on his knowledge to his grandsons. After he died, Uapui had no pajés. I was too young to learn. Time passed, and I always wanted to become a pajé, but there was no one to teach me. So I was sad. At the time Guilherme Garcia [or "Kudui"] was a great and famous pajé who lived on Eagle Creek at a place called Hamaraliana, in the middle of the forest. It was a little settlement."

[*Author's note: In the 1970s, Mandu said he began his apprenticeship as the result of a sickness, attributed to sorcery, that nearly killed him. He had a vision in his sleep of having reached the House of the Souls of the Dead of the Hohodene phratry. They told him to return home, for his time had not yet come to enter the House. On the way back, Mandu's soul encountered the soul of the powerful pajé Guilherme Garcia, who came to cure him and tell him to return home from his journey to the houses of the dead, for it wasn't yet his time to leave the world. After Mandu recovered, his parents sent him to learn from the same master pajé whom he had met in his dream.*]

"Time passed. Then my 'brother' [sib brother/parallel cousin] Eduardo Ferreira, father of Plinio, invited me to go to Guilherme Garcia's settlement in the middle of the forest. My father and mother went with us by canoe to Guilherme's place. It took one day by canoe and one day on foot through the forest. For the pajés, there is a certain time of the year when they prepare to do their work. At the time we went, Guilherme Garcia was prepared to teach. For the pajé, it's at that time of the year called *dzuruapi riko napadamawa dzuruapi riko*, in the time of the cicada, they transform in the time of the cicada; that is, the beginning of the dry season when the *dzuruapi* [cicadas] buzz and drone. The pajés transform into dzuruapi, we transform, and they transform in order to have more knowledge. At this time each year, the pajé transforms and prepares to teach. They transform to kill, to shoot darts, and to cure sicknesses given by other pajés, to close their bodies, to close the bodies of others who want their bodies to be closed and protected—in order not to get any sickness that might be thrown by other pajés or by the spell-blowers. At that time Guilherme Garcia was prepared to teach the wisdom of the pajés. Besides me, there were thirteen students who went to study with me: Eduardo, José Maximiliano, José Garcia, Augusto,

José Cornelio, Mário, Manuel, Erminio, Joäo, Matteo, Emilio, Janeroso, Graciliano. There were so many pajés who learned at that time. Today, among those thirteen people, there are only four who are still alive: Manuel, Mário, Augusto, and Emilio (José Garcia's brother who moved to Colombia). The other nine have gone to live in another life. This has been my life."

BEGINNING OF INITIATION AND SECLUSION

"How I became a pajé. When a person wants to train a pajé, the first step that he takes is to bless the *pariká* [shaman's snuff, made from the Virola tree] for the student in order to be able to snuff it without any harm. A person can't snuff it without having it blessed by the pajé because he could go crazy. Seriously, and this is what Guilherme Garcia did for the thirteen people. Second step: The master pajé prepares the student for seven days. In that preparation, the student must fast—can't eat meat, fish, or hot porridge. He only consumes cold water, everything cold. For the pajés, there is a reason why they can't eat hot food and can't drink hot porridge, or eat food made by pregnant women or women who are menstruating. There is a very important reason.

"The third step: after all this, the pajé talks with the person to see if he wants to continue or not, because the person has to remain separated from his family for thirty days. Thirty days away from the family and thirty days fasting. During the thirty days, the master pajé is working with the student. At the end of the thirty days, the pajé blesses food for the students to eat. Before a person eats anything after the fast, he has to go and fish, and he has to eat the fish that he catches because the fish has a meaning for the pajé.[1] The kind of fish that he catches has a meaning. If the student doesn't catch any kind of fish, he has to leave because he won't become a pajé.

"After eating, the master pajé accompanies the student for five months, watching him carefully. During the five months, the person has to remain separate from his family. He can't stay where there are children, and he especially can't be around girls. After that, the master pajé does an evaluation. Depending on the pajé, he may have to repeat the teaching. If not, then the teaching is done. After that, the students have to follow the advice of the pajé.

"This was the early learning of the pajé. It was like this that I learned. I had to suffer a lot, not a little, to get to where I wanted to be.

"This was the first stage of my life as a pajé. Then we returned to Uapui. When I was 17 years old, around 1950, I continued my training with several other pajés."

[Author's note: When I first worked with Mandu in 1977, he spoke a great deal with much more detail about the kind of instruction that Kudui gave to him. It is a very important statement of how a pajé is introduced to the "Other World." What does he see there? The following is a lengthy excerpt from my 1977 interviews with Mandu.]

"I first took pariká with Kudui. I did not eat any pepper, fish, or animals. Only cold xibé [cold water and manioc cereal]. Two months like that without eating. I started to take pariká—beginning with a little, and then more and more. It transforms our minds. And I dreamt well. I could not look at women. I had to stay secluded, *itakawa*, far from women. Because the women can affect the men, I was prohibited from looking at women.

"Then I began to take medicines. First, to suck out poison, manhene, then to suck out a stone remedy for rheumatism.

"Kudui and I took pariká. Kudui took a special stone from the sky, swallowed it, vomited it up, and put it in my mouth, and then tapped it down with the handle of his rattle. Then he got a special piece of wood for extracting sickness, then the "Jaguar cumare palm thorn" [*Dzaui kumale*] for extracting or giving a very serious sickness, then *uwa* [wood] extraction, then the magic stone *miyake* extraction.

[*Mandu then refers to a series of medicines, many of them in the form of hair; sicknesses sent by spirits of the forest or fish; strong-smelling leaves used by women to make a man "go crazy over her"; and kinds of kapuliro leaves which are used by the pajé to induce vomiting. The pajé mixes the kapuliro with water and drinks it before the work of extraction.*]

"I continued to fast, not having any relations with women, and only drinking xibé. Six years had passed since I'd started. By then I could already extract those sicknesses that I'd swallowed.

"After six years, I made marriages in the sky with the Vulture spirit and had six children with her. I then married a Kawawiri-fletcher hawk spirit in the place called Pulemakwa in the sky, and we had children. And finally the Tchitchiu sparrow spirit. These marriages are supposed to last forever. The sky has many rooms, and there is a separate room for each kind of spirit bird people.

"Kudui gave me more medicines to swallow: the crest feather of Kamathawa [harpy eagle spirit], which is a small piece of wood [then a series of different kinds of pieces of wood, all with names of the deities, great spirits and shaman spirits; then a series of poison darts].

"After that, the pajé has to go to the mouth of the underworld river, in his thought, and bring the wind. The pajé makes the wind blow over the heart-souls of the people who have just died; you push their canoes with wind. Everyone gets together inside a big boat, all the families that there are from every village, all in one boat called "Wind Boat," or "Pajés' Canoe," and other names ["Yumawa," "Uwa," "Mulema" canoes]—all of wood. Then comes the wind, and it pushes the boats.

"You have to ask Dzuliferi, who gives the pajé tobacco. Then you smoke it and wave it above the heads of the souls of the deceased.

[Dzuliferi is the deity whom the pajés call the "Spirit of Power," the primal shaman, the "owner of the pajés' pariká and sacred tobacco."]

And you say, "You have to leave your families behind, their heart-souls will remain happy." After that, the pajé says, "How are you, my family? Now the wind comes." And he blows with tobacco. People become more beautiful, and the pajé advises the family of this world that This World will continue to be well. And that's the end of that story."

EXPERIENCE OF KUWAI

"We had taken pariká, and I asked Kudui, "What does the body of Kuwai look like? Does it look like people?" He answered, "Do you want to see it? It's dangerous. You must die. You must take much pariká." So I did, and four of us fell to the ground [in a trance] after he had given us the songs. The pajé looked well into the sky. He found the place of the sky-door "where no one can die." Kudui showed it to me: the sky was closed, and he opened the door by spreading his arms. Then down came *Kuwai hliepule* [Kuwai's umbilical cord] with a kind of hook at the end. I sat on it, embracing it with my arms, and it took me up into the sky. Kuwai himself pulled me up. When I got there, I asked him, "Are you Kuwai? Are you really Kuwai? I've come to look for the soul of my friend." Kuwai then said, "No, I can't leave you with that. He doesn't have any payment. He has to pay." This is called *dawai*, payment for the sick person's soul. When Kuwai accepts the payment, he says, "I am the one called Kuwai. My body is all sickness. This is the sickness your friend has." And he plucks out some fur from his body and gives it to the pajé saying, "Now with this, you can cure your friend."

"But first, the pajé has to show that he can cure the sickness in the Other World. Kuwai goes out of the room and then enters back in as Dzuliferi's shadow-soul and lies down in front of the pajé. "Oooh, I am so sick," he says. "What do you have?" the pajé asks. "Manhene," he says. But it is really Kuwai who is lying there. He's just showing the pajé how to heal the sickness. The pajé must cure him by sucking out the sickness and by throwing water over Dzuliferi's shadow-soul. At the end, Dzuliferi sits up and says, "Ah, now I am better; if you had not come, I would have died." Kuwai then comes back in the room and says, "Now you are already taking out the sickness from the body of your friend. He will not die. He will get better."

"The pajé then returns to earth. He lifts up his cigar and begins to wave it, singing, and he slowly descends. When he gets to one world, he falls down and gets up again and sings—for each place of the Other World, he does the same. Until he comes out here on the earth. Every time he lands in one world, he makes lightning and thunder, announcing his return, like shotgun fire. People can hear the pajé returning to earth; his soul makes a noise like an airplane or motorboat. When he returns, he tells his friend that he has seen Dzuliferi and that he will get better. But the sick person can't eat animals or fish for so many months."

PAJÉ IN TRAINING

"The second stage of becoming a pajé: I lived in Uapui for two years after the end of the first stage. I already knew what pariká is. For six months, I studied the general knowledge of malikai [shamans' power] and general knowledge about types of sicknesses. Guilherme Garcia gave me knowledge of malikai and of sicknesses. For two years I could already start to attend patients. But I wasn't a pajé yet, neither to bless pepper nor to extract sickness. And I couldn't do water-throwing[2] because Guilherme Garcia didn't give me *Maliri-dakipe* [the body of the pajé, his rattle]. He didn't give me real knowledge. I asked my father and mother to take me to learn more. But Guilherme Garcia didn't want to teach me anymore. So I decided to ask my father to take me to learn more from another pajé.

"In 1938 my parents and I, together with my brothers, left Uapui paddling a canoe slowly to the place called Araripira, on the Aiary River, where we stopped to make pariká. There was no pariká where we were going, so we had to take prepared pariká with us. We stayed one week in Araripira making pariká to take to Venezuela. Then we continued on by canoe and on foot. We left there by river and got to a certain place where we had to get out of the canoe and drag it until we got to the place where we were going. On the way, the road from Maroa to the city, there were no cars at that time. So we had to go on walking, dragging the canoe to get there. It was a lot of sacrifice. There was no one we knew from whom we could borrow a canoe, so we had to take our own canoe to get to the other river. We got to the river, descended it, got to another river, and walked again on land.

FINAL INSTRUCTION AND SEARCH FOR POWER

"Since it had been a long time since we'd heard any news about the pajé we were looking for, we went around asking where he lived. This pajé was almost a kin of ours from the Dzauinai tribe. When we got to where he lived, the information we received was that he was not living there anymore. So we had to go in search of him again. If you don't search, you won't find what you want. When I go to look for something, I search until I find it. And so we found the place—called Uapassussu [Guapa Sucia, now an abandoned place, according to Baniva-Kuripako shamans] in Venezuela.

"This place is very special for me.[3] It affected my life deeply and even today it is a very special place for me. A place I'll never forget, it stays in my heart and in my memory. As soon as we got there, we found the pajé, whose name was Alexandre, a Dzauinai, who was very famous at that time in Venezuela.

"I went there in search of the knowledge of the pajé. He was very respected at that time. There my father spoke to the pajé and had to pay him, because one cannot fail to pay. He paid him. He asked me, "Do you really want to be a pajé? Can you really go without a woman for ten years?" I answered, "I can do it. I want to." "OK." But before starting, Alexandre let me relax for one month. During that month I didn't stay in one place. I went with my family traveling on the Guaviare River in Venezuela. We traveled very far by canoe. I didn't know why I was traveling with the whole family.

"Then we went to a place called Uwa. That was where I went to look for the handle of my rattle. The handle is very special, and the place was very beautiful. The handle is prepared at this place. It is not the pajé who makes it. But it's only there you can get the handle of the rattle. Alexandre asked me to go and find it. There it's a huge field and I went out to find it. I went out looking for it, and I found it. It's the same handle that I have today. It's very sacred. I got it there. Alexandre looked at it and said, "Yes, my son, one day you'll be a great pajé because you got this and you weren't supposed to. Now that you got it, it's yours." The handle of my rattle.

"Then we went back to Uapassussu, Alexandre's settlement. This was more or less in 1949 when I began to learn with

2. Mandu at the height of his powers, a "true pajé," in 1977.

Alexandre Jawinaapi, a Kumadene and Dzauinai [maternal and paternal phratric identities]. Alexandre began to teach seven students: Mário [Mandu's brother], myself, José Marcellino [his uncle], Maximiliano [brother-in-law Wanano from the Uaupés], Rafael [a Piaroa shaman], Emilio, and the pajé's grandson.

"When Alexandre was beginning to teach, a specialist pajé from the Piaroa named Fabricio was with him. They began to teach the advanced stuff of the pajés. Alexandre and Fabricio gave information on the origin of each kind of sickness. The pajé understands this. There are two main kinds of sicknesses that the pajé understands: *dzauinaipwa* and *yoopinai*.[4] When the pajé speaks of the dzauinaipwa, "Jaguar People's Way," he studies the *walama* [spirit darts], *haikuita* [spirit wood], *hipada* [spirit stones], types of yoopinai [spirits of the world, in the water, in the forest, in the animals — *hekwapi rikuperi, uni rikuperi, awakada rikuperi, yoopinai iarudatheta]*. These two types of sickness affect us Indians more, but for the white people, these two kinds of sicknesses don't have a cure. There I learned how to throw sicknesses onto enemies, how to kill enemies, and how to defend myself against enemies.

"The enemies of a pajé are other pajés. A pajé always has to be watchful when he does his work. If not, another pajé can kill him. And the specialist on that was Fabricio. That kind of knowledge a pajé only uses when it is necessary. It's not for just anyone. Fabricio was a Piaroa. I learned it well from him. The Piaroa pajé snuffs pariká at night. Why? Because at night it's easier for him to get the people that he wants to kill. When a person asks him to kill another person, it is very advanced learning. It is extremely tiring. You have to snuff pariká from six to seven hours straight and without eating.

"For the pajé, there's a rule, that within eight days, he has to pass on all of the information that he has to the students.

It can't be longer than eight days because when you get to the ninth day, you have to rest. If the pajé doesn't show everything in eight days, then he has to stop and begin all over again. In this case, Alexandre and Fabricio were able to teach everything in eight days. On the ninth day, they rested. On the following day, he took the students to fish. And, depending on the fish caught, the pajé gives it a meaning. If the student gets a swordfish (*duirita*), it represents a haikuita [sliver of wood] for the pajé. It's a dart. If he catches that, the student will be an excellent curer of haikuita. All the students got fish. Seven students got different kinds of fish. I caught four different kinds of fish: keredane, dzauira, duirita, carha (trairinha, acará, swordfish, piaba). The fish represent the knowledge and power of the pajé. With these four kinds, Alexandre told me I would become an excellent healer because they represent the sicknesses manhene, walama, hipada, haikuita, and fiukali.

"He said, "You're going to have a lot of work. These fish that you caught represent a lot of work that you will have. You will save many lives throughout your life as a pajé." And this is what has happened until today.

"Then he said, "With these fish, the two pajé masters will bless pepperpot [*kalidzamai*] for the students." After ten days, all of this time fasting. After that, the two teachers, the students, and the families commemorated: like graduating, they have a festival with caxiri. Each student has now become a pajé. Then he gives them advice. Alexandre and Fabricio recommended that each pajé had to observe restrictions for ten years. All the restrictions that I've already mentioned. You have to stay separate from others."

[Author's note: At the end of his training, Mandu says that he saw Alexandre in a dream, "inside a beautiful house. For there, the Other World

3. Mandu and José Garcia. The tobacco attracts the lost soul of the sick during a cure.

is all beautiful, and all people are shining white in color. He said, 'Now you are a true pajé. Now you know and you must live well with people.'"]

CHANGE AND SADNESS IN UAPUI

"In 1950 I returned with my family to Uapui. I was already a pajé. I attended my family and kin. I'd had four years of studying to become a pajé. After all of that, I stayed in Uapui. I lived with my parents for five more years. Always studying and practicing my knowledge. There was only one more year left to complete the ten years of restrictions when a tragedy occurred in my life. My mother, Nazaria, died in 1949. The next year, there was no one to make food for my father, me, my brothers, five men in all. So I married Flora. I'd already learned everything, so I married her. She was a Walipere-dakenai.

"After we'd married, I made several trips to Colombia to work in rubber-gathering. On one of those trips to work rubber, I remember very well, there was a place called Pakuwa. After my mother died, my family and I went there; I thought I would live there for the rest of my life. But Flora didn't want to live there. She said I had to go back and take care of the land where I was born. At the time I agreed with her, and we decided to return to Uapui. If we hadn't done that, I'd still be in Pakuwa in Colombia.

"I lived in Uapui, but I thought of going back to Venezuela. We'd already had three children. I didn't stay in one place; I'd always be traveling and then coming back to Uapui. Then I remembered I'm going to go back and visit Alexandre in Venezuela. It was then that I got news that Alexandre had died and Fabricio also had died. So I went back to stay in Uapui. Even so, I went to visit Alexandre's children and his widow. In 1968 I went for the last time. Then I lost contact with the children of Alexandre. I don't know where they're living. On the last trip Ercilia was very little."

"In 1970, we returned to Uapui and saw that my house was very old. My uncle José Cornelio, who was already very old, decided he couldn't remain as chief of the community of Uapui. So José gave me the post in 1972.

[Author's note: The old chief/pajé José and jaguar shaman of Uapui was born at Cará Stream on the lower Aiary in the late nineteenth century, first son to Marcellino Euzebio and Nazaria, founders of the village of Uapui in the early 1920s. His family moved to Uapui after his mother had

4. "Old pajé José" Cornélio (1890s–1978).

been killed by a jaguar when José was small. He married twice—the first time to a Wanana with whom he had two daughters, and the second to a Wanana who already had two Dessano sons. In the late 1920s he assisted the First Commission on the Demarcation of the Border Limits of Brazil. He worked many years at extracting balata and seringa latex at places in Venezuela and Colombia. In the 1950s he helped the Salesian missionaries to construct the first Catholic mission station on the lower Içana in an effort to stop the advance of Protestant evangelicalism. Later the evangelical pastors verbally abused him. As chief of Uapui until 1972, he prohibited the evangelicals from coming into Uapui. He was considered a great pajé,

having studied with his father, his grandfather, and other jaguar shamans.
He boasted of having taken the powerful niopo (ebena) with the Wanhiwa
pajé of the Guaviare. He was a well-known chanter whose services were
always being sought, whether to cure sicknesses or to officiate at initiation
rituals. He died in 1978 after he had taped a good part of his knowledge.
He left his most important knowledge, the kalidzamai chants, to Mandu
and to his adopted son, José Felipe, now a practicing pajé.]

"In 1973, the itinerant Salesian missionaries arrived in the
village: Father Roberto, an Italian; Sister Teresa, from Ceará
(Brazil), and Sister Inés, a Baré from the Rio Negro. These were
the first educators to help the people of Uapui. In Uapui there
were seven families. Then the people of Ucuqui upriver came
to live here—José Garcia and his family and other people. In
1974, the first little one-room school was built at Uapui. From
1972 to 1984 I was the chief of the community. In 1977, an airstrip was built behind the village, and I became the guide for
the military, who were opening up airstrips in the region: São
Joaquim, on the upper Içana, and at the mouth of the Querary
River, border of Colombia. Three airstrips were built; today two
are still open. Uapui is no longer open. I was employed as the
field guard to take care of the airstrip for thirteen years.

"Then in 1977 there was a great sadness in my life, for my
father died. And in 1978 I lost my uncle, José Cornelio, who
was a great pajé."

[Author's note: See my 1998 book, part 2, for the narrative of his father's
death, which occurred while I lived in the village.]

"By 1985, I was already tired of being chief of the community,
so I passed it on to my brother Mário, but he didn't stay very
long, just a few years. In 1989 my family and I went to visit friends
in Colombia and Venezuela. We went to Uacapana, where our

friends lived. It was soon after that that my son Jacinto died, a young man of 22 years of age. A lot has happened in my life, and there's been a lot of sadness.

"In 1990 I got very sick and went to São Gabriel da Cachoeira for treatment.[5] Six years later, I bought a piece of land in São Gabriel and made a house. Today I have houses in São Gabriel and Uapui. In 2001 I got so sick that I had to be taken to Manaus for treatment in the hospital. In 2004–2005 I had two surgeries, and with the help of the captain, a doctor, I recovered my health. So from 2000 to 2005 I wasn't able to do my work as pajé because I was very sick for a long time.[6] I was very weak in my spirit and my body. In 2006 I recovered and went back to attending patients. I even worked in the military hospital, although they didn't pay me anything for my work. I did my work as a pajé and chanter. A pajé can't remain without performing his rituals. He becomes sick if he doesn't work. His body wants it, needs it.

A RETURN TO HAPPINESS

Today I like doing my work, and I will only stop when I die. When I'm really sick, I can't work. Today I am healthy and attending patients, and I am very much sought out by patients. In São Gabriel I treat five to eight people per day. So, to conclude, that has been my life.

At the close of her translation, Ercilia added the following: "Today Manuel is eighty-nine years old. He has worked as a pajé for sixty-four years, working and suffering a lot to support his family. And today he is considered by the indigenous people to be a true and much respected pajé. He is proud of that. Despite his age, he still works."

"So that's his life, but there are other things to mention," Ercilia

5. Mandu and his wife, Flora, at their home in São Gabriel in 2000.

continues. "Dona Flora, his wife, is still alive. They had eleven children: four died, seven have lived. All of them have families. Only I am single, and that's because I decided to take care of my parents.[7] By 2009 they had thirty-three grandchildren and sixteen great-grandchildren. All of them dearly love their grandparents. That is all. I am proud to be his daughter, a Hohodene warrior and descendant of Keruaminali, our clan ancestor who was a great warrior. That's all."

2

Mandu's Apprenticeship and a Jaguar Shaman's Powers of World-Making

As part of my interpretation of Mandu's life story, I will integrate his narrative with an ethnography of the process of becoming a pajé, what the community expects of pajés, and what special powers and knowledge they acquire during their careers.

To understand shamanic knowledge and power (*malikai*) requires tools of interpretation, since we do not claim to fully understand their experience. We seek to understand what is involved in the pajés' construction of their new "shamanic" selves (*newiki*, person/self) through the changes made to the following aspects: sensory perceptions (sight, sound, smell); the heart-soul (*ikaale*) located at the center of the body, the source of all emotions, drives, and desires; the body (*idakipe*), especially the bones, viscera, fluids (blood, saliva, semen), body orifices (with their modulations: open/closed, permeability, porosity of the skin); the breath (*lipia*) and its relation to "souls"; and the shaman's external "soul" and "body," which are their sacred rattles (*kutheruda*), sacred stones, and their body coverings, called "mantles" or *maka* (which pajés translate as "shirts" or *kamitsa*, from the Portuguese word *camisa*). The last named are like jaguar pelts, by means of which the pajés manifest their transformations (*napadamawa*) into the jaguar shaman spirits (*Dzaui malinyai*). Each "mantle" is a distinct "shirt" the pajés acquire, empowering and protecting them in This World and the Other World.

SHAMANIC WORLD-MAKING

All of these elements undergo transformations during a pajé's decade of training. Buttressing these transformations are conceptual and normative frameworks within which sensual, bodily, and spiritual transformations and states are understood and transmitted. For us to understand this conceptual and normative framework, the notion of shaman as a "maker of worlds" is an important concept. This is a notion developed by British anthropologist Joanna Overing (1990), adapted from the philosopher Nelson A. Goodman, which presupposes "the reality of a multiplicity of knowledges" or "versions of the world'" (603) in any given society. This is distinct from the sense of "world-making" that David Carrasco (1990) has used for Mesoamerican cosmologies, which is more closely akin to Baniwa sacred stories of the first world (cited in chapter 4). The sense of "making the world" being used here is that of elaborating on a worldview, through the careful crafting of the "Other" world with the knowledge and powers the pajé has at his or her disposal, derived from training and years of experience. This world-making is adapted to the quandaries and dilemmas that Baniwa face today, especially given the increase in new contacts the Baniwa of the Aiary have had in recent years.

By seeing the pajés' journey as one of "making worlds," this permits us to understand the importance of performative acts such as "opening" the portal between This World and the Other World, which takes place immediately after he has inhaled the pariká. For then, the pajés begin to experience the "new Other World" in the sky, when the Other World "begins to show itself."

6. Jaguar shamans on their journey in the Other World.

It is a highly subjective experience that one can only know, Mandu stated, by feeling the emotion of "being there" in the Other World, which is above our own, the ancient or Before World, referring to the long ago past (*oopi*). The great spirits and deities of that time "never died," narrators say, and are now in the Other World, eternal (*midzaka*).

Apprentices are taught to interpret the shapes and forms of the clouds, which are, in their way of seeing, places of spirits or deities of the "Other World." From what they have learned, they give meaning to cloud shapes, their expansion and contraction, appearance and disappearance. This is one of their most important skills, for through it, they analyze the appropriate treatment to make and whether a treatment is even possible.

Through their skillful weaving of images appearing in the Other

World, the pajés are actually "making the Other World" come into being for themselves and for those who are observing. Hence their vision is constantly fixed on the sky during their cures, for it is said that their souls are "no longer in This World, but journeying in the Other."

What do they see as they analyze their visions? How do their discussions among themselves *as they are seeing* lead to a conclusion about the whereabouts of the patient's soul and which spirit took it away? Equally useful in Overing's work (in Santos-Granero and Mentore 2006) is the sense of ethnopoetics in shamanic chants, for the sensory images of the chants reveal the manifold ways in which the shaman's body, perceptions, and emotions are synaesthetically intertwined in knowing and making the Other World.

As their heart-souls journey to regain a "lost heart-soul," the words of their songs dramatize what the Other World is like, especially for those who came to be cured. The pajés represent the Other World through their actions and songs, which form a narrative of their encounters with the spirits, places, and deities that "come to them." Every journey the pajé makes brings to light a new aspect of the Other World.

A pajé's efficacy is judged by the community and other pajés on the basis of how well, and coherently, he represents the Other World to those who are observing and being cured. A complete cure proceeds by stages: after a person has requested a cure, the pajé takes pariká and, in his dreams (*itaponika*) prior to the appointed day of the cure, the "heart-soul" of the patient is located or the source of the sickness is determined. This is followed by the curing session, which is scheduled for noon the next day, when two or more pajés perform a song-journey as they slowly walk in file around the circular terrain where the cure is taking place. After singing, they proceed to extract the sickness and pain by sucking it out of the patient's body. The shaman then vomits out the sickness and casts it away where it will no longer harm the sick. This may take several hours, until the pajés have determined there is no more sickness to be extracted, whereupon their souls "return" to "This World," as the sun is setting. On the following day, the pajés chant prayers or orations, often in a barely audible voice, for several hours, over a remedy (*tápe*, herbal mixture, bottle of rubbing alcohol). These *iwapakethi* chants complement the phase of extraction by utilizing the power of verbal actions and breath to cool the fever, "sweeten the body," and protect the patient from any further spirit attack in the immediate future, preventing the sickness from returning after it has been expelled, blowing protective smoke over critical points (crown of the head, hands held together, feet joined together) on the patient's body, and renewing the heart-soul's strength. Finally, (4) the pajés give plant medicines or other materia medica that have been "blessed" with water to the patient with recommendations for post-cure health care. All of these procedures together form a total process, a thorough elimination of extraneous objects from the patient's body, reinforcing protection of the same, giving strength to the heart-soul, and offering a convincing performance of the pajé's knowledge and powers to heal.

In 2000, I underwent a treatment by three pajés for a fractured right femur. The head pajé was José Garcia, who informed me before the treatment began that he had dreamt and discovered that *umawalinai* spirits of the waters were provoking my pain because, shortly after my birth, my parents had not had the correct postbirth orations (*kalidzamai*) performed by an elder to "push away the gaze" of these spirits. This left me vulnerable when I was given my first bath. As a bearer of a so-called birth defect in my joints (Morquio's disease, a degenerative condition in the weight-bearing joints), I could relate my condition to his diagnosis; the fractured femur was a consequence of not observing a necessary

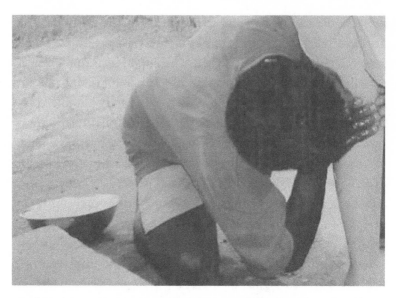

7. José Garcia extracting the umawalinai sickness and pain from the author's leg.

prophylaxis. The concept of "hereditary disease" does not exist in Baniwa medicinal theory. Thus the explanation interrelated a cognitive understanding with my personal situation and with the social unit responsible for the failed prophylactic practice.

The rite of extraction took place in the early afternoon of the designated day. José, Mário (Mandu's brother), and José Felipe (Mandu's son-in-law) worked together for more than two hours, taking turns at sucking out the material form of the sickness (pieces of wood characteristic of the umawalinai), vomiting them out at a short distance from where I sat, examining them, and throwing them far away. One comment that José made as he continued the extraction was that there was too much metal (prosthesis) in my leg, making it difficult to extract the material form of the sickness and pain.

The treatment continued the following day inside the infirmary of the Salesian mission center in São Gabriel. The three pajés performed healing orations (*iwapakaithe*) both on the ailing leg and on a bottle of rubbing alcohol. The words of their orations were blown with tobacco smoke on both. At the conclusion of this operation, I was given the plastic bottle of rubbing alcohol and instructed that it could be refilled any number of times afterwards, for the power of their orations had been absorbed into it.

I had received a "complete treatment," the three pajés said, demonstrating their satisfaction with a job well done. The payment for their services was quite high, commensurate with their certainty that the whole process had been done "completely," not halfway. I was both impressed and honored by the treatment. Each moment of the process involved the construction of a relation between the pajés, myself, and the Other World: first, the localization in time and space of the source of the problem, involving a distant moment in which a proper relation with the spirit world had not been respected. The result of that failure was vulnerability to the penetrating "gaze" of sickness-giving spirits. From that distant time on, I had suffered from the painful pieces of the spirits' palmwood stuck in my joints. The pajés reassured me I would not "die" from that sickness, but it was fortunate that they could treat it.

The extraction itself involved the pajés' pariká-induced mixing of the Other World with This World in which they transform into jaguar shaman spirits and suck out the pieces of wood. Once relieved of the visible forms of pain-giving elements, and with my heart-soul strengthened by the tobacco smoke blown over my entire body, the next step was to ensure that those spirits or any others that typically invade the bones would be prevented from further penetrating my legs. The orations named, one by one, all of the potential sickness-giving spirits and annulled their harm, cut their gaze, and threw them away to the Underworld, where all the remains of sicknesses are cast. More than that, the cure would last indefinitely; as long as the plastic bottle of rubbing alcohol remained in my possession, I should apply the empowered liquid to maintain a shield against any further harmful intrusions by the spirits of the waters.

The Other World is the "Before-world" (*oopidali*), which is of the ancient past but eternally alive, separate from This World but which the pajés enter once they find and open the door. In this living drama of the religious imagination that takes place before the community's eyes during a healing rite, pajés say that the pariká "raises a stairway" to the Other World, permitting their souls to enter and move about. Though their bodies are visibly moving about in the healing circle on the earth, they are constantly looking upward, examining signs in the sky, and singing with their heart-souls, as they seek the spirits and deities of the Other World who can help them in their search. The cures are performed only at noon, facilitating the pajé's passage from This World to the Other World.

Each shamanic soul-voyage during the act of healing can be considered a process of "world-making." The greatest power and knowledge that the jaguar shamans have, moreover, is that of "re-making the whole world and everything in it—water, stones, even people" (citing Mandu) in their "thought-song." The jaguar shamans, I was told, are supposed to reach a point in the cosmos where they are in a space "like a room next to" the universe creator, Nhiãperikuli, and can "open" or reveal the "ancient, hidden world of happiness and well-being," that is to say, sit in the place of the deity and produce a vision of the world as Nhiãperikuli did in the beginning, bringing that vision into This World. Often they provide a commentary on what the way to reach that world is like, a vision of a "world-without-sickness." When they reach this stage, the jaguar shamans are considered to be savants, wise men or women (*kanhenkedali, sábios*). Mandu is considered by many Baniwa to be one of these outstanding savants.

It is not clear under what circumstances the pajés actually do this, although it seems plausible that only the highest ranked of the jaguar shamans have this power and only in highly specific circumstances, as in the event of an imminent catastrophe (epidemics, a terrible famine, environmental disaster, or extreme reduction of population). The jaguar shamans' power to re-create "in their thought" the whole world and everything in it signifies that there is no distinction between "vertical" and "horizontal" shamans, as has been suggested for Tukanoan-speaking peoples (Hugh-Jones 1996).

The Baniwa jaguar shamans' power, nevertheless, differs from the related but distinct powers of the priestly chanters to re-create This World through the latter's "thought-journeys" chanted at the final stage of initiation rites. The priestly chanters exercise the "naming power" consisting of chanting the sacred names of all living beings in the world and "blessing" them to neutralize the harm they potentially do to the new adults.

"CALLING" AND INSTRUCTION

How does a pajé's apprenticeship prepare him or her for creating versions of the world to deal with contemporary problems such as sorcery? Why would a person wish to make a commitment to becoming a full-fledged pajé? What are some experiences that would impel a person to follow this path?

In Mandu's case, the experience of suffering was indeed what most propelled him to initiate his career as a pajé or, as is sometimes said, to become an "owner of shaman's knowledge and power" (*malikai iminali*). When he was twelve years old, Mandu suffered a very grave sickness. He said that he had been poisoned by sorcery, and he was practically making the final journey to the houses of the dead. In his dream, when he got there, the souls of the dead told him to go back home because "his time had not yet come." On his way back, Mandu recalls, the soul of the pajé

Kudui (Guilherme Garcia) suddenly appeared and said, "I have been looking for you." When he told his parents of his dream, it was a sure sign to them that their son should start training. More than anything else, he and his parents interpreted this as a sign that he had to learn how to protect himself from the attacks of sorcerers if he wanted to live long. Hence his decision to take up Edu's invitation to initiate their studies with the jaguar shaman Kudui.

Both Mandu's "calling" to "walk in the knowledge of the pajé" and the completion of his training were marked by dream experiences. At the end of the period of advanced training, as Mandu states, his master shaman, Alexandre Jawinaapi, who was reputed to be "even more powerful than Kudui," appeared to Mandu in a dream "in a beautiful house, a splendid place of beauty in the Other World."

THE FIRST STAGE

There is a specific time of the annual cycle that is propitious for the master shamans to transmit their knowledge. After the rains in June and July, when the trees and shrubs are in full bloom, the forest seems to change its aspect. This is the time when, long ago, it is said, the very first people, the "universe people" (*hekwapinai*), asked the stones, trees, and all beings how they wanted to remain in the world. Each replied, and when it came time for the universe people to respond, they said they would remain as cicadas (*dzurunai*). Thus the jaguar shamans today transform into cicadas, Mandu said, and drink the knowledge of the pariká flowers. So the teaching of an apprentice begins in the early dry season, when the cicadas regenerate their bodies, shedding the old ones and returning renewed.

Mandu, a young man in his late teens or early twenties, went with his sib-brother Eduardo Ferreira to request that the most powerful jaguar shaman of the entire region, the Hohodene Guilherme Garcia, Kudui, teach them the basics of becoming a pajé. Twelve other young men from various other communities of the Aiary went with them. At that time, the shamans' practice was still very much alive and thriving; belief in their powers was quite strong. Nearly every village of the Aiary had its own pajé(s), a situation very different from today when there are now only three or four left for the entire population and only one or two teachers for the new generation.

The initial period of learning lasts for thirty days with a short rest interval between the first and second halves. During the thirty days, the apprentices will take pariká, as the master-shaman teaches them general knowledge of the pajés, giving them some of the lightest powers and knowledge. The apprentices remain in the house of the master, whose wife prepares their food. They are otherwise isolated from any outside contact.

The pariká first has to be "blessed" through protective chants by the master shaman, for without that blessing, the apprentices could go mad, as the story of the first pajés recounts. As elsewhere in South American shamanism, the Baniwa tell stories of humans who used "unblessed" pariká and transformed into killer jaguars who roamed the forest at night, attacking and devouring people. They were eventually trapped, killed, and thrown into the river, but at each village where their bodies passed, the Baniwa took part of their pelts and brains and became jaguar shamans.

When pariká was first obtained in the first world, the tapir stole it from its rightful owner, Nhiãperikuli, the creator deity. The tapir began passing around pariká before it had been "blessed." Its potential to transform a person into a dangerous predator had not yet been neutralized, and so the tapir became a voracious jaguar. He was quickly subdued, however, and ownership of the powerful substance was restored to Nhiãperikuli. There is thus a deep link

8. Pot of reddish-brown pariká in preparation. (Photo by Ercilia de Lima da Silva.)

between pariká and jaguar transformation which demands further explanation. On the one hand, unblessed pariká can transform an animal or human into a violent killer; "blessed" pariká, however, under proper ownership of true jaguar shamans, transforms the destructive power into soul hunters.

Pariká (*dzato*) is considered by the shamans to be the "blood of Kuwai," the great spirit "owner of sickness," and the ancestor of all humanity. Pariká is made from the inner bark of four distinct types of Virola trees that the Hohodene know. The inner bark of the tree is cut into fine strips and soaked in water, producing a reddish liquid which is then boiled and dried until all the liquid has turned into a hard mass of reddish-brown resin. This resin is chipped away and broken into a fine powder that does indeed evoke an image of ancient blood, the blood of the Sickness Owner. How "Kuwai's blood" entered the Virola tree from which pariká is made is not known, however.

Inhaling this "blood" (a form of hematophagy) has the effect of producing a drunken state as the pajé manifests a trance, seen as the "death" of the pajé in This World, releasing the pajé's heart-soul to begin traveling in the Other World.[1] Pajés complement this internalization of the great spirit's "blood" by streaking their faces, arms, and chests with bright red *kerawidzu* (*Bixa orellana*), the vegetal dye that gives them the quality of being "live jaguars."

Another story, which is less commonly told to explain how pajés obtained pariká, states that it is the menstrual blood of Dzuliferi's daughter: Nhiãperikuli and Dzuliferi lived in the same house. Dzuliferi, the first jaguar shaman, had a daughter who one day was menstruating as she slept. Nhiãperikuli took some of her menstrual blood and "began to use it like pariká." He began singing like the pajés do after they inhale pariká. Dzuliferi found him doing this and reprimanded Nhiãperikuli severely, for he had used his daughter's menstrual blood in a totally inappropriate way.

Note that the two explanations for where pariká came from actually are saying complementary things about it: that it is "blood" which, when inhaled, transforms vision. For the pajés, it is the means for "opening the door to the Other World," going back in time to the primordial and eternal world, experiencing "death" and transformation, to meet with Kuwai. The daughter of the primordial shaman, Dzuliferi, menstruated, and her blood looked like pariká, but it was inappropriate for a pajé to use it because menstrual blood has a totally distinct cycle from that subsequent to sniffing the true pariká. The menstrual cycle is a short, periodic expulsion of blood; pariká is the inhaling of a "blood" of a primordial demiurge that opens up the "long cycle" between the Before, Other world of the ancestors, and the present generation of "descendants" (*walimanai*). Nhiãperikuli mistook the short-cycle menstrual blood for the long-cycle blood of the pajé.

The prohibition against a pajé's relations with menstruating women most certainly has to do with the idea of not mixing their bloods. Mixing implies the proximity of the two bloods—both of which have dangerous power (*kanupa*) to open or make holes in a person's body or vision; mixing together those who are in "open" states produces a wasting-away sickness (*purakali*) that could lead to death.

The pajé José velho stated that pariká is Kuwai's blood and his "dangerous openness" (*likanupa* Kuwai), which relates it directly to menstrual blood, for a girl's first menstruation is likewise called *kanupakan*. (See C. Hugh-Jones 1989: 130–31, for further discussion of this theme among the Barasana, Tukanoan-speaking people, to which we will return in chapters 6–8). In saying that the pariká is Kuwai's blood, this does not mean it is analogous to Kuwai's blood. The pariká that is derived from the inner bark of the tree is "sanctified," made powerful by the chants of the pajé before it is used.

At the end of the first two weeks, the inhaling of pariká is suspended for a few days while the master shaman observes how the apprentice is reacting to constant use. If the apprentice says he wishes to continue, then they go for another two weeks of inhaling pariká every day, learning more about the forms of sickness and medicines. Having completed the initial thirty-day period, the master "blesses" (i.e., intones the sacred chants over) pepper-pot and salt, making safe the apprentices' first food, which consists of fish that the apprentices have been told to catch. Then the restrictions on food—but not against celibacy—are lifted.

This diet, along with the consumption of the psychoactive pariká every day, alters their perceptions of the world, which are then shaped by the master shaman who, in a word, transmits a specialist's worldview to the apprentices: teaching them the names and places in the Other World, the significance of the sacred stories, the meanings of their instruments, kinds of sicknesses, and the powers associated with the stories in such a way that apprentices internalize the general knowledge and power of healing.

Until the end of their learning, the apprentices cannot eat any "hot" foods (everything must be uncooked), or meat or fish, and cannot have any contact with menstruating women or eat food prepared by them. All of these restrictions are for the purpose of dissociating the apprentice from normal social and sexual relations and purifying the apprentice from any potentially harmful elements. Mandu emphasized that "there is a very important reason why the apprentices consume only "cold foods" (manioc cereal, or mashed forest fruits mixed with cold water), and I believe that this has to do with their association with the "owner of sickness," Kuwai, who imposes on all initiates and pajé apprentices a diet of forest fruits and uncooked food.

Kuwai is a great spirit who is averse to all fire; he is of the waters, the forest, and the sky. The sacred flutes and instruments are his re-created body, and when not being played, they are wrapped and hidden at the bottom of certain creeks. The Virola trees from which the pajés extract the pariká grow in flooded lands, at the headwaters of small streams.

There is another rule imposed at this point to determine who can continue with the instruction. The master instructs the apprentices to catch fish for the meal consumed at the end of the first phase of instruction. If an apprentice fails to catch a fish, he has failed to demonstrate his "competence" to become a pajé and is advised that he must leave the school. He is not ready to receive the power to cure sicknesses, though he may try again at a later point. It is said that the primal shaman, Dzuliferi, makes this determination.

The type of fish the apprentice catches is directly associated with the type of sickness he will be good at curing later on; for example, the needle-nosed swordfish is linked to the sickness-giving spirit darts called *walama*. When I asked about the association between catching fish and continuing an apprenticeship, I was told that catching fish demonstrated the apprentice's competence. But we find some helpful leads to understanding why this is so in the sacred narratives, in which the fish are the affines of Nhiãperikuli. Although he is married to the daughter of the great "Father of the Fish," the Anaconda Umawali, whose real self is "Grandfather Piranha fish" (the latter wears an Anaconda "shirt" or *maka*, outer skin), the woman's father constantly is setting traps for his son-in-law, who nevertheless always outwits him.

In one of these stories, the creator introduces pepper as the "fiery arrow that burns," taking the life out of the fish that are caught so that people can eat them without harm; this is the basis of the kalidzamai chants. Thus, by catching fish, the pajé apprentice shows his competence to outwit the Father of the Fish, one of their principal enemies from the aquatic world. This hunter's image is completed by the priestly chanter's knowledge that employs the pepper as a fiery arrow that takes away the life of the fish, preventing harm to anyone who has undergone food restrictions and is now ready to be reintegrated back to social life. The association between fire and sociality is a very strong theme in the stories.

The pajé acquires a great deal of knowledge (*ianheke*) during the first period of his training, at the same time that his body becomes a repository of powers to cure, or "medicines" (*tápe*). Tápe are treatments to extract various kinds of sickness. His body is filled in several stages, accompanying the pajé's demonstration of competence, inner strength, and discipline.

The first hurdle, after receiving the pariká and becoming accustomed to it, is to swallow the four main types of sickness remedies — a small stone, a piece of wood, and two kinds of darts. The master shaman grabs these medicines from the sky and puts them, in their material forms, in the apprentice's mouth to eat. These will become lodged in the apprentice's heart-soul and be fed by the pariká, the blood of Kuwai, multiplying in the pajé's body. This act of ingesting the four principal medicines and sicknesses can only be completed if the apprentice has the courage to swallow their material forms; not all apprentices succeed in doing this the first time, and it may take time before that happens.

The new pajé has acquired the knowledge and power to heal certain sicknesses: the four types of yoopinai spirits (of the waters, of the forest, of the animal souls, and of this world) and the four types of dzauinaipwa or "jaguar peoples' way" sicknesses. He can never use that power, of course, to deceive or trick his clients.

The standard of truth imposed on the pajé is very high. Indeed, the distinction between "true" and "false" is a core feature of many aspects in Baniwa cosmology and knowledge: knowing what features distinguish a "true" plant remedy from its "false" look-alike is crucial. In the groups of boulders at the sacred site of Hipana, where the great spirit Kuwai was born, there is a "true Kuwai" boulder and a "false" one, recalling the sacred narrative of how Nhiãperikuli tricked the women into believing that the "false" sounds of instruments were her "true" son, Kuwai. Through this artifice, the men retained power over the sacred instruments.

In the pajé's practice, he must be able to distinguish between spirits who "deceive" and those who are "true" manifestations. This is an important element that contributes to the belief that community members have in them. It is an inbuilt means for denying any accusations of charlatanism. In their songs, pajés reiterate that there are those people "who don't want to know the truths" of Dzuliferi, but that they, the pajés singing, are "speaking the real truth." If a pajé diagnoses a sickness based on "false" information, and the sickness turns out to be something else entirely, his reputation is destroyed and he will be expelled from the community. If a pajé abides by the rules of long and frequent fasts, successfully supports long periods of altering his perceptions with pariká, and is able to clearly distinguish true and false manifestations of spirits, he is on his way to being considered a jaguar shaman spirit," *Dzaui malinyai*, whose principal duty is to protect his community from harm by sorcerers or sickness-giving spirits.

The new pajé then receives "the mouth of Kuwai" (Kuwai inuma)—bestowed by the master (presumably by the master pajé impressing the shape of Kuwai's jaguar mouth onto the mouth of the apprentice)—with which he will be able to extract the sickness from patients' bodies. It is, according to the pajés, the same as the mouth of a jaguar spirit that can become huge in one instant to engulf the sickness and instantly become small again when it has taken the sickness out of the body. We shall see in chapter 6 that when the baby Kuwai is born, its mouth is not like other babies—it is the jaguar's mouth with razor-sharp teeth that rip off a sloth's breast when it nurses. Kuwai's father, Nhiãperikuli, astonished by what he has created, sends Kuwai off to the Other World, the sky, to stay.

The "mouth of the sky" is also known as the "mouth of Kuwai," which is said to be "opening and closing" all the time, with razor-sharp teeth that can shred a pajé's heart-soul into pieces as it tries to enter. There is a clear enough parallel between the cosmic portal and the shaman's mouth, both of which are entitled "jaguar mouth" and "Kuwai's mouth." In short, the image of the devouring predator jaguar mouth dramatically heightens the jaguar shaman's extractive force and its capacity to rip to shreds all that enters its mouth, including whatever sickness the pajé is sucking out.

In all cases of curing, there is a payment that the patient, prior to the cure, gives to the pajé. This payment to cure is called *dawai*; depending on the sickness, payments could include anything from a matchbox to a sewing machine, depending on the difficulty of the task. The pajé will take it, in its immaterial form, and present it to Kuwai. The pajé thus opens an exchange relation with it; if

Kuwai accepts (but it is never assumed that he will), then Kuwai plucks out some fur from his sloth body, saying, "I am Kuwai. This is the sickness he has," and gives the immaterial form of the sickness to the pajé. If Kuwai does not accept the payment, it signifies that the sickness cannot be cured, and the pajé returns the payment, perhaps suggesting that the sick person procure another form of treatment.

If the exchange is accepted, the pajé then performs a cure on the "shadow-soul of Dzuliferi," Kuwai's father's elder brother and primal shaman in the Other World. The pajé could not perform a cure on Kuwai himself, because Kuwai is the source of the sickness. If the pajé succeeds, Dzuliferi's shadow-soul authorizes him to do the same in This World.

Before reintegrating the soul to the body of the sick person, the pajé extracts the sickness both from the "Other World" and from the patient's body, visibly vomiting out all traces of the material forms of the sickness and throwing them away. Then the patient's heart-soul is joined together from all its endpoints (blowing tobacco smoke from the tips of the fingers of both hands of the patient held together, and blowing down over the crown of the patient) to the body's center. The heart-soul is completely reintegrated within the body of the sick.

Sickness and healing are both processes that involve (1) the separation of immaterial from material forms in This World (soul from body of sick; immaterial form of payment from material; soul of pajé from his body); (2) in the Other World, an exchange of dawai for the sickness and/or soul of the sick; (3) in the Other World, the transformation of the Sickness-Owner into the "shadow-soul" of the primal healer; (4) back in This World, the reintegration of immaterial with material (soul of the pajé back to his body, soul of the sick back into the body, the immaterial form of the sickness into its material form, which is thrown away).

The master pajé continues to observe his apprentice for a period of five months after the first phase is over, during which time the apprentice must continue his restrictions. He must especially avoid the confusion brought on by contacts with girls or crowds of children. The master then evaluates how the apprentice has done, giving him counsel as to how he should safeguard his newly acquired knowledge and powers. This concludes the first stage of training.

The new pajé will work mainly in his community; however, he will only be able to handle the more serious cases of assault sorcery (*manhene*) after he has obtained "the pajé's body" (*maliri dakipe*), which involves a more advanced form of knowledge and power including transfiguration of the entire body and acquiring the perspective of a jaguar shaman.

HUNTERS AND WARRIORS

Shamans are, in Roberte Hamayon's phrase (1990), "hunters of souls." Sicknesses are understood to be detachments of the "heart-soul" from a person's body due to a spirit attack, the actions of sorcerers, or the appearance of omens of death (*hinimai*). The detached soul is taken away to any one of the Houses of the Souls of the Dead, or to the layers where Kuwai resides, where his "secretary" resides, or to any of the layers below This World. Sickness-giving spirits are found in the air, water, earth, forest. Over many years of practice, pajés acquire the capacity to recognize the signs of illness specific to each of the enormous variety of spirits. Acting on that diagnosis, the pajés' heart-souls undertake a perilous journey of hunting throughout the cosmos in search of the lost souls. It is usually in the pariká-induced trance that the pajé makes a diagnosis of the patient's problem, advising the patient before the cure that he has seen in his dreams where the soul was taken and by which of the spirits.

One of the most important services that the pajé performs is protecting clients from spirit attacks. As part of their warrior selves, the apprentices acquire a host of spirit armaments: an arsenal of spirit darts (*walama*); at least four kinds of "revolvers" that produce lightning bolts, which are supposed to mark the presence of the pajé to others but which can also be used as weapons; "swords" to decapitate the enemy; "boots" for long-distance travel; "clubs," and an array of hawk feathers, pieces of wood, and thorns attached to his body.

All of their perceptions are altered in training to support their system of defense: they are trained to see the double of any being (its invisible personhood and its shadow-soul; they see, for example, a sorcerer as a furry animal whose body walks in front of the sorcerer, but whose soul is *inyaime* (the spirit of the dead). Their sight is enhanced immeasurably through the use of crystals.

They learn the art of divining, how to interpret signs, omens, dreams, and unusual body sensations. It is said they are surrounded by "mirrors" (*likanaale*) that allow them to see the world from all angles. As long as those mirrors accompany him, the pajé's fractal vision renders him invulnerable to attacks by sorcerers. But once the light from their mirrors begins to fade, even the most powerful of the jaguar shamans is unable to protect himself from attack. Such has been the story of the jaguar shamans and prophets.

MALIRI DAKIPE: THE JAGUAR SHAMAN'S BODY, ALTERITY, AND INTENTIONALITIES

The process of the pajé's "becoming other" is the result of (1) the continued acquisition of knowledge and power and their icons, especially the rattle, the bone for inhaling or blowing the pariká, sacred stones, and a series of outer skin coverings, like shirts; (2) the experience of spiritual death, body detachment, and rebirth and learning to move freely between the Other and This World, through the mastery of song journeys; and (3) the highest degree of jaguar shaman holds the power of the jaguar tooth necklace. The complete alteration of the pajé's body (remade and adorned) produces the desired alteration in his perspective.

The pajé's "becoming Other" can be understood in several senses depending on the task at hand: in order to pass on knowledge, the pajés transform into other-than-human beings of the natural world that periodically change their skins and regenerate at certain times of the annual cycle. This is the importance of the cicadas. In the pajés' cycles of transformation, "the months of June and July are said to be the times for taking pariká daily, so that throughout the month of August, the pajé transforms into the cicada" (pers. comm., Alberto Lima da Silva, June 15, 2010); pajés become one with the "universe people" as they transmit their knowledge and power to their apprentices.

As the pajé's body fills up with medicines from the eternal (*midzaka*) Other World, he acquires a dimension that transcends human time and limitations. "He doesn't have anything more that is human," Mandu said, meaning that he "dies" (to his human existence), "exchanges his life" for that of the jaguar shaman spirit other.

The pajé is one who is constantly in the process of "becoming other," so we can hardly talk about his "being" in terms of fixed forms. It makes more sense to speak of the shaman as "a multiplicity of intentionalities," like the spirits and deities, constantly transforming ("*napadamawa dzaui malinyai*"): "the shaman is a multiple being, a micro-population of shamanic agencies sheltering within a body: hence neither are his 'intentions' exclusively his, nor can he ever be certain of his own intentions" (Fausto 2002: 121).

A jaguar shaman who has a "jaguar spirit" intentionality is in synchrony with the subtle changes in the environment, important for hunting lost souls. He is actually a force behind the cosmic, meteorological transitions that occur during the time of the pajé's transformation; with eagle feathers, he may help bring on the summer season. He has the vital role of guarding the food resources of the environment against potential attacks by sorcerers.

He experiences several worlds, conversing with the other jaguar shaman spirits of the Other World, the deities themselves, and the souls of the dead. Ultimately he transcends the irreversible death that awaits everyone. After physically departing This World, it is said that the heart-souls of the savants may return to their tombs and continue to counsel their kin.

The pajé learns what it means to "die" to This World, "become Other" in order to enter the Other World, and "transform" his heart-soul into powerful beings, such as the harpy eagle, jaguar, or serpent. Their acquisition of "otherness" is accompanied with many mantles or cloaks, thought of as clothing with which he can become a jaguar, for example, by covering his body with a multiplicity of animal spirit subjectivities. These cloaks allow the pajé to assume the perspectives and agencies of their otherness, often—but not always—predatory qualities as hunters and warriors of the Other World. At the height of their powers, the *maliri* may actually assume the subjectivity and agency of the Creator deity, the sun Nhiãperikuli, whose powers of vision, prescience, and moral counsel are sought especially during historical moments of uncertainty and disorder.

In short, the jaguar shamans have been an elite group with advanced knowledge and power, with access to the higher realms of the universe. On the lower levels in This World, the jaguar pajés of enemy tribes can act in devastating ways. The Tukanoan pajés to the northwest of the Baniwa, for example, are still said to be active, though much reduced in number, and are feared, for they may penetrate This World, where their souls are believed to incorporate the bodies of live jaguars to attack and take lives.

One extraordinary case of a Tukano jaguar shaman's attack on a Baniwa child occurred in the year 2000 at Tunui Rapids on the mid-Içana River. According to the old shaman Matteo of the Dzaui-nai phratry, in the upper levels of the cosmos, there are "Guardians of the Cosmos," pajés who are responsible for preventing food resources from becoming depleted. It is necessary "to open a small hole" in the cosmos, he said, so that the snakes, jaguars, beasts, and demons of This World leave, for otherwise they would eat all the food. Perhaps, the old pajé speculated, someone opened the way out but didn't know how to close it. For the Baniwa of the Içana River, in the past this could be a justification for warfare against whomever it was that left the way open. In this case, most likely enemy pajés from the headwaters of the Uaupés River came in to kill the girl. So, the old shaman warned people that "if you have a bad dream, don't go out at night, it's too risky." Such were the explanations of the elder jaguar shaman, which everyone took seriously, whether evangelical or not.

In one other case that involved Mandu, once a group of Tariana men visited Uapui village to film the rapids at Hipana, for both the Tariana and the Baniwa say that their ancestors emerged from the holes at these rapids. Thus the Tariana consider part of the rapids to be "theirs," so they got the idea to film the place of power and emergence. Mandu was not happy at all about the visit because of the possibility that the Tariana could put a curse on the river that would kill off all the fish, causing a famine for the villagers. Mandu sent his son to watch them (all of this is documented on film). Several years later, Mandu confronted the same Tariana, Pedro de Jesus, accusing him of having thrown a spell on the fish that killed them all, to which Pedro replied: "How could I have done that? I'm not even a pajé!" Whether he was or not is beside the point. The Tariana man's idea was the result of an external NGO and government incentive to establish a major culture center (Pontão de Cultura) that neglected to recognize that the Baniwa were caretakers of Hipana Rapids.

The advanced pajés learn to sing in the specific language and from the perspectives of the deities. These songs record their journeys in the Other World, and pajés say the songs are actually the voice of the "Spirit of Power," Dzuliferi, primordial pajé and master of all shamans' sacred substances (pariká and tobacco) who narrates the pajé's journey and encounters in the Other World. The songs are among the most valuable sources of knowledge we—as outsiders and observers—have for understanding what the Other World is like.

In a healing ritual, after snuffing the pariká, jaguar shamans immediately open the connection with the Other World. They arise from their seated position and begin to dance and sing in a circle around a designated space. It is said that, although we see them moving about inside the dance space, they are really "in the Other World," and their heart-souls are moving in the space/time of the Before World. Simultaneously, the Before World "turns around" and "comes to" the pajés.

The jaguar shamans and the spirits and deities of the Before World establish encounters, a meeting of two subjectivities through which communication and understanding are possible. Evidence to support the assertion that this actually happens comes first from the sacred stories and second from the pajés' songs.

Whenever, in the sacred stories having to do with shamans, a person of the story (*medzawaniri, -ro*, man or woman character) meets a spirit of the Other World, there is first a vertical displacement (down-to-up, or up-to-down, from one world to the other), followed by a horizontal displacement (from here-to-there), and the first question the spirit of the Other World asks the person of the story, "You were looking for me?" is answered by "Yes, I was looking for you," "Ah, yes, it is good." This establishes common ground for exchange to take place between the two, the starting point of spiritual encounters.

It is preceded by a desire of the person in the story to go between the two worlds, ultimately to "see" as the Other sees, "feel" as the Other feels, make powerful sounds (*khemakani*, of thunder), to "open the way" of the shaman apprentice to the Other World, and to hunt for the lost souls of the sick. Unless one can experience all of these alterations, one cannot fully understand the shamanic experience.

One of the key ways jaguar shamans "walk with" (or, it is said, "walk *in* the knowledge of") the spirits and deities is through the songs of their voyages and encounters with other jaguar shaman spirits, other spirit peoples of the cosmos, and the deities who entrust them to communicate their messages to humans. These messages are expressed in a certain way, for it is the voice of Dzuliferi that is constructing the terrain of the Other World.[2]

At the beginning of their songs, the pajés sing that they travel back "before us" in time (*waaka wapedza*) to the Other World, that the Other World "turns around" in space (*likapoko*) "among us," to face the pajés who behold the Jaguar shaman spirits, dzaui malinyai of the Other World. Their journeys are then sung, step by step, through the poetic and lyric reconstruction of all places they walk through in the Other World of the sky, the places where there are traps, the moment when they approach a deity's village or when they drink pariká with the other jaguar shamans. Above all, a question constantly motivates their search: "Is it here that I will find the soul of my sick companion/friend?"

Behold the village of the pajés' snuff,
Hee Hee Hee Hee Hee Hee (the transformative song of the jaguar)
Behold the Other Jaguar Shamans

We drink with them, we embrace them
There is the canoe of the pajé
That looks for the soul of the sick
We drink with them
We transform on pariká
We bring the payment
We place it in the Center
We the Children of the Sun (Heiri-ieni, sacred name for the
    Hohodene pajés)

The aesthetics of the pajés' powers to sing are most important to mention here. The pajés' songs may seem like freestyle, spontaneous creations, quite distinct from the *kalidzamai* litany-like chants sung at rites of passage. However, the pajé's chants are believed to be the voice of the deity Dzuliferi. The pajé "hears," "listens to" Dzuliferi's voice singing in him; it is Dzuliferi who "gives the pajé his songs," and this inspires the pajé. These songs appear to be like the *icaros* of the Ecuadorian shamans. The psychoactive DMT here again brings the spirit world into relation with the shamans. Pajés can only perform cures when they have "received the songs" from Dzuliferi about the sickness of a person to be cured. During their apprenticeship, the master pajé "gives" the apprentices the appropriate song for each task or action of the pajés' practice.

With time, the pajés grow in their understanding of the perspective of Dzuliferi, which enhances their abilities to translate and communicate their journeys to the Other World. This power is developed at a fairly advanced state of the pajés' training, when they hear the voice of Dzuliferi and accurately transmit it; the pajé "cannot deceive or lie about what Dzuliferi says," Mandu emphasized, affirming the truth-value of the pajés' journey.

The pajé has become sufficiently competent in his knowledge

of the Other World to be able to construct convincing poetic images of the Other World. Through a synaesthetic construction of hearing-seeing-singing-body choreography, the pajé communicates these images and information to the patients and observers who are listening and watching, reflecting on the pajés' voyage and confiding in his powers. It is in this way that Dzuliferi informs humans about their future, important events to come, anything having to do with Baniwa eschatology.

Carneiro da Cunha has argued that the most important labor of the pajé in Amazonia is as "a translator. It is suggested here that translation should be understood in its strong, Benjaminian sense, as a search for resonances and reverberations between different codes and systems" (Cunha 1998).

For Baniwa pajés, the poetics of the Other World as announced through the perspective of the shaman deity Dzuliferi are translated by the pajé into answers that humans seek for their dilemmas.

That is why it is forbidden for the apprentices to simply repeat what they have heard other pajés sing. In "giving the songs," the master-pajé will indicate key points that must be sung, but constructing the journey is up to the pajé. The songs have to be sung in a certain way—not loudly, screaming, or bellowing, but with a certain cadence and rhythm.

When a group of three or four pajés performs a cure together, their singing produces, to an outsider, a distinct echo-chamber effect in which the lead pajé guides the group's journey through the Before World, while the other pajés act as respondents, affirming what the lead sees and sings. Resonance and reverberations occur, like wave patterns, among the lead singer and the respondents, as well as—silently—with the audience. During the rite of healing, patients and onlookers listen or converse, commenting on what the pajés sing:

Where will it be that it will come back and stay with us, His
   World, Dzuliferi?
Where will it be, that it will come back and stay with us, this
   hidden place of long ago?
My grandfather Dzuliferi
My grandfather Dzuliferi
For now I come and open this hidden place of Long Ago
My grandfather, my grandfather . . . .
I will brush away and brush away their Tobacco Smoke,
   those Jaguar Shamans.

The singer leads the way through the Other World, where he
sees all the jaguar shamans together smoking tobacco. He clears
the clouds, their "smoke" (*kununu*, sweep away), so as to be able
to see clearly. The constant repetition of the song of the jaguar
spirit—"Hee Hee Hee Hee"—"opens up," "reveals" the miniature
and distant images of the Other World, bringing them into the
clear, life-sized vision the pajé reproduces in his songs.

EXPERIENCE OF DEATH-AND-REBIRTH

As is well known from shamanic experiences in various parts of
the world, the initiate reaches a stage when he passes through a
process of de-personalization, that is, he "dies" as a human and
is "reborn" into the spirit world. The death and rebirth experience may be thought of as a self-sacrifice (Sullivan 1988). In the
trance state, the Baniwa pajés say they see their bodies "become
skeletons"; then they descend to the netherworld of the dead and,
after performing certain operations there, emerge into the world
of the deities. It is a process of returning in time to the eternal
"Other World," the source of all creative power. Upon entering the
door of the Other World, the pajé "throws away his personhood"
(*lipeko linewikika*, including patrisib and phratric ancestral name,

phratric identity), is purified in a hole of "smoking resin" (*maini*), and then freely moves about, formless, in the Other World.

The pajé's soul journey is like the journey of the deceased, except that the pajé's soul continues onward past the Houses of the Dead to the places of the great spirits and deities of the Other World above the world of the dead. The pajé is a regular visitor in the Houses of the Dead. A more powerful pajé will know the Other World as far up as the level where Kuwai lives. Only a few pajés, men or women, have gone far beyond death and have "seen from a short distance" the house of the creator.

One of Mandu's most important experiences was his first encounter with the great spirit Kuwai, the owner of sickness. This occurred late in his training with Kudui and is part of what made Mandu a "real pajé," a high degree in the hierarchy.

For the Baniwa pajés, "real knowledge" comes from acquiring the "body of the pajé," *maliri dakipe*, with malikai and tápe (power and medicines). To acquire this "body," Mandu had to "die" to his former Self and Body, in order to "become Other," be reborn as another kind of being. After he had taken a large quantity of pariká sufficient for him to lose consciousness, he fell into a trance (*maliume*, "unconscious," "dead") and his soul began its journey. Then his soul left his body lying there, as though "in a coffin." Kudui had "left open the door of the sky" for Mandu to go inside and had "given him the songs" to sing while there, in other words, a map of the trails to follow and the important points to watch for.

Kuwai sent down his umbilical cord for Mandu to grasp and pulled him through the opening in the sky, a narrow and dangerous passageway lined with razor sharp teeth that keep "opening and closing" all the time. This is one of the trials the apprentice must endure in order to get to the Other side, thus crossing the passageway between the "here and now" and the "long ago" and "Before World" of the ancestral deities. There was a crosslike shape on the umbilical cord where he could sit as it pulled him into the "belly of the sky" (*eenu iwali*), "Kuwai's belly," taking him back into a prebirth state.

On entering the sky door, the pajé's soul jumps through a hole of burning resin. This is the place where souls are purified of their body-shaped souls; when they pass through this hole, they cry out as if they are being burned alive, a purification by fire, when, they say, they "throw off their personhood" (*lipekoka linewikika*). The incense-like smoke of the resin—which is usually brushed into the doors of houses after the death of a person in This World, "opening the way" for the soul to continue into the Other World—purifies the pajé's heart-soul of any trace of social and corporeal identity.

KUWAI AND DZULIFERI: SICKNESS AND HEALING

Mandu's heart-soul followed a trail to the house of Kuwai and announced that he had come to seek a cure for his friend's sickness. The pajé showed Kuwai the dawai, the required "payment for the soul" of the sick person, and gave it to Kuwai. The sick person's soul appeared to be "entrapped" in Kuwai's arms. Kuwai has the form of a giant black sloth, covered with fur, whose embrace can potentially suffocate the sick if the pajé does not succeed in releasing it.[3] If Kuwai accepts the dawai, he gives him some of the poisonous fur from his body, saying "here is the sickness that your friend has."

Then, Kuwai transforms into the shadow-soul (*idanimi*) of Dzuliferi. This transformation corresponds to the shift in the curing rite from localization of the soul of the sick and discovery of the sickness the soul has, to extraction by suction (jaguar mouth), water dowsing, and smoke blowing to revive the soul of the sick. This occurs first in the Other World; if successful, the pajé is "authorized" to repeat the process on the patient in This World of the descendants.

The pajé's body serves as a conduit for the sickness that passes through it and is vomited out in its visible, elemental form. What is accomplished in the Other World of ancestral deities is proof enough that the pajé can legitimately heal the patient in This World. The medicine is then transferable to This World.

Mandu remembered vividly what Kuwai's "village" looks like. There he visited the enormous plantation that Kuwai has near his house, where he found all sorts of spirit darts, the poisonous thorns of the great tree called dzaui kumale, "jaguar cumare." This is the moriche palm, widely known as "tucumã" and is used to make fiber, as in woven bags for the pajé's tools. It is dangerous to scale the walama tree, so the pajé scales one nearby and uses a long stick to tap off the thorns of the tree and put them in his bag for later use. Spirit darts such as these have far greater power than the thorns found on other kinds of palms at lower levels of the cosmos.

Further down the trail, the pajé sees multitudes of jaguar shaman spirits from all times past in the Other World. The names of these jaguar shamans correspond with sacred elements (kinds of sacred wood especially, which become the "bodies" of the pajés) in This World.

There is a reigning cordiality and camaraderie among them, as they chant, "embracing" each other, sharing their tobacco and "drinking" their pariká. For in the jaguar shamans' expression, the sacred "blood" is not only inhaled, it is "drunk" (*ilapa*) in a kind of hematophagous communion. (Fausto 2002 has noted a similar image of hematophagy among the Parakanã.) In the world of the jaguar shaman spirits, relations among them all can be understood as an ideal society of jaguar shamans, all of one spirit, among whom there is no conflict or strife. The pajés sing as follows:

Heeey Yaaeyyy
The Before-world will come and walk with us
Behold it will be, "Hee hee

Hee hee hee hee"
We will transform
Behold the Pariká stairway
It comes and journeys with us—Hee
Behold we will transform on it, among them
The Jaguar Shaman-spirits. . . .
We go to drink and dance together
Long ago
Before us
The Eternal Master
Behold he will come and drink and dance among us
The Eternal Master
Hee hee hee hee
Thus it will be, we are all the same as they, the Jaguar–shaman
    spirits
Hee
Thus it will be we are all the same as they—Hee hee—the
    Jaguar–shaman spirits.
Behold, then, the House of the Dead Kudamadali (the Cubeo
    House of the Souls of the Dead)
We go to dance and drink
The walama darts, the walama darts
We go to dance and drink
So it will be the Jaguars sing "Hee hee hee hee."

The "Eternal Master" (*midzaka thayri*) is Nhiãperikuli or Dzuliferi, since the first is the primal ancestor of all peoples and the
second is the primal ancestor of the Walipere-dakenai phratry, as
well as the primal shaman for all Baniwa people. At every place
the pajés pass through, they dance and drink as in a dance festival.
With the Cubeo, they dance inside the House of the Souls of the
deceased Cubeo with the dance masks (Goldman 1963).

The pajés follow certain paths in their search for the souls. In the above description, the pajés begin with the houses of the ancestors of the Hohodene and, in sequence, the Walipere-dakenai and the Cubeo. Each phratry has its own House of Souls located at the headwaters of small streams. They may look like hills, but inside there are all of the phratry members' souls, from the beginning of time, packed together "like white rice," one pajé said. At each one of the Houses of each phratry, the pajé asks the "chiefs of the Souls," the first human-like ancestor of each phratry, whether the heart-soul of his companion, the sick person, has entered there or not. The pajé's soul has to visit all five of these houses (Hohodene, Walipere-dakenai, Dzauinai, Adzanene, Cubeo) located at widely separated places in Baniwa territory.

If he doesn't find the soul in any of these places, then the pajé's soul goes upward to the worlds of the bird spirits and asks for their help in searching. The pajé is aware that some of them might send him off on the wrong trail. Nevertheless, the pajé has, during his apprenticeship, made a marriage with one or more of these bird spirits who have born offspring by him. He may call on these auxiliary children to help him in his search. The pajé searches everywhere he can, depending on his experience and knowledge of the different worlds.

When finished in the Other World, he returns gradually into This World, as if being reborn, passing through the same spirit house places until his soul reaches This World again.

The relation between the Other World of the spirits and deities and This World of kin and affines is marked by a temporal hiatus between the "Before" world and the future generations. This coincides with a qualitative difference between the "jaguar shaman spirits" of the Other World, who seem to enjoy a world of sameness with no hierarchical difference, and relations among pajés of This World, which is marked by hierarchical differences and disputes over power.

"Open" and "closed" bodies are conditions or states of being-in-the-world, equivalent to vulnerability and protection. When a child is born, its "body is completely open" (*idakithi madanhathaka dalee tsa*), it is said, along with the mother's and father's bodies. They are open to spirit attacks, so a chant owner is called to speak or chant the necessary orations with a tobacco cigar to close the body. The closed body is protected by a shield, the qualities of which are defined in the oration and blown over the person with tobacco smoke. At any moment in a person's life, sickness-giving spirits can penetrate the body, especially during moments of life transition when the services of the pajé are most needed.

A pajé is particularly susceptible to attacks by spirits and enemy pajés. "The enemy of the pajé is another pajé," Mandu stated, which means that the pajé must know how to protect himself. Whenever his soul is traveling in the universe in search of a lost soul or for whatever other motive, he is most vulnerable on his return. At this time, enemy pajés lie in wait and will try to kidnap the healing pajé's soul to take his powers away. The enemy pajé traps the returning pajé's soul, takes it to a cave, for example, in Cubeo territory where the "crime is to be committed," and there tears the soul into shreds. So the pajé has to be alert and have the powers to defend himself from enemy pajés at the same time he knows how to assault an enemy. Baniwa pajés say they only kill in extreme circumstances, but it is a part of the knowledge that they must have and will use when necessary.

In the past these wars among pajés of different peoples were more frequent, it is said, and often related to disputes over food resources. Even today a jaguar shaman such as Mandu is constantly watchful of the actions of outsiders that could affect, for example, the fish supply of the Aiary.

Throughout the pajé's apprenticeship, he is taught how to transform the states of his being, throw up a smokescreen, or divert the sorcerer's/enemy pajé's vision with his mirrors. There are several orations to protect oneself and village from sorcerers' attacks. One such oration creates a sort of "sanctuary" first by constructing an impenetrable fence of quartz and thickly woven thatch as a palisade around the settlement. The pajé then raises a long blowgun up to the place of Dzuliferi where "there is no sickness," and sends all the souls of the living (*hwekaale*), like the "cotton of a blowgun arrow," up through the tube to the Other World. He then diverts the vision of the enemy pajé who is searching, so as not to see where the children are. Using his mirrors, he deflects the light of the sun into the sorcerer's eyes to blind or distract him. Then when the sorcerer attacks in the form of a hawk, the pajé places a lasso on the trail to the longhouse in such a way that when the sorcerer's head passes through the loop, the pajé pulls the loop closed, instantly killing the sorcerer.

"Closing" the body can be both a defensive and an aggressive act. An enemy pajé can "close" a target pajé's soul completely inside a coffin-like trap. One time when the powerful jaguar shaman José Garcia was healing people in the city of São Gabriel, he failed to attend an elderly woman who had already paid him for the cure. Garcia returned to his village, exhausted after an intense period of treating patients. Suddenly he went into trance but could not return to This World; it looked as though he were "dead," but the pajés diagnosed that his soul was trapped inside a spider's web. He was unconscious for a month, people said. He later explained that his entire body had become encased in something like a spider's web but thicker, and that he could not see any hole or ray of light where he might try to escape. It took numerous chanters, other pajés each trying unsuccessfully their special powers against sorcery, until eventually one Wanano pajé broke open a hole in the enclosure.

In this case, it was explained that the enemy was the woman who had paid to have a cure performed, but José, exhausted by work, did not cure her and returned home with the payment. His condition was explained both in terms of his weakness and vulnerability as well as his failure to perform the cure, a breach in the rigid ethics of the pajés' practice. Nevertheless, after this bout with "death," he declared that he was going to regain the powers he had lost by taking even more pariká and becoming stronger than before.

ADVANCED KNOWLEDGE

After completing the first stage in his training, the apprentice may decide to deepen his knowledge through some specialization, in which case he goes to another pajé. As Goldman states, "The 'real' and the esteemed shaman is an educated religious savant, a member of what is in effect an academy of religious specialists with whom he is engaged in lasting discussion and studies. His curiosity, or perhaps his ambition, takes him to distant places, as far as the Guaviare River, for instance, to study with savants already esteemed for their specialties in healing or in sorcery" (2004: 300).

For the Hohodene pajés of the Aiary River, the most powerful pajés are of the "Wanhiwa" peoples to the north, who include the Guahibo, the Puinave, and the Piaroa (whose ethnonym is wóthuha). Mandu's second master was Alexandre Jawinaapi of the Dzauinai (Jaguar Peoples) phratry, who was of a long lineage of jaguar shamans going back to the time of the prophets Kamiko (of the Dzauinai phratry) in the mid-nineteenth century and Uetsu (of the Adzanene and Hohodene phratries) of the early twentieth

9. Shaman's rattle, snuff-bone, and cigar.

century. His narrative also referred specifically to a Piaroa pajé named Fabricio (now deceased), who specialized in the knowledge of killing enemies at a distance.[4]

When the master shaman agrees to instruct further, another group of apprentices is formed. Each apprentice prepares a large quantity of pariká to consume during the period of training, as payment for the master pajés. During the time of his instruction at Uapassussu (the real name for which is Guapa Sucia), under

Alexandre, Mandu learned more about sicknesses and the potential of sacred substances for opening his perceptions in the Other World. Alexandre was considered a great pajé of the Dzauinai phratry of the upper Guainia, around the town of Maroa. Mandu experienced the powerful hallucinogen caapi (*Banisteriopsis caapi*), which, like pariká, contains the psychoactive DMT, or dimethyltryptamine, which he took together with pariká. Mandu had many experiences, he said, of caapi, even in the 1970s when I first lived in the village, although he made no mention of this at the time.

Stories of the prophet jaguar shaman Uetsu mikuiri mention the mixture of caapi, or yajé, and niopo snuff (*Piptadena peregrina*), a psychoactive related to pariká. The special brew was called caapi ka yumpa, and its power enabled the "wise man" to have direct experiences with the souls of deceased kin, who showed him all around the Other World, even to the house of "our father" Nhiãperikuli. Yet what most marked Mandu's memory of his apprenticeship with Alexandre was the quest for his "shaman's body," the handle of his rattle.

THE PAJÉ'S RATTLE AND SACRED STONES

The pajé's rattle *kutheruda* is a complex synthesis of soul and body elements from the pajé's self and from the Other World, an icon of the pajé's alterity (other self). The rattle consists of the shaman's externalized body, which is the wooden handle of the rattle, and his soul, the globular gourd. The soul of the rattle contains pebbles called "celestial things" (*eenu ithada*). These are said to be "alive" and come from the primordial pajé's "head" (*Dzuliferi hliuidetha*). They are considered "medicines which the rattle has eaten." Just as, during the pajé's apprenticeship, he has consumed medicines from the sky that are lodged in his body, so, inside the rattle's globular gourd, his "heart-soul," there are living celestial medicines that the rattle has consumed. Engraved on the rattle's globular soul are "sky

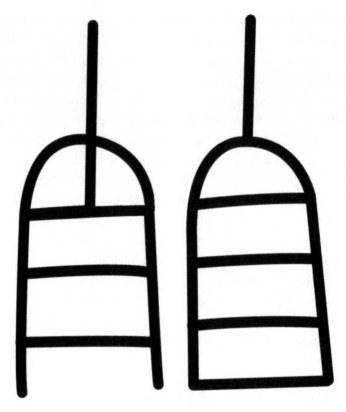

10. Drawing of sacred flutes incised on shaman's rattle.

trails" that the pajé's soul follows in his travels. Or there may be engraved images of the sacred flutes and trumpets of Kuwai, the owner of sickness, which he will encounter.

Sometimes holes are drilled in the rattle's globular soul to serve as the pajé's eyes for seeing far into the Other World. During the curing ritual, the rattle acts like a knife that, with the motions the pajé makes, cuts the sickness from the Other World in the sky, upon which the pajé sucks the toucan feathers at the rattle's head, ingesting the sickness in spirit form that he will later regurgitate in material form. All of the above-mentioned functions make the rattle a key instrument with which the whole process of the pajé's journey to the Other World and cure is realized.

In Jonathan Hill's work with the *maliri* of the Wakuenai, he discovered that their rattles serve to make alignments with the sun prior to a cure (pers. comm. July 7, 2011): "They would use the toucan feathers in their rattles to observe the position of the sun, and at exactly 12 noon they would begin working to heal patients. This spatiotemporal pattern was invariant, no matter where in the village the ritual was being held. Clearly the lidanam shadow-souls can only be 'seen' in the afternoon." Another way of saying this is that the alignment of the Other World with This World occurs at midday; it is a moment when—all of the sacred stories confirm—the passageway between the two worlds is open. The pajé's gesture seems to be aligning himself with the power sources of the cosmos.

Mandu's recollection of how he obtained the body of the rattle can be interpreted as a kind of vision quest, in the sense he received a sign, a gift from the Other World, which indicated the future power that he would have.

He and his family had journeyed a long distance into the Venezuelan Orinoco region, suffering a great deal, even dragging their canoe from one river to another, until they reached their final destination. This was the house of Alexandre at a very beautiful place (now abandoned), where they were received well by the shaman. Jawinaapi took the apprentices to a place on the Uwa River, where handles for rattles are found, and told Mandu to go out into the wide open field and find what he was looking for. It is, according to Mandu, impossible to explain—i.e., it is the pajé's mystery—how the piece of sacred uwa wood got to be where Mandu found it. Yet it was the sign that Mandu needed, for his master pajé interpreted it to mean that he had been accepted by the divinities.

Jawinaapi explained to Mandu that the gift meant much more

than simple recognition and acceptance: "You got this, and you weren't supposed to. One day you will be a great pajé." Mandu was to become one of those rare jaguar shamans who is also a "wise man" spiritual leader. The dzaui malinyai Uwa, a jaguar shaman spirit of the Other World, had sent a sign for Mandu, a living shape from the Other World, that materialized into the handle of a rattle that would be Mandu's shaman body (maliri-dakipe) representing his mission to save many people in This World.

It was understood that the jaguar shaman spirit had sent him an "agent" of his new shamanic power. The name *uwa*, besides being the name of the River Uwa and the wood of the handle, is the name of a jaguar shaman spirit who, from then on, was a connection for Mandu. This spiritual connection was materialized in the gift of the rattle's handle corresponding to the shaman's body, of both the Other World and This World simultaneously. The jaguar shamans of the Other World had chosen to send down a piece of themselves for Mandu, indicating his having been chosen to become a powerful healer.

What is the relation between the body/handle, the soul/gourd of the rattle, and the feathers at the crown of the rattle? A plausible interpretation would be the following: the body handle has the power to open closed spaces — as, for example, the wooden stick of the Jaguar harpy eagle Kamathawa, which pajés say is the body of the pajé that breaks open the hidden world of "happiness" (*kathimakwe*), and even — by extension — in the sacred story of Kuwai, the patauá log that penetrates the first woman's closed birth canal that brought Kuwai into being, the Other World into This World.

Its attachment to the gourd soul — inscribed with designs of the Kuwai flutes, with the trails of the Other World, with eyes that see great distances, medicine from the head of the first pajé — joins together the powers of the pajé's body to open the connection to Other Worlds with the soul that travels the sky roads, sees great distances, hears the voice of Kuwai (the trumpets) and Dzuliferi, and contains living remedies with which to cure. Coupled with the rattle's function in aligning the pajé with the powerful Other World, it is the synthesis of body and soul, Other World/This World connection that the pajé's rattle represents.

MANDU'S RATTLE AND STONES AS LIVING AGENTS

The pajé's rattle is a perfect example of "the occult life of things" as discussed with elegance in the volume edited by Fernando Santos-Granero (2009). The pajé's rattle is as much the pajé's alterity as it is his agency (his powers to act in the Other World and This World).

The rattle — as well as the pajés' sacred stones — are his soul companions, "like pets," the pajés say. They will even take care of the pajé's family in his absence. If one of the family members becomes sick, for example, the rattle will let the pajé know that something is wrong at home and that he should go back and see. This happened to Mandu a number of years ago, when he was living and working in São Gabriel and his wife, Flora, was at home in the village of Uapui. She got very sick one day, and it was feared that an enemy was attacking her. According to Ercilia, somehow the rattle and the sacred stones found their way back from São Gabriel to Uapui and came to lie underneath Flora's hammock.

Mandu looked for his rattle and stones, which weren't in the place he had left them. Then he received a radio message from the upper Aiary that his rattle and sacred stones were found in Uapui. Mandu quickly returned. When he saw that his wife was sick, he went directly to cure her. It was the rattle and stones that had gone ahead and drawn him back. "This is proof," Ercilia concluded, "that the jaguar spirit really is alive in This World."

The sacred stones are passed from father and grandfather shaman, master shaman to apprentices, or between colleagues. It is said that they can also appear in the dreams of the person who is becoming a pajé, indicating where they can be found. They appear of their own volition, seeking a companion shaman to work for, and they stay together even into the grave if the shaman has no one to leave them with. Ercilia recalled that her father often conversed with his rattle and sacred stones for hours privately before going to sleep for the night. The sacred stones are as important as the rattle and the snuff bone. The small stones in the shaman's possession thus embody "helper-spirit companions" with whom the shaman shares intimate concerns; they are among his multiple selves.

Knowing how powerful the rattles and stones are, Ercilia expressed her disgust at the evangelist missionary Sophie Muller's ethnocidal acts of ordering the pajés to toss their rattles and sacred stones into the river. She essentially told them to throw away their ancestral power, reducing the shamans' spiritual connections to nothing. Religious colonization deeply cut away a large part of the cosmology and metaphysics of the Baniwa pajés who, believing that Sophie was the one whom they had been waiting for, went into the *crente* faith. The New Testament became the primary source of spiritual "enlightenment," ultimately leaving the shamanic conversations with the icons of their spirituality far behind.

The jaguar tooth collar—the supreme symbol of a jaguar shaman's power—was another gift from Alexandre Jawinaapi, Mandu's greatest teacher. The jaguar tooth collar, which Mandu alone has today, is surely related to the jaguar mantle.

SHAMANIC HIERARCHIES

Based on their accumulation of knowledge and power, there is a strong sense of hierarchy among the pajés. Several degrees can be distinguished as follows: apprentice 1, "half-shaman," apprentice 2, "true shaman" with many years of experience, and "jaguar shamans."

The pajé's initial power derives from his abstinence from sexual relations, his fasting, and the constant intake of pariká, which transforms his body-soul entirely. Celibacy for ten years signifies a great deal of (libidinal) power or *likai*, the same word that is translated as "semen" or "essence of power," which, as one knowledgeable person stated, accumulates within his body to be transformed into shamanic spiritual power (malikai).

Another way in which the pajé obtains more power is through "marriages" with the bird spirits, the daughters of Dzuliferi, located in the lower levels of the sky. The bird-spirits not only assist the pajé in looking for the lost soul but they will also "bear many children" with him, extending his power in the spirit world.

MAKA, THE JAGUAR MANTLES

During his career, the pajé acquires a series of (invisible to us) outer coverings, called *dzaui maka* or *makkim*. Pajés refer to them as "shirts" (*kamitsa*, from the Portuguese), but they are not mere covering from the elements. These maka have several functions, the most important of which is protection against assaults by sorcerers. Mandu has more than thirteen of these maka, each of which adds a particular layer of protection against a specific kind of sorcery. In other words, each maka protects against its flip-side, inverse equivalent in a particular type of sorcery.

Beyond this, the maka are critical to acquiring distinct powers and qualities of the jaguar shaman. The maka are thus intimately connected with transformation in body and soul and the acquisition of Other subjectivities with accompanying power/knowledge. Body paint with red *caraiuru* and an owl feather headdress are spoken of, respectively, as the "jaguar mantle" and the "spirit-of-the-dead mantle."

PERSPECTIVES OF THE JAGUAR SHAMANS

With this entirely new body and perspective on the Other World, many jaguar shamans see that This World is a place of "wicked people," "pain," and "rot." They have a view of the world as a bad place to live, which has been ruined by the sorcerers and is rotten from the corpses buried under the surface.

In the next chapter, we discuss the "messages" of several "wise men"/jaguar shamans such as Uetsu, who repeatedly declared that This World is full of suffering that is the result of the actions of the sorcerers. José velho of Uapui also affirmed that This World is filled with conflict, and the only good place is that of Nhiãperikuli. For Mandu, people are in danger of losing their ways and the continuity of their traditions, opening the way for domination by those who seek the annihilation of the ancestral powers.

THE HOHODENE "POLICE": SHAMANIC RETRIBUTION

The practice of shamanic retribution at a distance is very ancient among the Baniwa and specifically links them with various indigenous peoples of the llanos in Colombia, especially the Guahibo of the Vichada River, who are known as powerful pajés capable of killing at long distances, and the Piaroa further north, who have specialized knowledge in killing.

One of several Hohodene stories explains how the Guahibo acquired their extraordinary powers to kill. A Guahibo jaguar shaman consumed so much pariká that he ultimately lost control of the changes that occurred in him:

The Story of Huiti wanakale
In ancient times there was a pajé called Huiti wanakale who looked for pajés' powers. He obtained much power but began to lose control and to kill people. He transformed into an enormous black jaguar. After he had killed people from other families, he went on to kill his wife's father and mother and then his wife and children. As he became more and more of a menace, his kin got together, ambushed, and killed him. It was

Huiti wanakale himself who recommended that they kill him. He instructed them to burn his body, but instead they simply cut off his head and threw it into the river. The head floated downriver still with its brains and the knowledge of how to cause all sicknesses but also how to cure them.

When the head reached a place a bit above Juí uitera (on the Içana River), the Guahibo sorcerers called Dzauinaikada got the head, took out the brains, and got all the sorcerers' powers in them, thus learning all sorts of evil things. After the Guahibo had taken out the brains, the head continued on downriver. In that time the Guahibo sorcerers were of a people called Padali. (Note: Koch-Grünberg's informant called them Pidzári.) They were affines of the Baniwa of the Aiary River. After they had learned all these things, they began to transform into jaguars, forest spirits, and other animals; they threw sickness-giving spirit darts onto people and ate people.

The story goes on to tell of a man who secretly overheard four of the Guahibo sorcerers planning to kill and devour all the people of his village. The man forewarned the people, who eventually killed the four sorcerers. Nevertheless, other Guahibo had succeeded in getting their power to kill. (My thanks to Luiza Garnelo Pereira for sharing this story.)

This story explains the dangerous potential that pariká has to transform a pajé into a killer black jaguar. That power ultimately ended up in the hands of the Guahibo sorcerers, who are those whom the Hohodene actually hire to do their vengeance killings. The power of these Guahibo as well as the Piaroa pajés to kill at a distance is held in very high esteem. The story suggests that these Guahibo may have been from the Dzauinai phratry, a sib called Padali, who according to oral tradition left the Aiary generations ago and went to an area to the north on the Vichada River in

Venezuela. (For further discussion of Cubeo sorcerers, see Goldman 2004.)

The story demonstrates how it is possible to lose control over the effects of pariká and the pajé then becomes a menace to society. It is as though the predatory "jaguar" power that pariká unleashes can potentially dominate one's thoughts entirely. By way of comparison, it is said that any sorcerer may likewise reach a point in his experience when "his only thought is to kill" (*manhekada lima*), that is, the repeated experience of practicing sorcery turns the practitioner permanently into a sorcerer, transforming his body and soul into a predator.

The commonly accepted discourse to explain why Baniwa pajés resort to the system of retribution through distance killings is that, while perfectly capable of undertaking vengeance killings, even at a long distance, Baniwa pajés do not do so out of fear of retribution by sorcerers against their families. Thus they seek other, distant, non-Arawak-speaking pajés to perform the rites. Underlying this justification seems to be that in such cases, resort is made to higher levels in interethnic vengeance killings; there possibly existed a very ancient web of interethnic relations focused on antisorcery retribution that is still activated as a last resort.

Hohodene pajés confirmed that the Guahibo and Piaroa are sought to perform this service for them. Cubeo and "true" Baniwa pajés could even produce more rapid results, but were more frequently hired by the Walipere-dakenai. The Hohodene preferred the Wanhíwa because, even though Hohodene pajés know who is responsible for a death or a series of deaths in their communities, they will never reveal the sorcerer publicly. Great power is attributed to outsider pajés, reinforced by stories of their origins that recall their indomitable knowledge of killing.

The means for undertaking vengeance at a distance through the use of the "filth" of the deceased victim (usually the hair, fingernails, or "dirt" from a corpse) is a form that is found in cultures the world over including among the neighboring Tukanoan-speaking peoples of the Uaupés (Buchillet 2004).

In chapter 3, I shall continue this discussion of what differentiates a pajé such as Mandu and a sorcerer such as the Guahibo. The term sorcery generally recalls the idea of killing, while the pajés' principal task is to heal. Shamanic killing is extremely difficult work, since, according to Mandu, one has to take pariká for seven straight hours, working at night. But there are important differences between this type of "sorcerer" who is a pajé trained in advanced knowledge of killing versus the sorcerer who is not trained in any way like the pajé but who learns through experience, beginning with the knowledge of a single sorcery chant and advancing to a state of constantly inflicting harm or death with no limits. These can represent even more of a danger than the trained sorcerer pajés.

In the story above, it is said that the Wanhiwa peoples obtained more of the jaguar's brain from which they got the power to transform and send their souls to kill at long distances. This affirmation (of which tribe "got more") evidently depends on which phratry the pajé-narrator belongs to. For the Hohodene, the Wanhiwa are their police who undertake long-distance vengeance killings for them. For the Walipere-dakenai, it is the Cubeo who received more of the black jaguar's knowledge and power and hence are their police.

Just as each phratry has its own set of enemy tribes, so each has its preferred group of external avengers. According to the story the Hohodene tell of the Wanhiwa, the latter once inhabited the Aiary, but at some point in time they became external allies who could be hired to kill. The Hohodene admit that in their own history, they too performed the role of "hired warriors" who killed enemies of their allies by direct warfare or shamanic vengeance (Wright 1998: chap. 3).

THE POWERS OF PRIESTLY CHANTERS VS.
THE POWERS OF THE JAGUAR SHAMANS

The chanters are in certain respects totally distinct from the healing shamans; nevertheless, both kinds of knowledge and power fall under the rubric of *malikai*. Instead of direct experience of the spirits and deities of other levels of the cosmos, the priestly chanters are masters of a knowledge that is canonical (Sullivan 1988), based on "thought journeys" throughout This World to protect (Reichel 1999), or lengthy chants of "heaping up" ("joining together") spirit names of all fish and animals (Hill 1993), and a "sacred geography," naming and "blessing" each place against harm (Wright 1993).

These chants, called *kalidzamai*, protect those undergoing life transitions during their period of "openness," to spirit attacks. The chanters invariably name all known spirits in the domains of food and place. The knowledge of the priestly chanters is "universalizing," all-encompassing, and critical for transition rites involving all the communities of the same phratry (Wright 2011). The chants at initiation rites are the most important of all, as they can be seen to re-create the world, all the places in it, with the ancestral power of the flutes, the body of Kuwai.

CONCLUSION OF TRAINING

In his narrative, Mandu states that at the end of his instruction in "advanced knowledge" with Jawinaapi and Fabricio, he caught four kinds of fish, which determined how his future work would be. It was unusual to catch four kinds of fish, each representing a specific and serious illness, against which the pajés' cures are highly appropriate. On those grounds, it was evident that Mandu would have a "lot of work to do," Alexandre said, for those sicknesses are what appear most frequently among the Baniwa. So Mandu knew he was being given a great responsibility to save lives. This has been his life's mission.

It is altogether in keeping with his pride in the warrior tradition that Mandu made a point of telling me to emphasize in his life story that he worked for the army as a pajé in their hospital, even though the army never paid him anything.[5] This is similar to the way many Native North Americans express their pride as war veterans, an adaptation of warrior traditions. His long associations with the white army, air force, and airstrip maintenance shows he played an astute politics, a strategy of working for the white man's authorities in order to be informed and to be well known among the white military. Above all, he had a charismatic way of commanding attention, of leading the community, and of intermediating for the community.

Hohodene express great pride in the warrior courage and resistance of their historical ancestor, the warrior Keruaminali. If it had not been for his courage and resistance, there might not be any Hohodene left, the story goes, because the whites had taken them all by force down to the lower Rio Negro. Similarly for the Walipere-dakenai phratry around the Pamaale stream. For the Baniwa, the white people, *yalanawinai*, are of two kinds—those who help, and those who exploit. Baniwa discourse on the whites is deeply embedded in the traditions of Kuwai, which is our focus in chapters 6–8.

Apprenticeship is a decade-long ordeal that the pajé has to endure. Mandu's power was put to the test during many years of his career by sorcerers of his own village who—he and his entire family believed—were responsible for many deaths that occurred over a period of twenty years. In the next chapter, we reconstruct

II. Mandu and his apprentices in 2010. (Photo by Euzivaldo Souza for *A Crítica*, 2010.)

the long story of his and his family's struggles against the sorcerers of the village.

Now that we know more of the pajés' perspectives on the nature of this world, and why humans will be in great danger if they abandon their traditions, we understand how important it is for Mandu to transmit his knowledge to new generations of apprentices. The project of constructing the House of Shamanic Knowledge in Uapui (see chapter 9) was a demonstration by Mandu's children of the great respect they have for their father's spiritual and political leadership. Today the Baniwa of the upper Aiary have a maloca-style longhouse where a whole new generation of apprentices is actually being formed among Mandu's sons, grandsons, and sons-in-law. It is located at the village where Mandu has lived almost his entire life. It is also the place where the world began for many Arawak-speaking peoples. There are very strong reasons to believe that the new Shamans' House of Knowledge and Power, built in 2009, will achieve its goal of strengthening shamanic traditions.

3

"You Will Suffer Along Our Way"

THE GREAT SUFFERING IN MANDU'S LIFE

In his life narrative, Mandu refers to periods of much suffering, and there are strong reasons to believe that his suffering was related to the deaths of many members of his family caused by a single sorcerer, who was a sib-brother, from the early 1970s until 1989. This story is now over, but it shows a long-term struggle for power between a sorcerer and a pajé, a theme that appears in many of the narratives about the "wise men" of the past. The final end of Mandu's struggle, however, is the triumph of the pajé over the sorcerer.

To fully appreciate the importance of the following story as paradigmatic of the battle of pajés and sorcerers, a battle of life and death, which ultimately can involve the whole community, political factions within a community, and intercommunity relations, we have to go back before Mandu's birth, when his grandfather Marcellino Euzebio opened up the forest around Uapui to start a settlement in the early 1920s. This is based on Hohodene oral histories corroborated in part by written documents of the period (see my 2005 book for complete documentary references).

Then as now, the Hohodene, Walipere-dakenai, and Maulieni were the principal phratries on the Aiary. Among the Hohodene, the local descent group at Uapui is today considered the "eldest brother" sib of the phratry. The Hohodene consider themselves to be the owners of the Aiary, having occupied that river for centuries.

According to their political history, the sib nearly became extinct during the period of Portuguese slavery and relocations in the eighteenth century, but their ancestral chief fled from the lower Rio Negro, where the entire sib had been taken, and returned to the Içana. Later the Walipere-dakenai made an alliance with the Hohodene chief by formally offering a daughter in marriage. Thus the Walipere became the Hohodene's principal affines.

In the Northwest Amazon, marriage is followed by a period of uxorilocality, a relation of temporary power of the wife-giving group over the wife-receiving group. The daughter's husband owes a period of service to his wife's father, which includes the cutting of gardens or building of houses. This lasts until the birth of the first child, when the natal family returns to the husband's descent group community. In the case of the ancestral Hohodene chief, he and his wife went to the headwaters of the Quiary River, a tributary of the lower Aiary, and had ten children, an ideal number of offspring indicating the sib had fully regained its social viability.

Over time the Hohodene settlements grew, occupying both the headwaters of the Quiary and Uaraná Rivers. Through an accord they made with the Walipere-dakenai, the latter also settled on the Quiary, and eventually both began making settlements on the banks of the Aiary. The Hohodene chief was killed by the Walipere-dakenai with poison [*manhene*], confirming the extreme ambiguity, already mentioned, perceived to be inherent in affinal relations: on the one hand, solidarity (dance festivals, marital ties, mutual support) and on the other, enmity and treachery (poisoning through sorcery).

By the time of the first extensive ethnographic reports on the peoples of the Aiary by Koch-Grünberg in 1903, the main riverbanks were inhabited by the Maulieni sib of the Hohodene phratry at the headwaters and the Walipere-dakenai and Hohodene from the middle to lower river. The Walipere-dakenai were politically the most important, with their center at the large and prosperous longhouse of Cururuquara on the mid-Aiary.[1] The chief of Cururuquara, according to Koch-Grünberg, was considered to be the general chief of the Aiary, and he served as an intermediary between the Indians and the rubber patrons. He was also considered a powerful pajé. Undoubtedly, the combination of these factors consolidated the power of the Walipere-dakenai of the village of Cururuquara over other sibs and villages of the Aiary.[2]

It also exposed them to the envy and sorcery of other communities. During Koch-Grünberg's visit, he witnessed the death of a Hohodene man in Cururuquara which the Walipere chief attributed to poison, given by "hidden enemies" from the man's "upriver kin" (most likely the Maulieni). Hohodene elders in the late 1970s said that the village of Cururuquara in fact had passed through a long history of sorcery killings between them and the Maulieni upriver—each giving poison to the other, in the context of dance festivals. The situation reached such a critical point that, according to one man, "the people of Cururuquara were nearly finished off." Indeed, when the ethnographer Curt Nimuendajú passed through Cururuquara in 1927 on a reconnaissance visit, he noted that the population had been reduced to about half of what it was at the beginning of the century.

Eventually, the survivors abandoned the longhouse and formed a new village slightly upstream, Kuichiali numana, which over time recovered its population so that today it is again one of the principal Walipere-dakenai villages on the Aiary. The important point is that sorcery is seen as the principal cause of the downfall of a large and prosperous village, a political center, reducing it to a few survivors. Envy at the prosperity of large villages and

12. Dyuremawa (Maulieni) Maloca on the upper Aiary River, 1927. (C. Nimuendaju, 1927, courtesy of the Museu Carlos Estevão, Universidade Federal de Pernambuco.)

treachery between affines are certainly motives for such historic sorcery warfare. On the other hand, it is important to note that external factors were also responsible for an increase in internal conflicts, for the early twentieth century was a period of extreme violence with the rubber boom and the aftermath of the bust as well as epidemic diseases (Wright 1998: part 4).

Similar processes were at work in the history of Uapui. The difference was that, surprisingly, sorcery literally tore away at the community from within, among descent group brothers (parallel cousins). Although affines were originally hidden behind the conflict, they were eventually openly accused as having been key intermediaries in the sorcery assaults.

Having followed this history for more than twenty-five years, I shall present my reconstruction and interpretation of these events based on Mandu's and other interlocutors' statements and my own observations. It is to me a paradigmatic case of the devastating role that sorcery can have in the history of a community; it is also exemplary for understanding how actors saw the situation escape their control. It raises key questions about the nature of sorcery and its correlates with tensions at different levels of social relations. Finally it illustrates the relations between external, imposed change (in this case, missionary intervention) and interpersonal conflicts expressed through assault sorcery.

As Cururuquara was gradually losing its political strength in the 1920s and 1930s, Uapui was emerging as a new center, but of the Hohodene. In the early 1920s, Marcellino Euzébio, grandfather of Mandu, cleared the forest on the banks of the rapids of Uapui and built the first longhouse there, larger than the one at Cururuquara. The place had not been occupied for many generations, although people often went there to sharpen their stone axes on the rocks of the rapids.

Uapui (Hipana) for all Baniwa was and is the sacred "center of the world, umbilicus of the world" where there are numerous petroglyphs that refer to the stories of creation. While it is a sacred place of origin, it is paradoxically considered also to be a place of poison; in the dry season, when the river is low, numerous holes appear in the rocks of the rapids, inside of which there are various kinds of poison—carbon, ash, "little stones"—that, according to the pajés, anyone may gather these and combine them with plant poisons obtained from certain hills in southern Venezuela to produce an arsenal of weapons.

By the 1950s Marcellino Euzébio had died, it is said, because of manhene given by the Walipere-dakenai. Shortly after his death, the unity of the longhouse (which Mandu recalled with much nostalgia) underwent some transformations. Several of Marcellino's sons moved away. With the second rubber boom, they migrated to Venezuela, leaving only three in the village: Keruami, Seraphim, and Joaquim. Salesian missionaries sought at this time to gain a foothold on the upper Aiary in order to stop the advances of Protestant evangelicalism, then a fast-growing movement among the Baniwa. Seraphim's sons (Mandu and his brothers Lourenço and Gabriel), Joaquim, and Keruami, then chief of the village, allied with the Salesian priests against the Protestants because, as Mandu said, the Catholic priest (Father José Schneider) was a worker and sent them material to build new houses. His sons had constructed three or four other longhouses on the locale, thus giving the place an air of prosperity.

In the early 1970s the Salesians sent an itinerant missionary to Uapui to start a grade school for the children of the upper Aiary. Many people from the upriver communities started sending their children to the school and even built houses in Uapui to live temporarily during the school year. Uapui thus became a political, social, and economic center of the Aiary. It was also a center of shamanic knowledge and power, with five pajés and some of the most knowledgeable Hohodene elders who had protected their traditions against the onslaught and repression of the Protestants.

Yet, as in the case of Cururuquara, this prosperity became vulnerable to the envy of those on the periphery, affines in particular. In this case, the enemy was the youngest son of Joaquim, named Emí, who for various reasons exiled himself from the rest of the community and resorted to sorcery to eat away at the prosperity of his own "brothers" (parallel cousins). In fact, Emí's use of sorcery against Seraphim's sons began at the time all of them got married. Mandu and his two younger brothers married three out of four Walipere-dakenai sisters; Emí married the fourth. However, Seraphim did not reciprocate the gift of the three daughters by giving one of his daughters in return to marry the only brother of the four sisters. Seraphim gave his daughter to the Wanano family from whom he had received his wife.

The father of the Walipere-dakenai women was enraged by this offense and secretly gave manhene to Emí, instructing him to poison Seraphim's wife. Her death was a major loss to the family, as Mandu said, for now there was no one to cook or take care of the gardens. It was a terrible emotional blow to Mandu, his brothers, and father. But it was only the first of a long series of deaths by manhene, all of which were attributed to the workings of a group of three sorcerers (Emí, Júlio, and João), all residents of the village of Uapui at the time of my first fieldwork there in 1976–77. None of the three are alive today.

Emí had publicly declared his intention to take vengeance against the entire community of Uapui, apparently in return for the death of one of his children in the rapids and specifically against Mandu and his family in return for a severe sickness (which he interpreted as sorcery by poisoning) which nearly killed his eldest son.

In all of these cases, we must keep in mind the whole drama from Emí's perspective: Emí's father, Joaquim, had been a shaman, but he was killed by a curse thrown by Cubeo shamans. Injury was piled on insult when the Catholic missionaries deprived Emí of the post of chief of the village—his by right. Finally madness overtook him, and "his only thought was to kill," as Mandu said. A few days before my arrival in the field, Emí announced in public that he intended to kill off all the schoolchildren of the village if his eldest son died.

Emí was thereafter marked as a sorcerer, *manhene-iminali*, who had poisoned several people in Uapui. Whether all the accusations leveled against him were justified was of less importance than the fact that, due to his public declaration that he would kill everyone in the village, he became the principal suspect in all deaths. It was only when I revisited the Baniwa in the 1990s, and after Emí had died of his own excesses, that Mandu and several other elders explained to me in greater detail the uncontrolled chaos provoked by his actions and the deeper and more sinister means he used to realize his objectives.

Emí and Mandu had been enemies since childhood, and it seemed as though every important moment in their lives was marred by their disputes. Mandu maintained good relations with Emí's elder brother, Edu, who was the one who invited Mandu to begin training to become a pajé.

Their perpetual conflicts were aggravated by a dispute over succession to the position of village capitão in which the Catholic missionaries had intervened, supporting Mandu. Emí, by traditional right of succession (he was the first son of the eldest of the male siblings still alive from the previous generation), had been capitão, but people complained to the missionaries that he was always away fishing and did nothing for the community; rather, the community worked for Emí's personal projects. Hence the missionaries decided to remove Emí from his post and put Mandu, then vice capitão, in charge.

During the 1970s, eight close relatives of Mandu were allegedly poisoned. Seven died and one survived, though severely debilitated. In all cases Mandu and other pajés suspected Emí; in several cases, the dying victims confirmed these suspicions by telling other family members who it was that they had seen put poison in their caxiri beer. As Mandu said to me in 1977, following the death of his father, "Emí has given manhene to six people already. He is the only one in Uapui who has manhene. His only thought is to kill (*manhekada lima*, roughly, 'in the manhene mode of thought'). He wants to kill us all so that only he remains. He sees the world that way and always has."

Besides being a clear statement of Emí's having lost control over his thought and ability to live together in the community, it was a clear reminder of the fact that Emí lived right next door to a house of the animal souls, powerful sorcerers who sought to kill Nhiãperikuli and his kin. Despite Mandu's skillful politics, none of his strategies (e.g., calling Emí to participate in community activities) seemed to work in controlling Emí's increasingly unbounded desire to create a generalized climate of terror.

It was only when two pajés decided to seek vengeance for their father's death by going to the Wanhíwa that Emí backed off on his campaign, but only temporarily. Their voyage had nothing to do with seeking retribution against Emí, since their father—a powerful prophet—had been killed by other pajés; nevertheless, since they did not make their intentions public until much later, it acted as a warning to Emí.

Mandu affirmed that things began to get out of hand at the time when an itinerant Salesian missionary took up residence in the village in the early 1970s. Before then, there had been cases of manhene, but they were very few and under control.

Shortly after the Salesian missionary began teaching in Uapui, she hired an assistant, a Wanana girl from the upper Uaupés who was Mandu's niece. It must have been during this time that one of Emí's children accidentally drowned in the falls and his eldest son suffered an attack of tuberculosis. Unexpectedly someone in the village gave manhene to the Wanana girl, and she died. Her father alerted Mandu that it was someone from Uapui who had given poison to his daughter, and he demanded that something be done to avenge her death. Mandu didn't know who it could have been. The girl's father eventually took a lock of her hair to the Wanhíwa shamans at the town of San José del Guaviare in Venezuela.

According to him, the Wanhíwa performed their sorcery and

showed them who was responsible: Emí had undertaken the killings in collusion with his brother-in-law, Júlio, a Walipere-dakenai, who had planned the killing with him and had involved Júlio's kin João, affine to one of the principal Hohodene pajés of the Aiary. It was discovered that it was the son of Júlio's kin João, also a Walipere-dakenai, who had poisoned the girl. Júlio had given poison to João's son, a schoolboy, to put in the girl's food; subsequently the boy, an innocent accomplice to the crime, was killed by sorcery. João was also involved, as the Wanhíwa inquest clearly indicated.

Once this became public knowledge, years after the Wanana girl's death, João was told by the community to leave Uapui. He decided to live for a while in São Gabriel da Cachoeira; later he moved to the Orinoco and then to the town of Puerto Ayacucho on the Atabapo River in Venezuela, where he spent the rest of his life.

Júlio also went to the Orinoco (not because of the inquest, he said, but rather because his son had "gotten a sickness" in Uapui). Júlio was ultimately killed by shamanic vengeance. In short, Júlio, a Walipere-dakenai, acted together with Emí and João in plotting and executing the death of the schoolteacher's assistant at Uapui. Mandu believed furthermore that his father and all the others of his family who had died in the 1970s and '80s were victims of this scheme. Another of his sons, Eduardo, was poisoned by Júlio, as determined by the inquest Mandu held shortly after his death.

According to Mandu, Emí was the first to use poison on others; then he began persuading Júlio to join him in his plan to "ruin the community." All the shamans of the upper Aiary, including João's and Júlio's affines, knew who was responsible for the increase in deaths at Uapui but could do nothing because of (1) their fear of reprisal by Emí and his cohorts against their families; (2) Emí was a sib brother (although this evidently was not a deterrent for Emí, whose "thought" by then was completely out of control); and (3) because the trip to the Wanhíwa to seek vengeance is costly and dangerous.

Emí's scheme was driven by a desire to seek retribution against Mandu for Emí's son's sickness. Resentment complicated the situation because the itinerant missionary counted on Mandu to undertake the mission's plans. Later, when Mandu was able to get a paying job to keep the airstrip clean behind the village of Uapui, Emí's envy grew deeper: how could one become so wealthy and prosperous, while he remained forever in debt to the merchants? It is not difficult to see how Emí's envy festered like a cancer.

Thus Mandu believed that it was for all of these reasons that Emí poisoned his mother, then his father, then his uncle. As his father lay dying, he warned Mandu that "this Emí has so much poison, if you don't kill him, he will kill all of you. Only he has manhene." Even Emí's elder brother, Edu, a pajé, confirmed this to Mandu: "Don't you know? He is a poison owner, he is full of poison." But the only solution to this problem was through the Wanhíwa because, as Mandu affirmed, "we of Uapui go to the Wanhíwa. It is they who kill for us." This was a local practice, according to Mandu, because the people of the comunity of Ukuki, a short distance upriver, go to *macumbeiros* (Afro-Brazilian assault sorcerers) of São Gabriel and even Cubeo shamans to perform such services.

It took several years for Mandu to get together the resources sufficient to make the journey in 1989, and even so, according to interlocutors, the Wanhíwa failed to kill Emí. The only sign that they sought vengeance was that a stone fell on the roof of Emí's house—nothing more. A full decade was to pass before the case was finally settled.

The date October 6, 1999, remains marked in the minds of all those who suffered and survived poisoning attempts by Emí, for it was when Emí died. According to Mandu, Emí's death was due to a "tumor" in his stomach. Nobody could say how it began. Months before his death, Emí discovered he had an ulcer and consented to be sent to the hospital in Mitu, Colombia, where he was admitted to surgery. People say that he was prohibited from drinking anything following the surgery, but he disobeyed orders. He fled from the hospital and went back by foot and canoe to Uapui. There, according to several people, he became "gluttonous," observing no restrictions on eating or drinking.[3] He resumed his previous way of life, again without observing any food restrictions (on pepper, for example), drinking manioc beer, and even doing heavy manual labor.

Predictably he developed a new problem. An external nodule on his stomach grew to the size of a small rubber ball. Advised that if he didn't take care of it, he would surely die, he went to the Protestant mission at Tunui on the Içana River and later to the Casa do Índio of the National Indian Foundation (FUNAI) in Manaus. By that time, the tumor had become impossible to control, and Emí soon died. The delegate of the FUNAI, who knew of Emí's long history of sorcery in Uapui, paid to have him buried in Manaus in the FUNAI cemetery on the banks of the Tarumã River. As in life, Emí remained an outsider to his community, this time permanently. He evidently died of his own excesses, not because of shamanic vengeance, or at least no one cited this as the reason. It was no doubt a relief to the villagers of Uapui that neither his shade nor any part of his being would affect their lives again.

It may be seen that Emí's actions were driven by motives that went far beyond vengeance for the loss of a child and his eldest son's sickness. After all, his elder brother, a pajé, who had suffered the loss of two sons by manhene, had discovered who was responsible and taken revenge (*likoada*), and that was the end of it. Nor did it have to do with his father's death by sorcery, which was attributed to the Cubeo and not to his sib-brothers.

First of all, there was Emí's incessant and intense hatred for Mandu going back to the time when they were boys—"they have always been enemies," people said. This enmity eventually extended to Mandu's entire family, fostered by his wife's father, a Walipere-dakenai, who "initiated," so to speak, Emí into the practice of sorcery, using the young man as fodder to return Mandu's father's failure to reciprocate his gift of four daughters in marriage.

Later, Emí's hatred was fueled by his "envy" (*likhema*) that they were the most numerous and successful family of the village. Mandu and his brothers had expanded the village, and in this they were supported by the Salesian missionaries and had greater success in negotiating with the whites. In other words, they had greater access to economic and political power within the village. Whenever people referred to Mandu, most said they "waited for" and "listened to" his words, his counsel, and assessments.

In the late 1960s and early 1970s, when his uncle José velho became too old to continue as chief of Uapui, he transferred the post to Emí, but Emí did not "work for the people." He would always be off doing his own work, or he got the community to do work just for him. The missionaries knew about this problem because Emí was never around when they visited. Mandu would respond, and he was liked by the Salesians, who deposed Emí and promoted Mandu. The Salesian bishop Dom Miguel Alagna had big plans to turn Uapui into another mission town like Jauareté or Pari-Cachoeira.

Mandu was confirmed by the community to be their new capitáo, and he exercised his leadership with great skill and competence. For many years he was an outstanding orator and intermediary with the white people. Villagers followed his orders to do community work, for he always spoke with certainty and vision. Coupled with his shamanic powers, which ranked him among the "true pajés" of the Aiary, Mandu had unequalled prestige, which was in large part why Uapui was for many years the political and religious center of the Aiary.

By contrast, Emí was unsuccessful in his relations with missionaries and with merchants, to whom he was always in debt. Ironically he was in constant debt because he would buy expensive new merchandise—such as battery-operated record players—that he thought would attract more people to his house for parties. Instead they looked on him with wonder and pity. How would he ever pay his debts to the merciless merchants? It was this "pity" which even some of the victims of Emí's sorcery cited as motives for not taking vengeance against him immediately. Why else would the people of Uapui allow this case to extend for so long, unless they were simply waiting for him to burn up in his own excesses, which seems entirely plausible? After all, he was a close kin, parallel cousin, and interlocutors were adamant in denying that they would never kill a sib brother or parallel cousin with poison.

For that reason, the expulsion of two Walipere-dakenai accomplices and their deaths by sorcery, together with Emí's death, represented the retribution that the family of Mandu sought.

Beyond their pity for him, Uapui villagers sought to treat Emí with tolerance and as an equal. For example, shortly after I first started living in Uapui, Emí had them help clear his gardens—as they did for anyone in the village who requested, on the system of *ajuri* work parties—although they never "followed" or "respected" Emí's freely given assessments. According to many villagers, he only acted in his own interests.

Frustrated in his inability to become a center of community attention, he resorted to resistance against Mandu by refusing to participate in community projects or, if he did, by turning them into disorderly affairs that accomplished nothing. In this resistance he had the support of his affine, Júlio, who likewise often refused to obey Mandu's calls to participate. There was always a rift between those who followed and those few who resisted Mandu, which produced considerable enmity.

Emí was forever suspicious that others might poison the food they offered him. Once while Emí and I were in a Wanano village on the Uaupés, our hosts offered us manioc porridge to drink. Emí made a point of showing what to me looked like a thorn floating on top of the porridge. To him this was clear evidence that the Wanano intended to put sorcery on us. His paranoia was most certainly connected to his suspicion that the Wanano would try to get retribution for the death of the young Wanano schoolteacher, who was the daughter of an important chief and pajé.

Emí was also a master at surprise attacks. Once when I was returning to my room at night, I was taken aback when I saw him in front of my doorstep with a strange expression on his face, which I recorded in my notebook as "the grin of a madman," chuckling cynically about how "we treat the white men well!" It sent chills down my spine, and from that moment on, I felt it best to keep my distance from the man.

Whether Mandu had a direct hand in Emí's sickness and death will never be known for sure. During the time I lived in Uapui, he never acted with physical violence directly against Emí. The most that I ever witnessed were some verbal exchanges of accusations. Years later, he told me that it was through the Wanhiwa that the Hohodene avenged their losses by shamanic vengeance. It seems more than likely that Mandu went to Venezuela in 1989 to seek the help of the Wanhiwa following his son's death by manhene. It was in this context that he met the Venezuelan anthropologist Omar González-Ñáñez, who interviewed Mandu for the film *Las Advertencias de Mandu*, a fitting title for that time of his life.

The sickness that led to Emí's death began many years after

Mandu's visit, however. With Emí's death, the community of Uapui now had a chance to rebuild the social fabric that had been torn apart by him and his co-plotters' sorcery.

MANHENE IMINALI (OWNERS OF POISON), ASSAULT SORCERERS

The sorcerer is a prominent figure in Baniwa traditions who merits a separate treatment. Unfortunately, I do not have sufficient interview material with the primary sorcerer in Mandu's life. I knew both Emí and Mandu at the time they were in dispute, and I witnessed several conflicts involving the faction within the village that supported Emí. My interviews with Emí were always very formal, on subjects unrelated to poisoning incidents. I found him to be a very agitated person during the interviews, but also very meticulous in giving information about parts of the house, body, kin terms, or drawings of the village croquis.

What is sorcery for the Hohodene Baniwa of the Aiary River? Elsewhere (1998, 2004a) I have characterized the sorcerer and the techniques they manipulate to kill. While this topic is full of mystery, it is accompanied by the real fear and dread of the violence of sorcery. Nevertheless those who have suffered from such assaults are more than willing to speak about them, analyze them from all angles, even if they refuse to openly accuse an author of the crime. "One doesn't know," they say, "one cannot know" who was responsible for the assault, and they prefer to leave discussions about such matters unspoken or veiled in mystery. They leave the inquests and justice to be undertaken by powerful sorcerers from a distant land, thus deflecting vengeance to outside their society and relieving themselves of any further reprisals.

"Poison owners," or *manhene iminali*, I translate as assault sorcerers. Poison and poisoning incidents are an important part of Baniwa politics and culture, central to their representations of sickness and death. Assault sorcerers specialize in the preparation and use of poisonous substances (plants, berries, resins, ash, etc.) to kill, and they are attributed dangerous powers associated with spirits of the dead and ancestral sorcerers.

This specialization in assault sorcery extends to various neighboring indigenous peoples of the Northwest Amazon, such as the Guahibo, Piaroa, Cubeo, Tukano—and also urban mestiços who have introduced the traditions and techniques of Afro-Brazilian sorcery, or *macumba*, into the region—forming a dynamic of aggressive and defensive actions. Guahibo shamans of the Vichada of Colombia, especially, have historically served to counteract or undertake vengeance on Hohodene sorcerers.

The word *manhene* means "one does not know" or "it is not known." It is translated into Portuguese as "*veneno*," poison (and in *língua geral* as *marecaimbara*) and refers to the practice of secretly putting toxic substances into the food, drink, personal objects, or natural orifices of an enemy with the intent to kill. Various forms of poisoning can produce such severe reactions (high fever, vomiting blood, diarrhea with blood) as to result in sudden death, while others provoke a process of chronic illness that slowly weakens the victim, leaving him pale, thin, anemic, and sometimes with behavioral disturbances similar to forest animal behavior and an incapacity to perform the normal activities of daily life. For all Baniwa, manhene is the most serious and frequent form of traditional sickness and explanation for death.

According to Mandu, there are at least fourteen kinds of manhene. Those most commonly used are the following three:

Lidzuna causes severe abdominal pain, followed by headache and vomiting. One can die from this after three or four days if untreated. I was informed that the incidence of this particular form was increasing greatly on the Aiary in 1999. In the pajés' cures, fur (*lidzu*) from the black sloth is the visible form of the poison extracted. The poison is secretly put in the victim's food or drink. While the actual poison may derive from a plant, when extracted it appears as black sloth fur. Why this occurs, we will understand only through the sacred narrative of Kuwai, whose body is covered by fur of the black sloth and whose liver transforms into poisonous plants.

Despite the common knowledge that it is a sorcerer who puts the poison into the victim's food, the poison transforms in the victim's stomach into black sloth fur. How is unknown. Its immediate effect is to make the person totally incontinent, vomiting and defecating with terrible aches and pains in the stomach and head, and burning with fever. This is consistent with what narrators frequently say of the spirit owner of sickness, who "makes holes in people's bodies."

The names of most other forms of *manhene* end with *-ikaime* referring to the sorcerer's power, the opposite of the shaman's healing power, the root for which has the same suffix, *-ikai*, as in *malikai*. The suffix *-me* seems to indicate a negative form of power, that which is the inverse and opposite of *-ikai*. Further on, we shall see other ways in which the sorcerer's power and the shaman's power are manifest through similar material forms ("bones," tubes) in which these "powers" are contained. (Thanks to Dr. Alexandra "Sasha" Aikhenvald, who had the patience to hear several of these linguistic puzzles over the years.)

Likaime is said to be an ash from the waterfalls at Hipana. It produces the same symptoms as lidzuna, but the pajé extracts "white hair" from the victim; another form is yellowish and is extracted as a yellow stone. Again, a transformation occurs in the stomach of the victim, from ash to hair/fur/stone. When the German ethnologist Theodor Koch-Grünberg visited the Aiary River communities at the beginning of the twentieth century, he witnessed a pajé's cure during which a man died from manhene, which the pajé showed to the ethnologist as a wrapped leaf bundle of "white dog's hair."

Puwekaime was more common in the past than it is today; *puwe* is the name of a monkey, and the victim is said to "go mad," "run into the forest, climb a tree, and stay there three days, then he goes back to his village." Remedies include putting a bark extract in the victim's eyes, apparently so that he "sees" as a human should.

There is one anomalous and particularly dangerous form of man-hene that is not put in the drink or food of the victim: a poisonous dart/thorn called *uephetti* (or *walama-kaime*, that is, the "sorcery power of the spirit dart") goes into the victim's canoe, and when he gets into the canoe, the thorn jumps up and into an orifice, thus penetrating its victim. Evidently this form of poison is considered to be a living agent independently capable of attacking its victims.

Throughout the cosmos there exists an enormous variety of spirit darts from the top of the Other World all the way down the central axis and into This World. They fly about in the air when there are storms. Or they may be sent by pajés who have a large arsenal of these. The origin of these spirit darts is also Kuwai because at the moment the women stole the sacred flutes, spirit darts shot out of the mouths of the flutes, turning the men back and helping the women to flee.

Poisonous berries are also included in the list, one of which is placed near the victim's nose as he sleeps, and its smell provokes headaches and weakness. Finally there is the swift-acting piranha leaf put into the victim's drink, which is guaranteed to kill within a few hours.

All forms of poison are classified as "unknown," which refers to the secret mode of its application in food or drink; the secrecy surrounding the figure of the sorcerer, in both the manner of hiding the poison (inside a bone, at the bottom of a stream) and the manner of attack (secret flight). All poisons enter the body through the orifices: they are consumed or inhaled. All produce intense physical pain often leading to the victim losing consciousness ("dying") and potentially transforming into (i.e., exhibit the behavior patterns of) an animal or otherwise losing all sense of self. Finally, most forms of manhene have their basis in Baniwa sacred stories of the constant struggles between Nhiãperikuli and the various animal tribes who in the primordial times attempted to create chaos and thus wipe out all people. Sacred stories of sorcerers are remembered in various petroglyphs and through real-life incidents that occur with frequency in Baniwa lives.

One important point should be stressed: the Baniwa jaguar shamans are the only specialists in health who know the methods of the sorcerer and the specific cures for each type of manhene. Certainly their extractions have produced vital results. However, one or two pajés cannot handle all of the cases that are appearing per year. Given that, the pajés express their worries that there need to be more apprentices trained, as well as a more fruitful exchange of knowledge to occur between biomedical specialists and the pajés as to the most effective treatment of these deadly ailments.

In contrast with other indigenous societies of Amazonia, Baniwa pajés say they do not double as sorcerers; in fact, pajés say they have the power to kill, but they adamantly deny they use manhene poison, affirming that their principal function is to cure manhene. The pajé's power to kill, I venture to say, is primarily through means other than manhene, in other words, *walama*, especially spirit darts.

While anyone can learn about poisoning and is capable of occasionally using sorcery, it is not just anyone who is considered to be a "poison owner," for this requires specialized knowledge of the location and preparation of poisons and their antidotes.

Not only this, a poison owner is considered to be "no longer like a person," for "his only thought is to kill." The body and soul of such a sorcerer differ from "normal" people. The poison owner's body, according to pajés who "see" their true nature, is like the ancestral sorcerers, a tribe of the tree-living animals called *eenunai*. Pajés see them with fur all over their bodies; they see the poison owner's heart-soul as a spirit of the dead, *inyaime*, which generally inhabits the periphery of This World: "When a poison owner enters a house, first inyaime goes in, then the body of the sorcerer," according to José Garcia. This image of the body of a monkey (or *idanimi*, shadow-soul, "that which walks in front") coupled with the spirit of the dead inyaime (literally, "the negative Other") is precisely the image we shall see in a crucial episode of the sacred story of Kuwai when he transforms into the monstrous demon inyaime and devours three children after they have broken the rules during initiation. Inyaime are a concern both among crente evangelical villages and the traditional communities.

Sorcerers usually live in separate, one-house settlements. Thus Emí lived with his wife and children in a settlement on the periphery of the main village of Uapui. Although it was on the same side of the river as the village, it was situated a good 100 yards away and down from the main village line of houses situated on the upper banks of the river. Emí built it near a rapids connected with the spirit house of the animals, whose chief is Iaradathita. Here were two clear signs to the villagers that Emí was in the fullest sense of the term a manhene iminali, because the chief of the animal souls is a powerful sorcerer to whom a human sorcerer can appeal for assistance in attacking a victim.

Another detail of importance: it is common knowledge that the sorcerers hide their poisons inside bones at the bottom of a stream somewhere in the vicinity of their village.[4] The sacred flutes and trumpets—the body of the great spirit Kuwai—are likewise hidden, wrapped in leaves, at the bottom of streams. The sacred flutes are considered poisonous for women and the uninitiated to behold, and the poison-inside-the-bone is an image of Kuwai, who left manhene in This World at the moment of his fiery death. Thus the sorcerer is quite literally the anti-pajé, for his heart-soul is said to "fly with the bone of manhene"—the counter-image of the pajé's soul flight upon having pariká blown through the bone called *maaliapi* (white heron bone) into his nose.

In the "nexus of religious knowledge and power" discussed in the introduction to this book, the various forms of knowledge and power are interconnected in numerous ways. The sorcerer and the healer pajé are opposing poles; thus we can expect that the symbols attached to their practices would be thoroughgoing inversions of each other. The pajé who exercises his power to kill, however, is not the same as the poison owner because the pajé does not kill for the sake of killing, nor does he use manhene but rather another part of the body of Kuwai, the spirit darts, *walama*.

Besides extracting poison, pajés usually recommend plant medicines (various types of roots called *kapuliro*, which counteract the gastric effects, as well as herbs to provoke expulsion of the poison in the victim's stool). While the Baniwa have also discovered a number of white man's remedies (liquid vitamins, for example) that help in cures for poison, many still seek the cures of pajés first.

What motivates a person to practice poisoning or even to become a poison owner?

1. Retribution (*lipuamina* or *liuma likuada*, exchange), vengeance for the death of a kin who is believed to have been poisoned or killed by sorcery. In this case, the person may either seek retribution through the Guahibo sorcerers or take vengeance personally, if the dying victim "tells" who is responsible for his or her murder.

2. Envy (*nakhemakan* or *maatchi likapakan*, he sees a person badly) at the success, prosperity, and well-being of others, relative to

one's own situation. Debt, rejection, isolation, and continued misfortune may fuel a person's desire to "ruin" the lives of those who are more successful and prosperous.

3. Resentment (*maatchi likaale*, his heart-soul is bad), for example, when a person does not live up to his or her part of an exchange (e.g., marital), producing an inequality, or when someone is known to have spoken malicious gossip.

4. The total loss of control over one's thought and emotions (*man-hekada lima*, someone whose only thought is to kill). This implies that the sorcerer no longer has any control over such emotions as hatred, anger, or envy.

In the past there were other motives for poisoning related to ritual transgressions, such as exposing the sacred flutes and trumpets to women, who would immediately die.

What are the social correlates of assault sorcery? That is, do certain social relations serve as conduits more than others? My initial idea, based on the counting of known incidents, was that it occurs more frequently among affines than among consanguineal kin, which would be consistent with sacred and historical narratives. When I pressed my interlocutors about this, they responded: "One doesn't know, one can't know." One man said, "It could be anyone, sib-brother, cousin."

My interlocutors agreed that manhene killings don't occur among members of a nuclear family, but as the circle of kin widens to include parallel cousins, sib-brothers, and at the extreme, affines (*imathana*) and potential affines (*itenaaki*), the probabilities become ever greater. With "enemies"—socially, geographically, and linguistically distant peoples—warfare (*uwi*) was waged in the past. With the abandoning of warfare, affines and potential affines are perceived as the greatest internal threat to kin groups.

This would be consistent with the hypothesis advanced here that the question of inequality is the crux of the issue: the sorcerer's ultimate objective is to redress imbalances in power relations in the community such that what he perceives to have been taken away is restored. A loss of a child is considered to be a source of imbalance demanding a redress by the removal of one family member of the accused. A failure to reciprocate in marital exchange is also a serious enough breach to warrant poisoning.

It is unknown whether there exists any internal differentiation among sorcerers as there is among the pajés. Minimally we can say that there are people who commit acts of sorcery for specific ends and no more. But if a person continues to practice it, it seems as though he is drawn into a state of "only thinking of killing" or killing until one's "heart-soul is satisfied" (*huiwa nakaale*). This could mean slowly wiping out a community. The only solution for that kind of situation is ambushing or killing at a distance. There are, in addition, numerous protective orations to thwart the attacks of sorcerers and, undoubtedly, orations to prevent sorcerers from stealing one's dream-soul during the night.

Are there other, more collective mechanisms for preventing manhene within one's community? One has to do with the deliberate shaping of community sentiment through discourse that downplays any and all discussions of, or references to, sorcery and its transmission. Such discourse could occur on the occasions of the elders' speech to initiates counseling them on the correct ways to live together. The Hohodene from the very large and prosperous community of Ukuki on the upper Aiary, for example, insisted that there were few cases of manhene in their community because the elders "only spoke of good things"—dance festivals and music, happiness—and frowned upon discussions having to do with poisoning incidents.

Another occasion for such discourse is the village chief's counseling or publicly haranguing the community on the occasion of some social transgression. In Uapui, Mandu frequently spoke to the community about living well together, not being sad, because sadness can lead to anger. However, rapid change provoked disruption and disorganization, and much conflict was translated into sorcery attacks. The case of Uapui was peculiar, however, because Mandu and Emí were parallel cousins, and Mandu was a relatively powerful pajé at the time of the killings.

In this regard, it is of great importance that oral histories point to the control of assault sorcery by poisoning as one of the most important objectives of historical prophets. Such figures sought to eradicate its use by publicly revealing those whom they knew to possess poisonous substances, exhorting them to throw their poison away. Their efforts worked to create community unity and discourage whatever would provoke misunderstanding and conflict. In the past, pajés say, sorcery cases were infrequent (a few cases per year or less), but the numbers increased along with a greater interference in their lives by external agencies. Independently of whether these agencies were of help or not to Baniwa communities, they did transform the indigenous reality in a number of fundamental ways.

Among the most delicate of the problems that have been created with increasing outside influence are wealth differences. For example, an NGO's policy of focusing initially on "pilot projects" for the implantation of experimental stations, or differential education, has created a distinction between those who have direct access to the benefits of these schools and resource tools and those who do not. This has given rise to resentment, lack of unity between community blocs, conflicts, and the increasing incidence of manhene, especially when projects do not provide for equal distribution of new resources among all communities, thus creating "excluded" communities. This has led to sadness, envy, and the desire to restore balance.

In Baniwa sacred stories of creation, there are numerous instances when something new is distributed relatively equitably among all peoples of the ancestral past. Frequently narrators claim that their own phratric ancestors received "more," but in principle, all peoples were present at the event to receive their share. This is one basis, then, for an ethic of "resource distribution" that has implications for contemporary circumstances. A group who receives little or nothing of a resource, while another receives much more, will seek to even out the differences, and sorcery by poisoning is one mechanism.

One case of a young evangelical leader, illustrated in the film *Baniwa, a Story of Plants and Cures* (2005), by Stella Oswaldo Cruz Penido, shows how the shift in power relations—from the elder generation to the younger—in a bloc of communities, resulting from intense involvement in the region's indigenous movement, did create tensions serious enough to have resulted in the poisoning of a young leader named André Fernandes. (Wright 2009b discusses this case in more detail.)

All forms of poisoning and sorcery began with Kuwai, who, according to the sacred story, taught Nhiãperikuli and humans how to chant at initiation rites and to cure, but he taught *hiuiathi* sorcery chants to Nhiãperikuli's younger brother, Eeri, who, thinking that they were to do good, transmitted them to humans. Eeri is the same figure as Mawerikuli, the first person to die as a result of manhene.

Other versions say that in the great fire that marked Kuwai's death, he passed all his knowledge about hiuiathi (which particularly affects pregnant women and their children, as well as extramarital amorous relations) to the spirits of nature called *yoopinai*; for this reason, they are the true sorcerers, or *hiuiathi-iminali* (sorcery owners) in the world today. Either way Kuwai, whose body gave rise to all the yoopinai, was the source of all forms of sorcery. Other spirit beings and humans learned and transmitted this knowledge over the generations.

The social and political dynamics of manhene, sustained by the sacred narratives on the origins of the world and the nature of conflict—are at work whether in progressive communities of evangelicals or in traditional communities. Behind the smokescreen created by the discourse of manhene, there is a logic that appears in Baniwa sacred stories in which, in order to realize vengeance for the death of his kin by his affines, Nhiãperikuli uses all manner of artifices to deflect the responsibility of vengeance to the outside and unknown. Nhiãperikuli is a trickster (Hill 2009; Wright 1998) who succeeds in killing his enemies by feigning, through magical and secretive actions at a distance, just as the Guahibo do. Such artifices and deflection to external causes are essential to Baniwa sorcery.

In regard to the principal motives for sorcery among the Baniwa, there do not seem to be any differences from those uncovered by ethnologists in numerous other societies of the world. Motives are passionate, and as others have observed, these motives can certainly be related to "structural tensions" within society, such as conflicts over the unequal distribution of resources.

One of the striking aspects of the stories of pajés' warfare among themselves, however, is the way in which the cosmos becomes a battlefield with various places for capturing and taking the soul of an enemy or unsuspecting pajé. One must always be on one's guard against these attacks, particularly if one has a lot of knowledge. Owning more shamanic knowledge and power is sufficient motive for an envious sorcerer to strike.

In rare instances, Baniwa assault sorcery today may assume proportions which know no limits in the sense that it becomes an insatiable desire to kill, until the enemy Other is demolished. In such cases as when the enemy belongs to the same sib, then the sorcerer is marked by the community as permanently peripheral, equivalent to a spirit of the dead. The sorcerer then exploits affinal relations to realize the deadly objectives of retribution.

Sorcery is another of the mysteries of the cosmos. "One doesn't know" and "one can't know" who is responsible, although an observer easily deduces that actors are perfectly well aware of all that is going on. "One doesn't know" is a cover that throws the responsibility of retribution up to the level of cosmological processes, that is, ultimate causes, referring to the spirit being who is responsible for the origin of all sorcery. In the story of Kuwai, retribution by sorcery killing and trickery are all part of a fundamental cosmic dynamic between kin and affines, fathers and sons, men and women.

To prevent manhene from taking hold of a community and destroying it from within, some elders reinforce a community sentiment of happiness, living well together, and avoiding discussions of sorcery incidents. The great Baniwa prophets of the past focused their messages and actions precisely against sorcerers who provoked discord, revealing their nefarious intentions in public, thus reshaping community sentiment toward a much desired harmony and unity.

DEFENDER OF MORAL TRADITIONS:
LAS ADVERTENCIAS DE MANDU

By the end of the 1980s, Mandu was considered by many Arawak-speaking peoples of the Amazon region in southeastern Venezuela and northwestern Brazil to be one of the truly powerful pajés of the entire region. A defender of the traditional moral order, Mandu became the subject of a documentary film produced in 1989 by Venezuelan anthropologists, indigenists, and the indigenous people of the town of Maroa on the Venezuelan Guainia.

Las Advertencias de Mandu (*The Warnings of Mandu*), was made while he was in Maroa, the municipal capital, where he received many people of different ethnic groups who came to consult with him. They alerted him to the fact that many individuals were using the teachings and knowledge of their ancestors improperly. The "crioullo" population (non-indigenous or of mixed descent) in particular, which was growing in number in towns such as Maroa, was using shamanism for political purposes, and consequently the indigenous peoples were losing their traditional cultures. If the indigenous people didn't react, Mandu warned, the result would be disastrous, and they would only experience misfortune and ruin.

He spoke especially with the elders and revealed the names of numerous individuals who were using sorcery to kill their enemies or harm people who did not support them. Like other Baniwa prophets since the mid-nineteenth century, Mandu publicly warned that these were the errors that had caused the destruction of the world in past times and the disappearance of the "ancient peoples" who had once populated the earth. Whole families had been devastated by shamanic attacks, and thus the crioullos were able to dominate the indigenous population as slaves and take their lands from them. Mandu emphasized that it was necessary to "continue following the traditions and the healthy customs of the ancestors" because these were the key to cultural survival and the continuity for all those who followed them. As he said: "Indian people have to live in harmony, no more sadness; show respect for and observe the ways of our ancestors; if we move away from these ways, we will suffer catastrophe. This is what happened to the ancestors in the past."

JAGUAR SHAMANS AND HISTORICAL PROPHETS AMONG THE HOHODENE

Cosmogonies of many native peoples throughout the Americas express the belief that the world was destroyed and remade several times before the creators were satisfied (Sullivan 1988). These cosmogonies foretell that other destructions and reconstructions will occur in unspecified future times. In such cases, the sacred stories of the primordial times may become the source of action in the sense of realizing popular hopes for "concrete utopias" (Barabas 1987). The movements associated with them therefore should not be considered simply as the consequence of external pressures but also of dilemmas and paradoxes internal to indigenous cosmogonies. In some cases emissaries of the deities have acted as interpreters of the signs of the times, foreseeing the end-times as a necessary passage for the regeneration of the world.

In the sacred stories of the Baniwa of the Aiary River, the world was destroyed by conflagration and flooding on several occasions. Thus it is entirely possible that some of the historical prophets did foresee cataclysmic events, as alleged in the written historical documents. In fact, the Baniwa have a long prophetic tradition dating to at least the mid-nineteenth century, the history of which is told in detail in several of my and Jon Hill's publications. The first was Kamiko, a Dzauinai prophet who emerged in 1858 and, according to the written documents, preached the end of the world by fire and the descent of God to earth, while his disciples sang and danced the songs characteristic of the Kwaipan initiation rites. If the documents are correct in what Kamiko stated, this would be entirely consistent with Baniwa cosmology in which all of these things did happen in the sacred myth of Kuwai, the moment when he was burned in a huge fire and the world shrank back down to its miniature size. It was Nhiãperikuli, or Dio, who made this happen.

Kamiko's influence was widespread among indigenous and mestiço communities of the upper Guainia and its tributaries in Venezuela, the Içana River up to about the community of Tunui, and the Xié River. The numerous oral traditions about Kamiko state that he began a tradition called the "Song of the Cross" and that his principal message was the elimination of sorcery and the installation of a society based on harmonious conviviality. There is variation in the traditions from one phratry or ethnic group to another, but most state that Kamiko had miraculous shamanic powers to escape all attempts by the white military to kill him and that he even foresaw the whites' own destruction, a prophesy that was realized when the military commander at San Fernando de Atabapo, the rubber baron Tomás Funes, was executed in a rebellion by his own soldiers in the 1920s (Hill & Wright 1988; my thanks to Jonathan Hill for showing me a photo of Funes' tomb at San Fernando).

Written records indicate that Kamiko died in the early twentieth century. Other prophets emerged, including Uetsu mikuiri, said to be Kamiko's "son," who was from the Adzanene sib of the Hohodene phratry on the upper Guainia. In May 2010 my field assistant from the community of Ukuki interviewed Laureano, chief of the community, whose father, Ricardo, was one of Uetsu mikuiri's canoers. This man did not know the prophet personally, but his father had told him many stories of his miraculous cures. In response to my question, "What was his message?" Laureano answered:

He said to the people: "You will suffer on our way"—*hirapitina wapuwa* in Baniwa. When it was the night before a festivity, he looked for people to celebrate together, and at the same time he helped people in their difficulties, telling them how much time that person would remain alive with their families, or with regard to a sickness that he was about to get, like poison and other kinds of sicknesses of indigenous peoples, Uetsu would help those people protect themselves.
[As with Kamiko and Mandu, it is said that he would pray every night, "in a very reserved way":]

He sat in his hammock, and during the prayer he would lie down for a long time, during which time he would converse with Nhiãperikuli, and when he returned from his dream, he would come back praying silently until he woke up. When he came back, he would always ask for water to quench his thirst, and then he would say that the way was difficult to be able to get to Dio Nhiãperikuli.

I asked, "So he gave counsel in the same way the pajés did, by payment (*dawai*)? How did he die?"

With poison (manhene), he had no more power to defend himself. According to the story the pajés always tell, all around them there are mirrors through which they can see an enemy from all sides, but when his time comes, the pajé's powers of vision no longer work.

The next prophet was the jaguar shaman Guilherme Garcia (or Kudui), who knew and worked with Uetsu mikuiri and likewise was a great healer. According to Laureano, Uetsu mikuiri and Guilherme "walked together in knowledge. Uetsu would confirm for people that, after he left This World, there would be a person with the same knowledge as he had, but after the death of that person, there would be no other successor to him in his knowledge. But it would be very difficult for there to be another person who was as wise as he. Now in our times, I don't know whether José Garcia [deceased in 2009] was one, or whether another one will come later. Let's wait and see what's going to happen."[5]

Kudui died from sorcery in the early 1970s and was buried in the cemetery on Warukwa Island. Before he died, his sons related, the Salesian nun Irmã Teresa from the state of Ceará had bought Kudui's sacred rattle. She gave him a shotgun for it. What she did with the rattle is unknown.

This is as colonialist a story as one can find, and indeed the Salesian Missionary Order was found guilty by the Fourth Russell Tribunal in 1980 for the crime of destroying indigenous cultures in the Northwest Amazon region, as was the North American, fundamentalist evangelical New Tribes Mission, who had Christianized the Baniwa in the 1950s. Kudui also resisted the intrusion of the evangelical pastors into the villages of the upper Aiary (Wright and Ismaelillo 1982; Wright 1998, 2005).

Why did Guilherme Garcia trade away his sacred rattle? She insisted, he said, but he had warned her that if anything happened to him afterward, the roof of the house wherever she lived would come crashing down on her head. Shortly after he gave up his rattle, it is said that Guilherme began to get very "sad and sick" because he was without his kutheruda. From what we have said, the kutheruda is the "Other self" and companion of the pajé; it protects his family. Kudui was killed by an enemy pajé's manhene, it is said.

Pajés and many people believe that the heart-souls of the prophets return to their graves and stay there to attend their families of kin. For that reason, people today still visit these graves and place coin offerings, requesting their protection or intercession to prevent adverse situations, especially following an omen. The prophets were great diviners (*linoparotaka*) and had the power to intercede with the deities to prevent a tragedy or terrible sickness from striking.

On the Aki River, indigenous people of the upper Guainia similarly continue to visit the tomb of Kamiko. In some ways like the "saint cults" of popular Catholicism, the prophets Kamiko, Uetsu, and Kudui are believed to protect their communities even after their departures from this physical world. Their graves are places where the living converse with the souls of these immortal shamans. Their teachings continue to circulate as an underlying theme in conversations today. Their messages of living well

13. The tomb of the prophet Kudui on Warukwa Island (d. 1974). (Photo by Isaias Fontes.)

together, in happiness, without sorcery, revealing the secret evils in society, are among the most important moral guidelines the jaguar shaman prophets have taught.

Mandu da Silva is considered by many peoples of different communities and by his clientele in the city of São Gabriel to be a "wise man" (*sábio*), and he has already added his wisdom to a long line of counselors and great pajés before him. He was a charismatic chief of the community of Uapui for many years. He is a *kalidzamai* chanter as well and knows a large repertoire of chants. It wasn't difficult for the Foundation for Shamanic Studies to grant him its Living Treasure award in 2009.

TABLE 2: Prophetic Traditions of the Northwest Amazon (including Tukanoan and Arawakan prophets)

Year	Prophets	Group	Following	Locations	Oral Traditions	Written Sources
1857–1902	Venâncio Anizetto Kamiko	Dzauina Baniwa	Baniwa, Baré, Tukano	Içana (Brazil), Acque (Venezuela)	Dzauinai, Hohodene	Wright 1981; Wright & Hill 1986
1858	Alexandre, Basílio Melgueira, Claudio José, Cypriano Lopes	Baniwa Baré	Tukanoan and Tariana	Lower/Mid-Uaupés (Brazil)		Wright 1981; Wright & Hill 1986
		Wareken Wareken	Baniwa and Warekena	Xié River (Brazil and Venezuela)		
1858	Caetano	Baniwa	Baniwa	Uaupés		Wright 1981
1875–1903 +/-	Anizetto, *Uetsu mi*	Baniwa Adzanen	Baniwa, Tukano, Kuripako	Cubate River, Upper Guainia, Aiary		Wright 1981; 1998; 2002; and 2005
Late 1870s–1880s	Vicente	Arapaço Tukano	Indians of Uaupés	Japú Igarapé (Lower Uaupés)		Wright 1981; Hugh-Jones 1989
*	Joaquim Parakata	Tukano	Tuyuka, Karapaná, Tariana, Dessano, Pira-tapuya	Papuri, Tiquié Rivers		Hugh-Jones 1989

Year	Prophets	Group	Following	Locations	Oral Traditions	Written Sources
End of 19th century	Maria	Dessano	Tukano, Dessano, Pira-tapuya, Maku, and others	Papuri, Tiquié, Uaupés Rivers	Dessano	Panlon kumu & Kenhíri 1980; Freitas 1983; Bruzzi da Silva 1977
End of 19th century	"Bishop" Paulino	Tukano	Idem.	Turí igarapé	Tukano	Freitas 1983
Beginning of 20th century	Yewa, or Lino Sêwa ("Santo Lino")	Tukano	Tukanoan	Montfort (Papuri River), Uaupés, Tiquié	Dessano	Hugh-Jones 1989; Panlon kumu & Kenhíri 1980; Bruzzi da Silva 1977
Early 20th century	Raimundo	Tukano	?	Turí igarapé	Dessano	Hugh-Jones 1989
1948–1950 (+)	(Sophie Muller, et al.)**	(North America Curripaco)	Kuripaco, Baniwa, Cubeo	Içana, Aiary, Cuiary, Querary, Guaviare, Guainía	Baniwa	Wright 1998
*	Tukanoan and Bará emissary	Tukano	Barasana, Bará, Arapaço, Tatuyo	Pira-paraná (Colombia), Tiquié	Barasana	Hugh-Jones 1989
1960s–1970s	Kudui	Hohoden Baniwa	Baniwa, Wanano	Aiary River	Hohodene	Wright 1998

** No specific information available; information is obtained from oral traditions. (Source: R. Wright 2002.)

Table 2 summarizes the most up-to-date information on the wise men and women, except for one story of a Cubeo wise woman.

MANDU'S CONCERN FOR THE DESTRUCTION
OF THE WORLD BY INDUSTRIAL SOCIETY

In early July 2010, shortly after the BP Gulf oil spill, I asked Mandu about the disaster, framing my question by remembering first the other natural disasters that were occurring at that time, such as the floods in northeastern Brazil. Did he think that the world was nearing an end? Familiar with this notion through his people's cosmology, he replied that, yes, the end-times were "almost" coming, adding:

> They've [the oil company, British Petroleum] penetrated the first level below This World which is the home of the Iaradathita, the place of the animal souls which humans cannot (or should not) disturb; the second level likewise cannot be disturbed by humans; and now they are at the third level, which is the place of the Chief of the Animal Souls, the owner of all the worlds of the animal souls. For that reason, humans cannot disturb it. . . . They have to stop. Tell them they have to stop!

Baniwa cosmogony recounts several times in the past when the world was destroyed by fire and by water in order to cleanse it of sorcerers, cannibalistic animals, and demons, which are believed to have plagued humanity in primordial times.

Indigenous Amazon jaguar shamans are considered to be powerful seers who know of events that are about to occur by direct consultation with the divinities in their cosmos. Dzuliferi, the most ancient of the pajés, the spirit of shamanic power, is said to know everything about the future of every human being on this planet. Mandu is well known throughout the region for his deep understanding of cosmology and sacred narratives and his ability to foresee events that, sooner or later, have actually come to pass.

Although Mandu has never seen a mining or exploratory oil rig, he knows firsthand the rubber camps of the 1940s and 1950s, and he has heard the explosions of dynamite behind the city of São Gabriel, where a company hired to build a hydroelectric dam for the city's energy is removing rocks to prepare the construction bed. From his people's cosmology, immediately beneath our earth is the world of the animal souls, which has three levels, the most important being that of the chief, who is the spirit keeper (guardian) of these worlds. What BP did was to invade the territory of the animal spirit worlds, destroying their habitat. Mandu believes the spirits can be expected to react by sending catastrophic sicknesses and epidemic diseases. Mandu said there would be an "explosion that will kill thousands" because people were not respecting the territory of the animal souls. The drilling provoked an explosion that killed thousands of fish, birds, wildlife.

News photos showed the terrible holocaust that befell the animals. The jaguar shamans are trained to understand this world of the animal souls. They understand through long experience that the world of the whites is dominated by technological and industrial thinking, which is directly opposed to a worldview that believes in the active presence of spirits and deities in this world. The result of the BP's invasion was a disastrous slaughter of thousands of living beings.

Concluding, the wise man or woman is recognized as being a true emissary of the divine based on information about the community the pajé has served, the specializations of knowledge the pajé has acquired, and the moral counsel the prophet has consistently taught. Thus Alexandre Jawinaapi's foretelling that Manuel was destined to be a great pajé was a prophecy fulfilled; it was knowledge that came from Dzuliferi. Mandu has been seen as a strong leader for more than three decades, and until 2010, when I last saw Mandu, he maintained his message of the search for happiness and commitment to continue the shamanic tradition in his family. The prophet's time on earth depends on his being able to see his "mirrors," for those are what protect him from enemy assaults. When the prophet's time in this world is nearly over, the light in the mirrors fades.

In oral histories, the prophets emerge as great counselors and diviners, struggling against sorcerers. Their common objective was that of creating a harmonious community, and for a while they succeeded, but when they were no longer able to see the mirrors and their powers no longer worked, it did not take long for the sorcerer enemies to react. Nevertheless, the prophets are considered fundamental models in Baniwa history, like the historic ancestors of the phratries. More than that, they are considered to be much like the creator deity, who outwits the enemy by mastery of strategy. They are, seen from one angle, the historicization of the mythical models, the intervention of the sacred in history showing that the Baniwa understanding of their history is far from being a closed account (Sullivan 1988). Rather, it is one that permits the intervention of the deities into human affairs through the wisdom of the prophet.[6]

The life story of Mandu and the memories of the prophets raise critical questions regarding the nature and sources of shamanic power and knowledge as well as assault sorcery. To understand these more deeply, we have to go back further in time to the first creation and present a more or less coherent view of the cosmos, the knowledge and powers of the deities and spirits, and their relations to temporal cycles, sacred geography, and human history. This view ideally should emerge from the ethnography itself. When we reach an understanding of the universe as a whole, we will then be in a better position to understand the most important of the sacred stories, the epic of Kuwai, the Sickness Owner, the Poison Owner, whose body became the sacred flutes and trumpets that initiate the children into adulthood and whose chanting knowledge was transmitted to the elder men at the first rite of initiation. Nearly everything about the jaguar shaman's knowledge of sickness is related to Kuwai and his place in the cosmos.

Part 2

Shamanic Knowledge and
Power in the Baniwa Universe

4

Creation, Cosmology, and Ecological Time

This chapter discusses the metaphysical and ecological principles through which the Baniwa pajés of the upper Aiary River understand their universe (Hekwapi). The most knowledgeable sources on this are the experienced and powerful jaguar shamans. Here I seek to build on and revise previously published versions of cosmology (Wright 1998) with the information provided by several of the highly respected and powerful jaguar shamans still alive at the beginning of this century. Two of them have since died, one through old age and the other because of a serious accident. It is important that their versions of the universe, complementary to Mandu's, be known.

First, the stories of creation published in Cornelio et al.'s *Waferinaipe Ianheke* (Wisdom of our ancestors, 1999), based on research with Baniwa elders in the 1970s and 1990s, did not contain the story of the first universe and the universe child, Hekwapi ienipe. This evidently did not please some Baniwa elders, who pointed out this error and wanted the "correct" version to be published in its entirety. The opening episodes of that version are presented here.

Second, I am convinced that a different way of seeing the inter-relations among the levels of the universe could better reveal several principles that dynamically give it shape. This chapter is especially indebted to Irving Goldman's *Hehenewa Metaphysics* (2004). This work provides important insights and ethnography about a people who are neighbors to the Baniwa of the Aiary and who share many aspects of cosmology and shamanism. For the purposes of this chapter and this book, Goldman's work is the most significant ethnography of indigenous religions of the Northwest Amazon ever published.

Third, this chapter develops more deeply an ecological under-standing of the universe and its relation to shamanism, building on a long line of research among the neighboring Tukanoan-speaking peoples by Reichel-Dolmatoff (1985, 1989, 1996), his daughter, Eliza-beth Reichel (1999), Janet Chernela (1993), Kaj Arhem (2001), and others.

Finally Hill's book on the Wakuenai (Kuripako) "trickster" myths (2009) about "Made-from-Bone" presents versions that are, in many aspects, similar but distinct from those told by Hohodene and Dzauinai jaguar shamans of the Aiary River. Thus it is appropriate to present the two traditions as variations and seek to understand their differences in relation to distinct historical contexts.

What this chapter attempts to do is systematically think through key features of the Baniwa cosmos: (1) relations among the worlds above and below the world of humans, (2) the kinds of knowledge and power attributed to the creator deity and to the great spirits of the Other World, (3) the material and nonmaterial forms this knowledge and power take and how these are transmitted from ancestors to descendants; (4)the pajés' powers in universe-making, as evidenced in the sacred narratives; and last but not least, (5) the "ecological metaphor" inherent to the arrangement of levels of the cosmos. The ecological metaphor assists in understanding the arrangement of critical norms and values situated at different levels.

One of the points to be examined is how and why the jaguar shamans' views of the cosmos show an asymmetry between the "Other World" (Apakwa Hekwapi or Apa-kuma), the primordial and eternal world, the world of the deities and great spirits, and the "World Below," called "Place of Our Bones" (Wapinakwa), the world of the bones of the deceased, the souls of the animals, and a series of worlds of different and strange "peoples," all of whom are images of a proto-humanity that may come into existence "in another end of the world," as the Baniwa pajés say.

The nature of this asymmetry can be understood through the qualities of the different "peoples," spirits, and deities of the Other World. These qualities are expressed in shamans' exegeses about each level of the universe. The levels of the Other World can be seen as "magnified versions" (Fausto 2008) of each of the principal "specialists" outlined in table 1 (chapter 1). Apakwa Hekwapi and Wapinakwa are normally accessible only to the pajés.

The importance of presenting the universe as a whole is in placing humanity (or This World) in proper perspective both spatiotemporally and as part of an interrelated process between the highly developed and ancient forms of Apakwa Hekwapi and the unfinished proto-forms of Wapinakwa.

The relation between the sacred stories, which recount events of the "Before World" (*oopi*), and the eternal Other World that pajés continue to visit today is that the narratives are about the time-spaces of the first ancestors who prepared This World for humanity. The stories reveal how the complex structure of the universe came into being, with each level being the subject of one of the major cycles. The memory of the events that occurred in the Before World are inscribed on stones (the petroglyphs) that were at one time "wet" and are believed to have been the work of Nhiãperikuli, the creator, who wanted to leave a record for future generations by drawing images on the stones. Those stories and their material manifestations serve as constant reminders to humanity of conditions that came into being, lessons learned but also as models by which to guide human action. They are, as one Baniwa leader said, "stories that we live by," and they are understood as guides to moral behavior.

After the deities and spirits created the conditions of This World for their descendants, they went to live in the eternal Other World, accessible only to the pajés. The deities and spirits there, nevertheless, are "alive" in different time dimensions from humans. To them, humans belong to the "new generations" (walimanai), and to humans, the deities and ancestors belong to the Before World. Each of the principal deities and spirits also has its own peculiar spatiotemporality, although to humans, they are all old (oopi).

By attempting to see the universe holistically, we reaffirm the findings of earlier studies (G. Reichel-Dolmatoff 1976; E. Reichel 2009), which demonstrate how shamans are responsible for environmental cycles and sustaining an ideal ecological harmony. Ecological knowledge is systematically organized and follows certain principles of "energy exchange," as in the exchange of souls of animals for the souls of humans (Arhem 2001). While I do not focus on the food chain as such, it is important to recognize that the jaguar pajés have always been seen as the caretakers of seasonality and are thus the indigenous ecologists. Indigenous ecological knowledge is sacred knowledge in the sense used by Fikret Berkes (1999): a knowledge-practice-belief complex consisting of local ecological knowledge, social institutions, and worldview.[1]

This chapter begins by presenting stories of the creation of the universe, followed by a panoramic view of the universe and the twenty-five worlds it contains. In seeking to understand the metaphysical principles and ecological relationships among the levels, our focus will be on some of the principal forms evident in the representations of the cosmos and their qualities of "fixity" or "fluidity." One form in particular, the tube, has been examined by previous scholars (Hugh-Jones 1989; Hill 2009) as characteristic of Northwest Amazon cosmologies, but it has not been shown how a single form such as the tube is a vehicle for several kinds of knowledge and power that are critical to life-giving and life-taking processes in the universe: healing, sorcery, chanting, initiation, and dance rites. The umbilical cord, for example, is one of the primordial images of the tube through which flows ancestral power. The bone is another concrete image in shamanic practice that is a vehicle for the transmission of primordial powers. The bone is also a place for hiding poison used in sorcery. Each combination of tube plus spiritual power can be understood by the different kinds of knowledge and power that shape Baniwa perspectives on their universe. These kinds of knowledge and power are complementary, overlapping in many ways, yet distinct in others, since each serves a different purpose. All of them together form the nexus.

This holistic view of knowledge of the universe provides us with the proper perspective for understanding the sacred story of how the pajés originally obtained their spiritual powers. This story should be considered as being among the important cycles that come immediately after the story of the very first universe. From the story of the pajés' powers, it is easy to see how temporal flows and spatial movement acquired shape and form through the calendric cycles related both to shamanic transformations and food-getting activities, as well as to the sacred geography or "mythscape" inscribed with the meanings of the primordium found throughout Baniwa and Kuripako territory.

In 1998, one of the young leaders of the Baniwa on the Içana
River decided he wanted to find the most complete version possible of his people's creation stories. The young Walipere-dakenai
leader had raised a question about *Waferinaipe Ianheke*, a book of
sacred stories of the Hohodene and Walipere-dakenai organized
with several narrators (Cornelio et al. 1999) from the Aiary River,
because the story of creation began with an episode about the
universe people, or Nhiãperikunai, the Cricket Brothers, which
he said came much later than the episode below.

The oldest of the few remaining Baniwa jaguar shamans at
that time agreed to record this "true" version, which is quite different from those that have been previously published. To the
young leader's prompt—"tell us how the universe began, Grandfather"—the old pajé replied as follows (my translation):

In the beginning there was only a little ball, Hekwapi.
Nothing else around. A vast expanse of nothing around the
little ball.
There was no land, no people, just the little ball of stone.
So the "child of the universe" looked for earth. He sent the great
dove Tsutsuwa to find earth for him,
and put it all over the little ball. He made that stone ball become
the earth.
The name of the universe child was Hekwapi ienipe.
He made the sun rise up then above the new earth, above the
hole in the earth Hipana, the umbilicus of the universe.
The universe child was all alone, so he went to look for people.
He went to the universe-umbilicus at Hipana, the celestial
umbilicus.
He heard people coming out of the hole.

They came out one after another, and he gave them each land.
Then he looked for night. It was inside a small, tightly sealed basket.
On his way back, he opened the basket just a bit, and night burst out, covering the world in darkness,
and the sun fell away.
He waited for the sun to return.
He and the birds waited for it to return.
When they saw the sun entering the sky, the birds began to sing, for it was the beginning of a new day.

The version cited here goes further back to when there was only one being, the universe child, Hekwapi ienipe, who was an orphan (*pawaada*) — no one existed in the universe before him. Nothing else existed before the little ball of the universe and the universe child. The universe was then floating in the emptiness of space, "nothing else around." The body of the universe child was the sun; in the primordial universe, there was always light.

The story begins with three connected elements: (1) the miniature stone ball, Hekwapi; (2) the space all around it, *lipukuthawa*, a vast expanse of light all around, for the universe child's body is the sun; (3) and the universe child, Hekwapi ienipe. No one knows what the universe child — who was the maker/transformer of the universe — really looked like as a person (*newiki*). José Garcia declared that in his many years of soul travel, he had reached a place near Dio and that he had experienced a brilliant light flashing back and forth in a room surrounded by mirrors. This image of Dio is clearly associated with the prophetic leaders of the past, but the basis for it is the original shamanic power of light reflecting from all angles, illuminating all around the universe. Garcia referred to Dio Nhiãperikuli as the Illuminated one. He describes the universe child, Nhiãperikuli, and his world as beautiful, luminous, eternally young (*waliatutsa*), and shining like silver (*paratutsa*). The importance of this power of light for the prophets is that it dispels what is hidden (*lidawanikwa oopi*), reveals the secret, and brings back the primal state in which there was nothing unknown, nothing dark as in the powers of sorcery.

The body attached to that light was the sun at the top of the universe. Dio was situated much further beyond or above the primal sun (Kamui), but still attached to it as an illuminated source projecting a visible "body" (in contrast with the relation of body-and-shadow among present-day humans). This idea is found often in Baniwa religious thought, expressing the connection between a body and its shadow-soul. Hill agrees (pers. comm., February 16, 2011) that

> the idea of shadow-soul (*idanam*) is quite central to all shamanic ritual practices. In my experience, shamans (*maliri*) will "set up shop" in the morning, always facing east and using *dzaato* [pariká] and *dzeema* [tobacco] (as well as songs and rattling) to establish their contact with Dzuliwherri [*sic*] and other powerful spirit beings (or, alternatively, to take on the characteristics of these powerful spirit beings). But they never worked on healing any patients until after noon.

The body/shadow-soul connection is of great importance to cosmology. Many spirits have bodies of animals, birds, or insects, and these bodies are called their *idanami*, meaning "shadow-soul," "body-shaped soul," "that which walks in front." From the point of view of normal humans, for example, the chief of the *yoopinai* (spirits of the forest, air, and water) has a material body that is visible to humans as the lizard (*dopo*). Its shadow-soul (or dark interior) is projected as its body shape, the lizard.

The "personhood" (*newiki*) that humans do not usually see (only the pajés see) of the chief of the yoopinai has the form of a dwarf, with long hair and white skin, wearing a golden necklace and smoking a huge cigar. He is a pajé as well as chief of the yoopinai. From the human point of view, the visible body shape of the lizard and its shadow-soul are both connected to its personhood as pajé/chief of the yoopinai. Its features define its agentivity. The long, loose hair, the golden necklace, white skin, oversized cigar, undersized body—all cohere in meaning: whiteness (= spirit), golden necklace (the white man's power, contrasting with a true pajé's jaguar tooth necklace), undersized body (characteristic of beings from the World Below, chief of the animal souls).

Later on, we shall see how the sacred flutes and trumpets are Kuwai's material body (*dakidali*) in This World and, when played by the men, how the breath that flows through them brings them to life; they then are people. The great spirit Kuwai lives in the Other World and has an animal body shape entirely covered by hair, which is projected in its shadow-soul form both as a black sloth (*wamundana*) and as a little red-tufted white sloth (*tchitamali*), "secretary" of the large black sloth. The name *wamundana* can be broken down into its components: *wamu*, black sloth, and *idana*, shadow-soul; thus a translation of his name would be "black sloth shadow-soul." Kuwai's shadow-soul form is the sloth.

As "spiritual animal," Kuwai's body is a combination of the two-fingered sloth (*Chloepus sp.*) and the three-fingered sloth (*Bradypus sp.*), one very large and the other tiny. Thus on the petroglyph of Kuwai at Pukweipan, the two appendages for his arms have two and three fingers on its claws. The mask that the Tariana once used for their figure of Kue or Izi is supposed to have had a similar configuration of fingers on its hands and feet:

> The Tariana Yurupary myth ... states that the child Yurupary wandered around dressed in a monkey skin and that it is for this reason that the masks are used as his symbol.... The men

who wore the masks had visible only four fingers on each hand and only three toes on each foot; both the fingers and the toes were armed with long claws like the culture hero Yurupary of legend. (S. Hugh-Jones 1989: 194)

The Baniwa story of Kuwai states that, when alive, Kuwai transformed into various kinds of spirit beings whose body shapes are animals that live in trees, among which are a big-bellied monkey and the two types of sloths. Wamundana is of the Other World. *"Kuwai idanami wamu"*: Kuwai's shadow-soul is *wamu*. Kuwai's fur penetrated the sloths (Cornelio et al. 1999: 137) of This World, which is why the sloth's fur is the icon of poison (*manhene*).

The universe child is light, formless, and shapeless (a spiritual power), and his features are brilliant luminosity, reflectivity (light rays bouncing off mirrors), and intentionality (he "looks for" people, "looks for" night, etc.), while his sun body is the corporeal manifestation of that light. In speaking of spirits and deities of the Other World, nearly all have "bodily shaped" manifestations as visible beings in This World that humans today see, although the "people" sides of those manifestations are only visible to shamans.

Reichel-Dolmatoff in his *Amazonian Cosmos* (1969; original title is *Desana: Simbolos de los Tukano del Vaupés*) translated the word for the Tukanoan Dessano first deity as the "yellow intention," which has some merit when compared to the features of the Baniwa universe child, who also exhibits his "intentionality" and suggests the synaesthetic image of color plus power, attribute.

This sun deity is also called "our orphan father"; he is not the result of any prior reproductive process, but rather embodies the idea of self-generation. How did the universe child come into being? There is no answer; it always existed, along with the little stone ball and the vast expanse around. In one sense, the universe child means the universe as child, which throws a new light on the nature of the first being. The universe was not a bone—not yet at any rate—it was only the illuminated intention, the universe child, which later transformed into a bone from which three creator brothers emerged to put order into an already chaotic world. The light of the sun and the bone of a devoured person are two features of the creator deity that appear at distinct moments of the coming-into-being of the universe.

There is a hole located on the little ball, Hipana, an opening from which ancestral beings emerged from their virtual existence into the first world. This opening is the universe umbilicus, the primal cord of birth. When the universe child "looked for" the ancestral people, they were "born," dancing round and round at the opening until they finally jumped out of the hole. In the narrowest sense, the universe child is thus the first ancestor of all Baniwa and Kuripako, for which reason they call him "our father," Nhiãperikuli. In a wider sense, he is the father of all humanity (including the whites) and, most inclusively, the father of all living beings. In sum, Nhiãperikuli is a self-generated and self-generating principle that brings into the light of day the first generation of living beings and distributes them on parcels of land all over the earth, which was at that time still miniature.

These first beings, ancestors of various peoples, were not at all like human beings today. Nor were they shaped like animals today. Their forms and shapes were completely different; they appear to be shapes derived from concepts, as the body of the sun was derived from its self-generating light reflected by mirrors in a circle (the jaguar shaman's "mirrors," *ikanaale*). We can often see those forms of the first beings engraved on the petroglyphs throughout the region.

At the beginning of the Universe, there was no water anywhere. By contrast, today Hipana is the major waterfalls on the Aiary River and a place of great importance. Many universe-forming events particularly having to do with birth took place there. The rocks and boulders at Hipana are inscribed with the memory of these events as well as bodily impressions of the primordial beings cut into stone.

At Hipana, there is a large, perfectly round hole, called "the pot of the sun" (*pot* is commonly used to refer to circular depressions in the stone), which pajés say leads down to the worlds below and connects with the worlds above. This is the navel, also known as the celestial umbilical cord (*hliepulekwapi eenu*, from which the ancestors were born. Nhiãperikuli, the universe child, went to this opening, and when the sun was at its zenith, the ancestors of the phratries came out of the hole. Some narrators say that Nhiãperikuli let his saliva (*liahnuma*) drop into the hole, which is evidently a creative act of conceiving the ancestors, for saliva of the great spirits and deities has the power to generate new life.[2]

The words for "day" and "universe" in Baniwa are the same, *hekwapi*; thus another translation of *hekwapi ienipe* is "child of the day." The first temporal distinction came into existence when Nhiãperikuli went to look for night, since it was always day, and the sun did not move from its position at the zenith. There was no motion in the first universe, no water flowing, no time passing. It happened that Dainali, the spirit owner of night, gave Nhiãperikuli a "little basket" with instructions that the basket should not be opened under any circumstances until he returned home. The basket, however, was extremely heavy, for apparently unknown to him, all beings related to the night—birds, insects, animals, and the powers of sorcery—were contained inside it, in a state of virtuality. Like the opening at Hipana, inside the basket was a virtual kind of reality waiting to be brought into existence. The difference here, however, was that the container was sealed. Halfway home, Nhiãperikuli's curiosity ("what could be so heavy inside such a small container?" he asked) got the better of him; he disobeyed the instructions and opened the lid "just a little," but it was enough for the pressure of such a vast potentiality of nocturnal existence to burst out and cover the nascent universe in darkness. The sun suddenly dropped through the western door, "where the sun goes out" of the sky vault, bringing in its wake the state of darkness called *Deepi*, night.

It is significant that the gift of night came from an outsider, a spirit owner who is Nhiãperikuli's affine, his wife's father. From the beginning of the universe, the Other (affine) "owns" and transmits life-giving and life-taking powers to the (son-in-law) creator.

Nhiãperikuli's wife told him that her father had something good for him that would allow people to rest from their work, but the gift of night is double-edged. Because it came from the affines—the most ambivalent of all the categories of Other beings—it also brought sadness, creating the Village of Night in which sorcery prevailed, the pajés explain.

What is the significance of opening the basket "halfway home"? The sun was at its zenith, a moment that prefigures transformation in all Baniwa sacred stories. The sun—which up until then had remained immobile at the top of the universe—is suddenly set in motion, and daylight suddenly comes to an end. Day and universe come to an end. Darkness covers the universe. The birds and other animals begin to ascend the trees. Nhiãperikuli—as invisible intention—remains at the top of a tree on the eastern horizon while the sun, his body, moves beneath the universe and reenters the eastern sky vault.[3]

That this first long night is seen by the jaguar shamans, who understand its meaning, as intentionally catastrophic is revealed in their song "*Deepi karumi oopi*" (The first long night), about the Night Village (Wright 1998: 43–45). As Mandu explained, in the darkness of the night, there is the Village of Night (Deepi dzakale), where there was much sorrow and people were afraid of animals roaming around wanting to "eat people with poison," that is to say, use assault sorcery against them. This is the first reference we find in Baniwa world-making to a primordial form of poison, called *likurumahe*, and the predation of the animal sorcerers. Mandu explained this moment in the following way:

> The world ended once. Night covered the whole world. Nhiãpe-rikuli himself made this happen. Later he saved the world with his song. Then he asked the animals, "So you are not going to remain like animals, killing and eating people with poison?" Nhiãperikuli saved us.

Evidently the story relates how the alternation of day and night was set in motion, along with a set of other dualities — Nhiãperi-kuli/affines, light/dark, work/rest, and [the doors where] "the Sun enters"/"the Sun leaves." Night entered the world as the result of desiring a better condition, when people could rest half of the day and work the other half. This major transformation set the basis for an entirely new social order. The primordial division between an unchanging condition (always light) to a hoped-for "better condition" brings with it a situation of uncertainty ("how will it be for us now?"), followed by a transformation full of dangerous elements and a final resolution accompanied by a new order of space, time, and relations among living beings that is then "given" to all future generations, the *walimanai*.

During the first long night, Nhiãperikuli's wife threw poisonous ants at him in the darkness. But Nhiãperikuli transformed every poisonous ant into a harmless moth. Finally the day began to return, when the body of the sun returned through the eastern door to be reintegrated with Nhiãperikuli waiting in the treetop to begin a new day. (Note how "body" and "immaterial form" are separated and reunited, an important movement repeated throughout cosmology and shamanic rites.) From the "new universe" to the "new day," motion and time passage defined a new world order.

All the birds and animals announced the return of the day. The usual greeting at the beginning of the day is "*Haale waikahle!*" or "the white [sky] comes to us" as in the white, cloudy dawns of the Aiary and the brilliant whiteness (*haliapi*) of the Other World.

WHAT IS MEANT BY "THE COSMOS"?

In the sense we adopt here, the cosmos, or universe, is the temporal and spatial framework within which people seek to live a meaningful existence. (Sullivan 1988). The deities, demiurges, and spirits associated with different levels of the universe provide a set of fundamental values through which people understand and orient their activities.

In all cosmologies, there are at least two senses of spatiality: horizontal and vertical. Native Lowland South American cosmologies also show a feature that we might call "curvature in space/ time," for example, where the sky and earth meet, the sky being a rounded dome at the tip of which is a door leading to the other primordial worlds above.

Often each of the multiple worlds in the universe is thought of as a round disc, relatively flat, bounded by water, covered by the sky vault. Some versions represent This World as an island of earth surrounded by a body of water and connected to the other worlds above and below by tubes running through their centers.

Critical horizontal spaces include world centers, where typically the most important values and meanings of existence cluster in key symbols. Around these are frequently found markers of the main directions (mountains, lakes), as well as one or more interconnected spaces in which different kinds of beings make their homes.

Vertically the universe is composed of a series of interconnected layers, more or less one on top of the other. Each layer is a different world in which distinct kinds of beings live. The vertical dimensions of the universe vary widely in composition from simple three-layer arrangements (upper world, middle world, underworld) to massive twenty-five-layer compositions inhabited by a great variety of beings.

In general, the upper worlds are associated with creative and life-renewing forces of light, lightness, and liquids (rivers, lakes), and also with places of soul transformation, the ancestors, order, beauty, and happiness. In contrast, underworlds are associated with places of darkness, netherworlds of the dead and animal spirits, monsters, and inverted beings who can put sickness on humans. The middle world, the center of the universe in both vertical and horizontal senses, is the place of human life.

The worlds above and below are connected to one another in such a way as to constitute a whole. For example, the water cycles define the origin of rivers or bodies of water, the directions of their flow, their connections with the rain — all of which demonstrate how the planes of the entire universe are interconnected by aquatic cycles.

Certain kinds of landmarks, such as trees, mountains, waterfalls, and vines, are reminders that in the Before World there was always communication among the spatial and temporal planes. When the sun is at its zenith in the center of the sky, its rays penetrate through the centers of each world and alignment occurs from top to bottom. In sacred stories, references to the sun at midday often coincide with the descent of a deity from the upper realms into the world of humans, a mixing of worlds which is usually of great importance to both.

Introduction to the Levels of the Baniwa Universe

I present here a perspective on the universe as it developed from its very origin — when there was but one being, the universe and child — to the grand model of the universe today as narrated by the jaguar shaman José Garcia in the year 2000. Unlike the drawing

14. Kaxadadali, a Baniwa basket.

of the universe by Mandu, which has been published in several other works (1992b, 1998), the drawing presented here is based on Garcia's statements; he indicated how it should be, and I drew. His remarks were based on his extraordinary experiences of the universe, coupled with what he had learned from his father, widely recognized to be the most influential "wise man" and prophet of the recent past. It is by far the most elaborate schema ever documented of the Baniwa cosmos.

As Garcia spoke, I drew each level of the universe as a disk-shaped form with a tube running through the centers of each disk. Each disk is a "world," inhabited by a different tribe of people. The worlds can be seen as stacked one on top of the other, with the overall shape—according to Garcia—like a large woven basket called *kaxadadali*.

Garcia demonstrated how he "saw" the worlds below our earth

by looking down through the mouth of such a basket. During their cures, the pajés constantly fix their gaze upwards at the sky where the Other World is located, revealed after the pajés have snuffed the psychoactive powder called dzato or pariká.

The Other World is extraordinarily top-heavy, while the world below is an "undeveloped" version of the worlds above. A simple comparison to the jarlike basket shows how the shaman's vision can take in, as they say, the entire group of worlds above or below our earth "all at once." Being in the center positions the shamans to have this holistic view of the universe. Not only is their capacity to see-all-at-once important, but the feeling of wholeness is also essential to the shaman's perspective, Mandu emphasized. In a letter written by Mandu's daughter to the author (August 28, 2008), she explained:

> It is difficult to explain the wisdom of the pajé to another person who is not a pajé. For the person will not see what the pajé is seeing and will not feel what the pajé feels. We need time to explain each word and each level of the stairway that the pajé goes up to the Other World.

With that caveat, the following reconstruction is based on the conversations that Ercilia, Mandu, and I have maintained over the past several years (see figure 15).

The connecting tube from top to bottom is the "universe way" (Hekwapi iapuwa), a trail, which to the pajés is a "stairway," by which their heart-souls journey up or down. It appears to coincide with what is known as the celestial umbilical cord, which passes through the center of each world, beginning in the world of Nhiã-perikuli and extending down to a river of cold, fresh water (uni hapepawani) at the bottom of the universe. To understand how this could be so, we have to know that a single form can have many analogous meanings; in this case, each form consists of multiple spiritual connections. Thus the single tube form connecting all worlds may be a "stairway" for the pajés, a celestial umbilical cord down which the souls of newborn children descend at birth, or a tube (called *Dzuli-apo*) through which the souls of the recently deceased journey to their soul-houses in the Other World (Wright 1998: 208). All are connections, forms in this space-time, which are not fixed in the sense of a single, solid, material shape. Rather they may assume, in appropriate contexts, many analogous material shapes having to do with life-transmitting processes.

The notion of "center" is of utmost importance in the cosmos. There can be multiple centers of the world, in different physical places on a geographical map, but having the same name, Hipana, which signifies "world center." Thus the Hipana of the Aiary River is known by all Hohodene as the "center of the world" in both vertical and horizontal senses; however, the waterfalls have another name, Kupikwam, referring to a kind of forest vine that is found hanging from the trees around the falls. That forest vine came into existence at a certain moment in the myth of Kuwai. There are several other sacred places in the Arawak-speaking northern Amazon region that bear the name Hipana (on the upper Guainia River, for example, and on the upper Içana) (Journet 1995; Gonzalez-Ñáñez 2007).

Further, Baniwa and Kuripako elders confirmed that the best-known "sacred places"—where the universe began, where the first rite of initiation took place, where the women hid the sacred flutes and trumpets, and perhaps others—have local physical referents for them. The Kuripako affirm that the center of the world is the "City of Nhiaperikoli" (Xavier Leal 2008) on the upper Yawiary stream, off the upper Içana; the Baniwa of the middle Içana River region affirm that the center of the world for them is Jandu Falls (Ehnípan) near the mouth of the Aiary. In short, there exists what we may call an "ideal arrangement of sacred places," or "mythscape," that is mapped onto distinct geographical spaces (see chapter 5, below; Wright 1993; Hill 1993) and that corresponds to the worlds of different phratries.

At the borders of each circular world, sky and earth meet; each world is covered by a sky vault, like a dome. The opening of the vault—called variously "sky-door," "beginning of sky," "mouth of sky," "mouth of Kuwai"—is a narrow passageway leading into the Other World (Apakwa Hekwapi).

The point of junction of earth and sky on the horizontal plane is known as *eenu táhe* or *tsuwai*, "where the waters no longer run." The curvature of space-time is reflected in how people also understand spatial and temporal proximity and distance. The verticality of the universe drawn here should not be understood as fixed, however. The locations of up and down are relative to positions of the speaker.

At high noon, the sun's rays align with the center of the universe, producing the sun's reflection in the river of cold, fresh water that flows from west to east at the bottom of the universe. This is the most potent of the vertical positions that the "up-down" axis can assume. It is also the time when the pajés usually begin their cures (as they do among the Wakuenai in Venezuela; pers. comm., Jon Hill, June 10, 2011). The position of up and the location of the sky (*eenu*) and the Other World, however, can also refer to the top of a hill, for example, in relation to the shaman's position "down" on the ground. Or sky is the top of a tree, where a tribe of ancient tree animals (called Eenunai) once lived. The meaning of *eenu* is thus deictically dependent on the position of speaker and referent.

The axis of the universe can also be understood in relation to the water circuits, for example, in which vertically up or down may refer to upriver or downriver, respectively, coinciding temporally with before and after. The Before World, the world of the deities, besides being straight up above in the sky, can also refer to sacred places on the horizontal plane (This World) at the headwaters of the Içana and Aiary Rivers or at the tops of the few hills in the region, which are understood as the sources of rivers or as primordial lakes.

According to the stories, the Uaraná stream, off the upper Aiary River, is the place from which all water on this earth began to flow, from east to west, downwards until it reached the extreme downriver connection with the "great sea" where sky and earth meet, *eenu táhe*. There the waters of the world "no longer flow." At the bottom of the underworld, the waters reverse direction and flow back from west to east in an upriver direction, all the way to the upper worlds. From the upper worlds, water falls back to the earth as rain. This water cycle, besides being a major connection among worlds, provides passage for the souls of the deceased in their journeys, with the pajés' guidance, to their phratries' soul-houses in the Other World. This journey at the end of one's lifetime on earth ultimately becomes a return to the beginning of all life in the Before World of the deities.

The curvature of space from the top of This World to the place where the speaker is at a given moment is a way of marking spatiotemporal reference points from the distant to the proximate. In other words, the furthest away in time-space is straight above, coinciding with the origin of the universe. Tracing an arc down to the horizon brings the Other World closer in space-time to where he or she is located. A pajé once measured the distances in space-time from the zenith to about a 60° angle, where, he said, my family lived—very distant, still an Other world; continuing downward to about a 45° angle, where the city of Manaus—the world of the whites, likewise Other, yet close enough that Baniwa remember the place from their historical narratives—is located; and eventually to where we were at that moment standing in the middle of the village plaza. Similar ways of deictically connecting space-time to social distance can be seen in many phratric oral histories and in the movements of spirits from the Other World to This World in sacred stories (Wright 1998, chap. 3).

THE UNIVERSE AS GREAT TREE

The most significant vertical forms visible to everyone in the world of the Upper Rio Negro today are the great trees, magnificent beings that cross through many layers of the sky. It is little wonder that in Baniwa sacred stories, great trees also mark important periods in the construction of the universe. When in sacred narratives major trees are cut down, critical transition periods occur from one cosmic age to the next (end and beginning).

Hekwapi, the universe, is today structured into three main parts, each part being divided into various layers. The history of the cosmos is the story of how the universe expanded and grew from its miniature, undeveloped state, as a ball of stone floating in eternal space, to the height of its complex, diverse, and dynamic powers, as represented in the ideas supporting figure 15.

Thus in one of the most important creation stories that relates how Nhiãperikuli obtained pajés' knowledge and power, Kaali ka thadapa is an enormous tree bearing all food, as well as the fruits of shamanic power, the pariká beans, inside a hole midway up to the top of the tree. As a great symbol of primordial unity, we may call this the Tree of Sustenance, as it is the origin of all food including pariká, the pajes' sustenance. Like other great trees, in Baniwa cosmology, it is a marker of one major period in cosmic history, when there was a direct connection between worlds. When the tree is cut, the first period of cosmic history comes to an end.

The act of felling or "breakage" of such connections in Baniwa sacred stories, whether as one piece or into many pieces (parts of the tree), brings some "vehicle" (or sacred power) contained inside the tree down to the level of This World. Through that power (pariká),

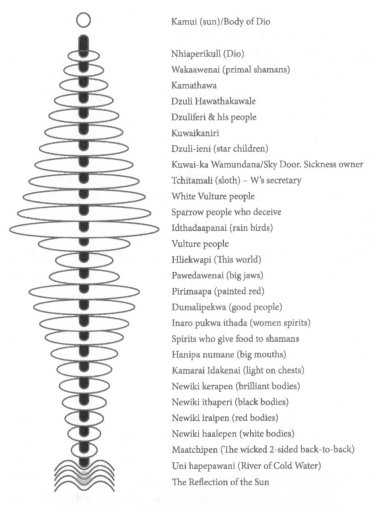

Kamui (sun)/Body of Dio

Nhiaperikull (Dio)
Wakaawenai (primal shamans)
Kamathawa
Dzuli Hawathakawale
Dzuliferi & his people
Kuwaikaniri
Dzuli-ieni (star children)
Kuwai-ka Wamundana/Sky Door. Sickness owner
Tchitamali (sloth) – W's secretary
White Vulture people
Sparrow people who deceive
Idthadaapanai (rain birds)
Vulture people
Hliekwapi (This world)
Pawedawenai (big jaws)
Pirimaapa (painted red)
Dumalipekwa (good people)
Inaro pukwa ithada (women spirits)
Spirits who give food to shamans
Hanipa numane (big mouths)
Kamarai Idakenai (light on chests)
Newiki kerapen (brilliant bodies)
Newiki ithaperi (black bodies)
Newiki iraipen (red bodies)
Newiki haalepen (white bodies)
Maatchipen (The wicked 2-sided back-to-back)
Uni hapepawani (River of Cold Water)
The Reflection of the Sun

15. The universe (Hekwapi), according to José Garcia in 2000. The celestial
umbilical cord runs through the center of twenty-five "worlds" (kuma) to the
bottom of the universe where a river of cold, fresh water flows. Actually this
river is part of the water cycle that connects all levels of the universe in one giant
circuit. (Drawing by M. C. Wright.)

it is possible to reconnect to the Other World. This is the basis of the shamans' use of pariká. In Mandu's version of this story, for the pajés, after the Tree fell, each large branch became a riverbed, and the smaller branches were the communities of people all over the world, who received their original plants from this tree. The Tree was the body of Kaali-thayri, the Master of the Earth; thus each community shares in his body, which is manioc bread, the basic sustenance among all Baniwa and other peoples of the upper Rio Negro. All of the knowledge of planting was likewise distributed throughout the world. Besides the knowledge of the planting and harvesting cycle, Kaali is the owner of a huge plantation at a place called Waliro, a hill in the depths of the forest.

The felling of this tree coincides with the beginning of planting cycles, seasonality, and other important modes of temporality that structure people's livelihoods. Thus the tree marks the end of one time-space during which there was no separation between the Before World and This World, no pariká with which the pajés moved between worlds—and the beginning of the next when they do.

Another tree of major importance is the paxiúba palm tree, likewise a great symbol of primordial unity which emerged from the earth after the "death" of Kuwai, child of the sun, whose body was the source of all the sacred flutes and trumpets representing the first ancestors, with which the elders initiate the children into adulthood today. When this tree burst out of the earth at Hipana, it shot straight up to the top of the universe. After the tree was marked and split apart, Nhiãperikuli transformed its naturally hollowed-out pieces into sacred flutes and trumpets, and these became the means by which humans today connect their children to the Before World of the ancestors.

In other words, the ancestral past from that time forward became the sacred source which produces future generations. A major circuit of temporality connects humans with their first ancestors and the source of all life. In both cases, the great vertical tree is the connection between one world and the other, between primordial past, present, and future. The two major "vehicles" for transformation "back" into the past derive from trees, inside of which there is a potent power for transcending time. These instruments of time travel (pariká and the sacred flutes) are essential for humans to periodically reestablish their connections with the great powers of their primordial past, eternally present in the Other World. The pariká, as we discussed in chapter 2, is the "blood of Kuwai," and the sacred flutes and trumpets are his "body" (*lidaki*) through which Kuwai is revived in the initiation rites.

Figure 15 looks very much like an upright tree paired with its inverse reflection in water. The vertical axis is the celestial umbilical cord, a flexible tube that connects all beings to the Before World, to the beginning and their ancestors, and inversely, the Before World to the future world of the descendants.

I shall now show how the universe can be understood through the meanings attributed to each level of the Great Tree at the world center. This image organizes the multiple levels of the universe, the spirit-peoples and their animal avatars (*nadanami*, their shadow-souls) that inhabit each level, and meteorological phenomena. The Great Tree image can be understood as home for these spirit/animal/meteorological beings, as the universe is home for all life; at each level there are villages—sometimes with only one house. A pajé's journey is like ascending a stairway and then walking along trails through the Other World, stopping in each village along the way.

The Baniwa understand the universe in this way as demonstrated by their placement of appropriate animal avatars in each level of the cosmos. Especially important are (1) the birds, auxiliaries of the pajés and guardians of great power, who make their nests at various levels above This World; (2) the tree sloths and monkeys, animal avatars of Kuwai and the powers of sorcery and sickness, as well as announcers of seasonal transitions, particularly the beginning of the rainy season; (3) the bee-spirits and cicadas, guardians of shamanic remedies and seasonal cycles. In particular the beginning of the dry seasons and the flowering of certain trees are times when the pajés transform into cicadas and prepare to transfer their powers to their apprentices; and (4) meteorological phenomena: clouds (seen as places in the Other World) and astral bodies (sun, moon, stars).

The upper world (Other World) is a hyperdeveloped world of owners and masters, where the powers of the deities and their animal avatars are the fullest possible expression of shamanic knowledge, while the underworld (Place of Our Bones) is populated by the dead, numerous spirit peoples, and animal souls. Immediately underneath the earth are several layers of the souls of animals, called Iaradathe, the chief of which is the keeper of animal souls, who is particularly important for the hunting of animals and protecting animal souls from any harm. The other kinds of spirits, however, are individual creatures with distorted or inverted body shapes. These can be friendly and helpful in the pajes' quests for souls, but some can harm humans by giving sicknesses. At the very bottom level is the spirit-with-two-bodies stuck back-to-back, considered to be dangerous and wicked.

Of the master and owner relation between the deities, spirits, and humans, their "pets," Carlos Fausto clarifies that it is inherently ambivalent:

> In Amazonia, mastery relations produce magnified persons, which contain in themselves the device both for generating potency and for undermining power. The fact that the master is necessarily affected by his pet, combined with the plurality of

the relationships he contains, produces a relational dispersion and an instability in the ownership relation. This may help to explain why mastery has seldom crystallized into an institutional locus of power in Amazonia. (2008)

In this sense Baniwa cosmology appears to be hierarchical, where the masters and owners can accumulate great power. The owners are all shamanic beings with great knowledge and power who are responsible for the creation of the world that humans, animals, and spirits live in today.

Baniwa history is testament to the emergence of prophetic leaders, considered to be "wise men and women" all of whom were jaguar shamans, priestly chanters, and dance leaders. The stories of the prophets' lives, however, consistently show how they refused to consolidate the centralization of those powers. The prophets are, instead, more concerned with the well-being of all their people. They are highly respected and admired, yet vulnerable to the attacks of sorcerers. Their mission has been to warn people of imminent self-destruction if they continue to live by the ways of sorcery. In the Other World, the villages of the jaguar shamans are exemplary for the kind of ideal egalitarianism that all people should wish for in This World. The Other World is the beautiful sky of the deities, shining silver, like the dawning of a new day. This world of humans is called *maatchikwe*, bad place, due to sorcery that ruins people's lives.

In figure 15, at the very top of the universe is the place of Nhiãperikuli, with the sun "his body." How did Nhiãperikuli create the world and all that was in it? Mandu stated that it was through his "vision," that is, "how he saw the world in the beginning." Nhiãperikuli sat and looked out over the vast expanse of nothingness (*lipukuthawa*) and "saw" things come into being. The place where he sat and thought was at a large boulder overlooking the Surubim stream, off the Yawiary River, on the upper Içana, according to information that Xavier Leal discovered from a Kuripako elder and printed in his master's thesis (2008). It is this power that the pajés with the greatest knowledge have, to see/make, to remake the world ("the stones, trees, and everything in it") in their thought, envisioning how a new world might be.

Living together with Nhiãperikuli is Kamathawa, the harpy eagle, the avian symbol of shamanic power everywhere in Amazonia and the Americas. Harpy eagles make their nests in the tops of the forest canopy, the highest places in the forest, in solitary family nests. About these eagles, the narratives say that in the beginning of time, before the Other World became separated from This World, the great harpy gave Nhiãperikuli's younger brother shamanic powers to see, to sound thunder, and to become invisible.

Harpies and other eagles are major avatars of the pajé, the avian equivalent of the jaguar; one sacred title used for the great harpy is "Jaguar Kamathawa." They are predatory birds noted for their incredible strength, long-distance vision, whistling, and piercing cries; they are sentinels who guard the box of infallible medicines in Nhiãperikuli's house. The harpy Kamathawa has in its power crystals with which the pajé sees great distances. Harpy feathers have the shamanic power to "sweep the skies clean of clouds," thus bringing on the clear summer season if the rainy season becomes prolonged. The eagle feathers are believed to have the power to open what is closed and enable clear visions, which are of utmost importance to curing.

One important story explains that the harpy was Nhiãperikuli's younger brother slain by the treacherous affines. This confirms that the themes of the conflicts between kin and affines and the treachery of the affines come from primordial times. As the affines were preparing a cannibalistic feast of the younger brother's body, which they had transformed into a surubim fish, Nhiãperikuli transformed into a wasp and managed to retrieve his younger brother's heart-soul. Nhiãperikuli cooked the heart-soul in water, and as foam appeared in the boiling water, out stepped a series of hawks, one larger than the other, ending with the great harpy whose strength Nhiãperikuli tested by having it carry heavy logs while flying in great circles until the bird was ready to take vengeance on its killer. The harpy then avenged his death by killing and eating his father-in-law, Grandfather Timbó (Fish Poison), whose body transformed into fish poison plants and curare. By trickery and many shamanic acts, Nhiãperikuli turned the tables back on the enemy tribes (Cornelio et al. 1999).

This story may explain many other questions about pajés and their powers: the pot in which Jaguar Nhiãperikuli cooked his brother's heart-soul, producing a "foam" from which came the powerful Jaguar Kamathawa, reminds us of how shamans actually produce pariká, the blood-red exudate derived from the inner bark of the Virola trees. The blood-red foaming liquid, as it is cooked, becomes "the blood of Kuwai," the "Owner of Sickness."

The world immediately above the harpy—seemingly, the clouds from a non-shaman's perspective—is actually the place of the village of the primal shaman tribe called *wakaawenai*, who helped cut down the Great Tree of Sustenance separating the Other World from This World. Once their task had been completed, these shamans ascended to the Other World without passing through the separation of body and soul at the moment of death. They sang their way up, body and soul, to the Other World, and there they now dwell in "villages of pariká" (*dzato dzakale*); they are also known as the "owners of pariká" (*dzato minanai*). Whole villages of jaguar shamans (magnified shamans) exist at this level, only visible to other jaguar shamans. The clouds the shamans see are "their tobacco smoke."

The most important and ancient of all pajés is Dzuliferi, the owner of pariká and sacred tobacco, whom the pajés call Padzu (Father), the same way they address Nhiãperikuli. He is Nhiãperi-kuli's elder brother, a very ancient spirit, "the Ancient One," as is the shamanic use of pariká and tobacco, according to the sources Kapfhammer (1997) examined.

In the few stories there are about Dzuliferi, the "owner of tobacco"—of which there are numerous kinds—he gave fresh, green tobacco to Nhiãperikuli at the beginning of time, long before the first ancestors of humans were brought into being. Each phratry has its own ancestral, sacred tobacco, given to the souls of their ancestors, along with sacred pepper, when they emerged from Hipana.

Tobacco is present in all curing rites because the sweet smell of its smoke attracts the souls of the sick back to life (see Wilbert's classic 1993 work, *Tobacco and Shamanism*, for further discussion). A pajé blows tobacco smoke over a patient's hands joined together, and the crowns of the heads of fellow pajés and the patient, to strengthen and protect the body, concentrating the life force, that is, the patient's heart-soul at its central place. Smoking freshly grown green tobacco makes the soul "content" and the body "strong." Passing a fresh cigar around a circle of people is a mark of harmonious sociality in the sacred stories and in real life. "*Alira*," the Baniwa say, as the tobacco cigar goes around, leaving each person with a strong and contented heart-soul. The evangelical missionaries, who condemned tobacco smoking as being "of the devil," in reality were condemning Baniwa souls.

Dzuliferi is an impressive deity who, it is believed, watches over humans, knows when they will be born and when they are to die, can intercede in a person's fate and change the time of death, or make someone change his mind and not commit acts of sorcery. We might say he is the powerful spirit of one's destiny. Humans may "pray to" and "pay" this deity to intercede on behalf of their kin or themselves when they feel threatened. The pajés sing to Dzuliferi, and Dzuliferi inspires (in the etymological sense of the word) the pajés' songs.

Unlike Kamathawa and Kuwai, who have animal bodies living in distinct levels of the universe tree, Dzuliferi—as far as can be deduced from the narratives and shamanic discourse—has no fixed animal body form clearly associated with him. (There is a hint of his association with the shamanic birds, since his "daughters" are the "Vulture-spirit-women" of the lower sky-worlds.)

Rather, Dzuliferi is strongly associated with sacred plants—tobacco, pariká, and pepper. He is called the "spirit of power," shamanic power in the plants, the transformative power of pariká, the "fiery arrow" of pepper that cooks the rawness out of live game or fish so they can be safely eaten. In the story of how Dzuliferi gave tobacco to his brother Nhiãperikuli, the former becomes a "ball of celestial fire" which descends at his brother's house and plants the tobacco; overnight, the few plants blossomed to the size of a huge plantation full of tobacco. Priestly chanters make their thought journeys throughout the world today with tobacco smoke during rites of passage. In the Other World, he is a "very ancient" deity, a hyper-shaman, always transforming.

In This World, it is said, Dzuliferi has the form of a large boulder with petroglyphs located immediately above the rapids of Hipana. The jaguar shaman and "wise man" Guilherme Garcia designated this boulder as the "true center of the universe" and not the holes in the rapids. Mandu likewise identified the great boulder as Dzuliferi (Gonzalez-Ñáñez 2007: 63). One Hohodene young man recently wrote that "Dzuli [sic] (one of Nhiãperikuli's brothers) is also a huge boulder in the Aiary River. People who pass by it converse with it, you know? Because he [Dzuli] is alive in the form of the boulder" (pers. comm., I. Fontes, July 2010).

All of the principal Powers—Nhiãperikuli, Dzuliferi,

Kuwai—have multiple sides to them, each of which appears at a different level in the drawing of the universe. There is Dzuliferi, as chief of all pajés, and there are "his people," the jaguar shaman spirits. On another level, there are "Dzuliferi's children," referring to the first ancestors of the phratry called Walipere-dakenai.

Today the Walipere-dakenai are the principal affines of the Hohodene. From the Hohodene perspective, their own ancestral place in the Other World is near the "primal sun," *Heiri*, because their first ancestor emerged from Hipana when the sun was in its zenith in the sky; hence they are known as the "children of the primal sun" (*Heiri ieni*).

In This World, affines are among the most significant yet ambivalent Others; in the "Other world," we find the ancestral jaguar shamans of both the Hohodene and Walipere-dakenai, the two most numerous of the phratries that are found among Baniwa of the Aiary River, in distinct but proximate worlds. This spatial separation of the two in the Other World is reflected in two separate emergence places in This World, of the first ancestors of the two phratries: the Walipere-dakenai ancestors are said to have emerged from a place called *Enukwa*, the "pot" (i.e., depression in the stones) of Dzuliferi, located slightly downriver from the "pot of the sun" at Hipana where the first ancestors of the Hohodene were born. The name Walipere-dakenai means "descendants of the Pleiades constellation."

According to the Walipere-dakenai today, when their ancestors were "born," Dzuliferi watched them emerge. Later he gave them their sacred names, tobacco, pepper, and other ancestral property. The narrator of the story cited above (p. 152), Matteo, a member of the Dzauinai (jaguar people) phratry, stated that the Walipere-dakenai ancestors emerged immediately following the Hohodene but from the same hole.

Most narrators, nevertheless, do recognize distinct ancestral origin places of the three principal phratries that appear in both This World and the Other World, as perhaps a way of marking their affinal relatedness and distinctive attributes. While all phratries are located along the "celestial umbilical cord," there is no fixed ceremonial or political hierarchy among them in This World. To the contrary, as affinal phratries, their relations are defined both by respect and harmony, on the one hand, and tension, treachery, conflict, and competition, on the other.

A different aspect of alterity is represented by the trickster sides of the celestial powers, a feature that has been explored well by Jon Hill (2009) working among the Wakuenai (ethnonym for the Kuripako of Venezuela) in relation to Nhiãperikuli. The Hohodene jaguar shamans stated that there is also a "trickster *Dzuli*" as well as a trickster Kuwai—both are shamanic beings. The name of the first is Dzuliferi hawathákawale, the "deceiver," the trickster. There is Kuwai, the owner of sickness, whose Other side is Inyaime, an "other Kuwai," who is the demonic spirit of the deceased. Inyaime is dangerous because it has a trap at the vault of the sky that takes souls away to its village, a world much like our own, where there is suffering and thirst but no water.

The idea of the trickster can be seen in another way as consistent with the hyperdevelopment of the warrior who outsmarts the enemy. That is, the trickster manifestations of a single deity enhance that deity's powers to ward off enemies or provoke confusion among enemy pajés.

Nevertheless, their alterity belies their own enmity. Both the "other Dzuliferi" and the "other Kuwai" who deceive, manifest themselves as white men in cosmology and the sacred stories. The first is two-faced (*dthamekwali*), one-legged (*apemakawali*), and has a shotgun or poison dart in place of his other leg. He is "white" in color and communicates with the religious leaders of the "white people," the pope in particular. This "other" Dzuliferi is constantly watching over the white people, sending messages on paper to the pope to transmit to the white people "in order for them to have greater intelligence" and to know how to live.

The trickster Dzuliferi is potentially a "deceiver" and may send false pajés to cure people: "He sends a pajé to tell humans they will get better, but he is deceiving them," as José Garcia said—evidently an artifice to trick an enemy. Rather than being totally negative features, deception and ambiguity can be important powers for the jaguar shamans, for the purposes of protection and for eliminating enemies who seek to cause harm.

The figure of Kuwaikaniri (also called Eeri), or Mawerikuli (an alternate name adopted from the Cubeo), the next level descending, is the thoughtless younger brother of Nhiãperikuli and Dzuliferi, who was responsible for bringing death into life. Kuwaikaniri is called the "unfortunate one," because it was through his inexplicable error that death was introduced into the world for all future generations. Kuwaikaniri represents both irreversible death and the vertical separation of body/bones from heart-soul at the moment of death. According to Mandu, during a pajé's cure, he looks for the spirit of Mawerikuli in the Other World. If the sick person that the pajé is trying to cure will get well, then the pajé will have a vision of Mawerikuli's rising from his tomb. If the patient will not get well, he will see Mawerikuli remaining still and motionless in his stone tomb.

Kuwaikaniri/Mawerikuli thus represents both the fatality of death and the possibility of reversing death by returning to the center of the universe at Hipana. An important healing chant relates how Kuwaikaniri, having been swallowed by a serpent and brought downriver to the city of São Gabriel, was able to return to life, because he used preventive shamanism correctly and, with the help of bird spirits, killed the serpent and began a long voyage back to his elder brother's home slightly above Hipana.

Hill (1993) has convincingly argued that Kuwaikaniri's mythical return journey from the city of the white people back to the home center may be understood as a "historical metaphor" of the return journeys of ancestral leaders from the devastating effects of epidemic diseases on indigenous peoples of the upper Rio Negro. In fact, the narratives about Hohodene and Walipere-dakenai warrior ancestors both recall a process of historical dislocation from the Upper Rio Negro, a descent to the place that the Baniwa consider an ancestral town of Barcellos, or the Fort of Barra, the seventeenth- and eighteenth-century capital of the captaincy of the Rio Negro (Wright 1981, 2005). After several years working for the whites, the ancestral leaders fled from the colonial towns, seeking refuge in the ancestral territory, where they could recover from their losses. A process of ethnogenesis ensued in which the two phratries, the Hohodene and Walipere-dakenai, initiated a marital alliance resulting in the repopulation of their villages.

Another indication of the historicity of this story and accompanying chant is that the serpent's rotting corpse gave rise to the white people and that Kuwaikaniri "nearly died from poison" in the city of São Gabriel. These are clear references to deaths from assault sorcery in the city both in the past and present. They also affirm a historical truth that the center of the universe at Hipana is considered a "sanctuary" from the devastating epidemics in historical contact. The Kuwaikaniri chants, called "bringing the heart-soul back home" are, in a broad sense, a form of healing from the traumas of historical contact.

The Bone and the Spirit Inside

Nhiãperikuli, Dzuliferi, and Kuwaikaniri are brothers, collectively known as the hekwapinai (universe people). One of the best-known stories about them explains how they came into being from inside the bone of a person (who perhaps was Hekwapi ienipe, the universe child all grown up) who had been devoured in the primordial times, presumably during the period following the end of the first world (after the felling of the Great Tree of Sustenance). Animal tribes then roamed the world, still small, killing and eating people until it appeared as though all people of an ancient tribe called Duemeni, the Jaguars, would be wiped out.

An elderly "grandmother" of the tribe wept and implored the animal chief, Enumhere, to spare the finger bones that he was then gnawing. The chief threw the bones into the middle of the river and told her to fetch them. She retrieved them in a fish net, but the bones had the forms of three crayfish, inside of which there were three beings, the "universe people," "those inside the bone," which is translated in Baniwa as Nhiãperikunai ("Bone-inside-they"). The "bone" refers both to a finger (three pieces of bone connected into one finger) that the animal chief was gnawing on and also to the exoskeletons of three crayfish, which were the three brothers. (See Wright 1998 for complete version.)

There are petroglyphs on the Içana River that show three crayfish joined together. This could easily be a graphic representation of the three brothers. The "crayfish" constellations, Dzaaka manaapan (Crayfish with no arms) and Dzaaka Makapali (Crayfish with two arms), appear during the short dry season of February and March. The story of the crayfish inside the bone, the reappearance of the Nhiãperikunai, can be correlated with the ecology of this period, for the plot coincides with the end of one garden cycle and the beginning of a new one. Thus the beginning of the story takes place in an old garden; this is followed by the three brothers tricking and killing animals in revenge for the killing of their kin, and it ends with the burning of a new garden in which the heroes outwit their animal father-in-law's attempt to kill them off once and for all.[4]

The bone, in short, is a form through which this narrative presents the reconstruction of the universe after near-total demise. I suggest that the bone is one more manifestation of elongated tube forms found in several sacred stories, and that whatever is inside it, or goes through it, is the life-giving and life-taking power that is at the heart of shamanic *malikai* and of the universe itself.

At this point, it is important for us to recall Mandu's warning to the people of the upper Guainia River, that they should remember what happened when they nearly lost all of their traditions: the enemy peoples came to dominate them. Mandu's warning referred specifically to domination by the whites. This is another clear parallel that Mandu made between catastrophic moments of the Before World and imminently catastrophic moments of the present-day world.

It is perfectly in keeping with the death-and-rebirth theme of shamanic imagery that Nhiãperikuli—who in his first appearance was the child of the universe—now reappears from a dismembered body, a piece of which is thrown into the waters of the river. Inside-the-bone came back to life in the form of three crayfish, followed by three crickets, followed by two types of woodpeckers, and finally emerged as a person all grown up. This story is perfectly consonant with the shamanic being of the three brothers. The bone was the three hekwapinai, universe people. From one being (Hekwapi ienipe), three brothers (elder-middle-younger) were regenerated, a triad of knowledge and power. In the universe, the three brothers can be seen as the three highest layers.

The symmetrical use of numbers throughout Baniwa sacred traditions can be directly linked to patterns in social and "natural" cycles. A minimum hierarchy, for example, consists of three: elder-middle-younger, which can be expanded in ancestral creation stories to five (original ancestral agnatic siblings in the Hohodene phratry). Although this may seem marginal to the topic at hand, the themes of symmetry and asymmetry are basic building blocks of the universe. Their appearance in different sacred stories is never by chance but rather is a fundamental part of the central theme of the creation story.

If we now compare all the most important forms of bone-tubes and their relations to themes of birth, death, and rebirth in Baniwa stories and shamanic practice, we find the following:

1. The very first tube of creation was the umbilical cord of the sky, which came into existence at the birth of the universe, when there was no division between worlds. Like the universe, the first soul a newborn child has is the umbilical cord soul, which is believed to connect the newborn to the celestial umbilical cord and thus with all other living beings through the one collective *Hwepule*, "our umbilical cord soul," the celestial umbilical cord. At a person's death, the first soul to leave the deceased's body and return to the Other World is the umbilical cord soul, which goes up to the Houses of the Dead in the Other World. It is a spiritual cord, invisible to all but the shamans, which is always there at Hipana, and which connects this world with the Upper World.

2. The pajé's snuff-blowing bone (*maliapi*) is the tube through which pariká is blown, and pariká is the means by which the pajé's soul travels back and forth through time. The pariká opens the pajé's vision to the trails that lead to the world of the dead, the ancestors, and the deities.

3. The paxiúba tree is a hollow palm tree that is the source of the sacred flutes and trumpets, collectively called Kuwai, which are parts of the body of the owner of sickness. Breath is blown through these tubes, bringing Kuwai's voice back to life, the ancestral music that makes the forest fruits and children grow, connecting the primordial past with all generations.

4. The human bones are the elongated forms through which a person's soul circulates. The heart-soul and human bones give

life and mobility to a person; at death the person's heart-soul detaches from its bones and makes a journey up to the Other World as the bones lie horizontally in the "Place of Our Bones."

5. The sorcerers popularly known as *manti* hide their poison inside a bone, and it is said that the sorcerer can fly with this bone to wherever he wants to go in order to strike a victim with the poison.

6. The collective umbilical cord soul is the only soul that can be invoked to reverse the destruction of poison; to pajés, it is a protective remedy against lethal sicknesses.

It is for all these reasons that the bone of Nhiãperikuli's name is a tube inside of which the creator deities are reborn. The sacred flutes and trumpets are the body parts, especially long bones, of the child of Nhiãperikuli through which the "powerful sound that opened the world" (Hill 1993) is blown or, as the Hohodene say, *limale-iyu*, the sound that made the world increase in size. The bone of the pajé, *maliapi*, transmits the blood of the child of the sun, Kuwai, which allows the pajé to transform into a jaguar shaman spirit and to intermediate for humans. A bone is used as a container of deadly substances in sorcery. And finally the soul inside the bone separates from the body at death and journeys to the worlds above where part of it will "wait for its kin" when they die, and part returns to the source of all ancestral souls where it will be regenerated into the souls of future children to be born. All of these meanings together form part of the complex nexus of religious power and knowledge.

All of these are themes related to shamanic "death" (or trance) and the reversal of time. Without understanding why and how, we cannot understand the first mystery of the jaguar shamans, the first mystery of the universe. The transformative power of the soul inside the bone is what sustains the universe and resists the destruction of Other tribes or peoples, such as the enemy affines, or whomever alterity may refer to. It also resists the destruction of time and death by its immortal forms (somewhat along the lines of what Viveiros de Castro and Carneiro da Cunha were referring to as *aletheia* in Northwest Amazon notions of temporality).

The Knowledge of the Universe Owners

The transformative power of the "soul" elements in the universe is intimately connected to the forms of knowledge (*ianheke*) that brought the universe into being and that overcome all attempts by enemies to destroy it. It is critical to understand how the knowledge and power of each of these deities is distinct but complementary. These forms of knowledge were transmitted from the original owners to their descendants, who then became guardians of that knowledge in This World.

Nhiãperikuli's knowledge is that of the warrior pajé. Stories of social conflict, poisonings, and deaths abound in Baniwa traditions of Nhiãperikuli and his kin. There were numerous enemy animal tribes, frequently affines (*nalimathana*), that sought to destroy the universe in the Before World, but there are equally numerous allies (*ikitchina*)—especially the birds—without whose help Nhiãperikuli's plots to thwart the enemy animals' attempts to kill him could never have been realized.

Dzuliferi knows the destiny of all humans. His knowledge is more of the priestly, "canonical" type, defined by precision of language and thought, which is critical for the reproduction of the universe. Thus the elder chanters at rites of passage have the most important function of annulling the dangerous powers of all the ancestral spirit names of all the fish, animals, and places in This World to protect the new persons who have emerged from seclusion (Wright 1993; Hill 1993). The "other Dzuliferi" is said to periodically send messages on pieces of paper to the pope at the

Vatican, in order to "educate the white people" on proper ways to act in This World. This can be understood as a way of affirming the superior knowledge of indigenous shamans, consistent with themes in the stories of historic prophets (Turner, in Hill 1988).

Kaali, the "Master of the Earth," is the guardian of sustenance in the plants of the earth, food that sustains society, festivals of exchange, and manioc beer offerings that celebrate sociality among kin and affines.

Kuwaikaniri is the younger brother, the tricked one, the unfortunate one who, acting on impulse, brings on not only his own death but also the deaths of all people after him. If his brothers are known for their foresight, vision, and precise knowledge, he is the "unknowing one" who, by his failure to foresee the consequences of his actions, produces disaster. Humanity was condemned to die from then on, having lost its immortality. It seems that only pajés do not die "irreversibly," or at least the most powerful of them return as souls to stay by their graves and give counsel to their kin.

Finally, Kuwai is an extraordinarily complex and mysterious spirit. One of his animal avatars is the black sloth, whose fur contains an enormous variety of insects, fungae, and viruses. This is undoubtedly one reason why the Kuwai black sloth, or Wamundana, is known as the owner of sickness, the owner of poison and the power of sorcery. According to the sacred story, at Kuwai's fiery death, the poisonous fur of his body ran and entered the fur of the black sloth. What, we might ask, is it that makes the black sloth such a powerful image to the Baniwa, of the same intensity as the powerful harpy eagle or the jaguar spirits? Second, what kind of knowledge does Kuwai have or leave for humanity? Third, do other Northwest Amazonian indigenous peoples have similar notions about the sloth?

The sloth seems like the most harmless leaf-eating animal in the forest, more like the victim of other predators, especially the

16. Wamu, a black sloth with whitish stains on its pelt. (Thanks to R. Duin.)

harpy eagle, the anaconda, and the jaguar. It is paradoxically the sloth's lifestyle that caters to its ability to avoid being killed. The sloth's slow and silent movements make it almost impossible to be seen from the ground, and the greenish tint within its fur gives it added camouflage (Mendel 1985; Montgomery 1985). The sloth's fur and movements do not prevent it from being attacked from the sky, but sloths take special precautions to stay out of the sunlight at dawn and dusk when the eagles are hunting.

Further, the sloth manages to live on various levels of the trees, from canopy to lower branches, thus being in between several of the vertical worlds. It descends to the ground to defecate after periods of continence lasting up to ten days. It is a supreme example of one of the most highly valued lessons that the Baniwa teach their children and that master shamans teach their apprentices: to exercise continence and fasting for long periods.[5]

The sloth's symbiotic relationship with plant algae makes it unique from a biological point of view.[6] Its body can function as host to as many as 10,000 beetles, "whose life cycle is completely reliant on the sloth's daily routine" (Davis 1997). The sloth's feces are similarly perfect places for beetle and moth larvae to mature. In all, the sloth has an important place in maintaining equilibrium in the ecosystem, and its body—much like its spirit namesake—combines both animal and plant features.

The calibration of the sloth's descent from tree to ground with seasonal changes is but one analogy that shows how shamanic knowledge is linked to seasonal cycles, and vertical movements from the sky to the earth are equated with movements between the Other World and This World.

I agree with Stephen Hugh-Jones (1989) that the sloth's sluggish movements and long hours of sleeping recall initiates' behavior. Indeed, one of the early historical representations of Kuwai in initiation rituals among the Arawak-speaking Tariana of the Uaupés

River was a mask, called Izi, woven from the fur of the sloth and the hair of young girls at menarche. The mask had three large holes for the eyes and mouth and innumerable small holes.

Kuwai evidently has a great deal to do with changes that take place at boys' initiation and girls' menstruation. These can be dangerous, for as Baniwa men say, "Kuwai makes holes in the initiates," referring among other things to the dangerous "openness" of sexual orifices, from which blood and semen flow, coinciding with changes that take place in the universe from the dry season to the heavy rains, the scheduling of the initiation rites, and the ripening of forest fruits. All of these are critical, interconnected aspects of the pajés' knowledge of sicknesses that occur during these times. These interconnections among important biological-ecological-meteorological-zoological cycles are elaborated in the most sacred of chants, called *kalidzamai*, with pepper and salt at rites of passage.

Why are pepper and salt so important? Because the kalidzamai chants present them as the principal "weapons to kill" the potential danger that animals, places, fish, and ancestors could present to those undergoing passage. Restoring a normal diet is equivalent to being integrated back into society, which is symbolized in the sacred narrative as an enormous fire when the great spirit Kuwai was burned to death.

Returning to our panoramic perspective on the universe, the sequence of four bird spirit worlds below the "door of the sky" includes both black and white vultures, the high-flying sparrowhawk, and the scissor-tailed kite. All are the "daughters of Dzuliferi." In Hohodene cosmology the vultures have huge houses (*wadzulikadapan*) in their worlds to which souls of deceased humans are attracted. When pajés of the past used *Banisteriopsis caapi*, the psychoactive more commonly known as *yajé* or just *caapi*, their souls followed a vine to these houses where the souls of the dead could be found. As in various other parts of South America where the "visionary vine" *ayahuasca* is used, there is an association of the "vine of the souls" (its meaning in Quechua) with the souls of the deceased.

Frequently pajés "make marriages" with bird spirits, living in different worlds, with whom they will have children who will assist the pajés in their search for the lost souls of the sick. Evidently this increases the range of movement that the pajé has in the Other World. The birds are messengers who advise, inform, and warn.

From the beginning of the universe, women collectively called *Amarunai* have exercised a vital role as agents of change, intermediaries who frequently are from affinal tribes and are spouses of Nhiãperikuli and his younger brother. Their connections with other, often enemy tribes, place them in an intensely ambivalent position. As wives, they bring about irreversible changes in the order of life; as elderly "aunts" or "grandmothers" and kin of the creator-brothers, they are salvific heroines, guardians of powerful remedies, nurturing the dead back to life. Their most important roles, however, are as mothers, especially of the child of Nhiãperikuli, Kuwai, and of all the "white people" in This World.

The mother of Kuwai, Amaru, is remembered in the narratives as the source of all flowing river water in the world, which was produced from her menstrual blood. She is also remembered for having taken away the sacred flutes and trumpets, the body of Kuwai, from Nhiãperikuli, beginning a long chase throughout This World when she became a powerful adversary to the men, playing the sacred instruments everywhere, in the final opening up of This World to its present-day size. According to Mandu, after the men regained possession of the instruments, the first group of women, Amarunai, remained at the "ends of the world," Tsuwai, "where the waters no longer run," and there they made "industries" producing poisonous air that provokes contagious sicknesses among humans today. This story will be discussed more fully in chapter 8.

POWER AND ECOLOGY AMONG THE UNIVERSE OWNERS AND CEREMONIAL CHIEFS

At this point, it is appropriate to elaborate on the notions of owners and masters among the spirits and deities of the Other World and contrast their ownership of powers with the shamanic functions in This World.

The notion of the owners of the universe is explicit in phrases which the Baniwa use to refer to their deities, as owners, guardians, or patrons (*iminali*) and ceremonial chiefs (*-thayri*). Nhiãperikuli, Kuwai, and Dzuliferi are all considered the owners of the universe (*hekwapi iminali*). Kuwai is called Waminali, meaning "our owner," during the Kwaipan rituals.

Abstractly this proprietary relation seems to refer to the fact that, through their actions, they saw things come into being, leaving them for posterity, as the legacy of the ancestors—the powers themselves—for their descendants. Nhiãperikuli made "everything in the world" and gave it to the Baniwa with instructions on how to live well on it. Dzuliferi is the owner of pajés' snuff, pariká, and tobacco; he gave them to Nhiãperikuli, who left them to posterity, especially for the pajés "to know the world." Kuwai is the owner of sickness and the owner of poison who left all forms of them in This World, but he also gave the pajés the material and instructions on how to cure them.

From the perspective of humans today, Nhiãperikuli, his brothers, and Kuwai are considered to be our owners, for humanity lives and prospers according to the order and the conditions inherited from them. The relation of the deities to humanity is brought into experience through the pajés, who request from the owners remedies with which to cure. This involves bargaining, for the sick person has to "pay" for his or her soul in order to bring it back to This World. The patient must supply the material offering or payment (*dawai*), which the pajé then takes in its immaterial form to Kuwai.

The relation of owner is also brought into experiences through the sacred flutes and trumpets, which are the "body" of Kuwai and played only by the men at initiation rites (in the past, also at whipping rites and prewar ceremonies). Each phratry is the guardian of a particular flute or trumpet that is its Kuwai-first ancestor, which emerged from the hole at Hipana at the beginning of the world. The men call these instruments their "pets" (*wapira*). In initiation chants, the pet relation refers to Nhiãperikuli and Kuwai. Nhiãperikuli was Kuwai's father; Kuwai (as instruments) became his pet (*lipira*).

Here Carlos Fausto's observations are again relevant, that the master/ownership relation to a pet is "the device both for generating potency and for undermining power, due to their relational dispersion and an instability in the ownership relation" (Fausto 2002). The Baniwa universe we have so far described seems to centralize a great deal through the universe's umbilical cord, from which all things begin and return. Nevertheless, the peoples of the world, with their ancestral instruments and knowledge, are dispersed over a vast territory, which makes the centralization process emerge only when there are collective rituals, notably the rites of initiation, taught to humanity by Kuwai. Outside of this kind of supra-local centralization, concentrating peoples of many communities in the initiation rites, each community has its own sacred flute or trumpet linking it to a particular place and ancestral identity.

Among pajés a similar kind of dynamic occurs, for the accumulation of shamanic knowledge and power can certainly produce the "wise men and women" at the apex of this hierarchy. However, according to the narratives of these prophets, they resisted accumulating this power; they do not wish to become kings or presidents or powerful leaders. Their stories show how much their families suffer from attack as a result of their spiritual leadership. Nevertheless, if they have important messages to deliver that offer divinely inspired guidance to their followers and all Baniwa communities, they carry through their mission until they no longer can.

The title of ceremonial chief or master (*-thayri*) in the Other World is applied to the same triad—Nhiãperikuli, Kuwai, Dzuliferi—all of whom are considered the ceremonial chiefs and priests of the world. Another deity, Kaali, is also called a ceremonial chief because he gave to humanity knowledge of the planting ceremonies. He gave people the songs to sing at the *pudali* exchange festivals. In some respects, Kaali is like an earthly form of Nhiãperikuli, and some narrators are more explicit when they say that Kaali is really Nhiãperikuli. This makes perfect sense in terms of the nexus of religious power and knowledge. Kaali is the original dance owner, *mandero*, whose dance knowledge and power, *manderokai*, are part and parcel of the dynamics of Baniwa social and ceremonial life.

In the story of his life and death, Kaali sacrifices himself in a huge earth fire, and from the white earth that was left at the place where he was burned (the word *kaali* also means "white clay earth"—again, whiteness and spiritualization correlate), the first manioc tree emerged, from which humanity obtained all the plants they needed. In other words, he gave his knowledge and his body for the needs of others. His body, the Baniwa say, is manioc bread, a basic ingredient of every meal.

Kaali is the deity who taught humanity how to plant gardens, to sing and pray at the time of planting, and to celebrate at the *caxiri* festivals. He controls the weather for planting and establishes a calendar for agricultural activities. The great manioc tree, which sprouted from his body, as well as the plenitude of his plantation recall the story of the Great Tree of Sustenance, Kaali ka thadapa, which was cut down at the end of the first era of the cosmos. Kaali ka thadapa contained shamans' powers, which Nhiãperikuli disputed with the animals. This story is the very beginning of shamanism. That the Tree of Sustenance contains pariká indicates that it is considered to be the food of the shamans.

It seems as though the story of the Great Tree of Sustenance precedes in cosmic history the story of how Kaali later sacrifices himself in a garden fire in order to relieve the hunger of his family. While the first story "takes place" in the Other (First) World, before there were any people in This World and is the source of shamanic power, the second story takes place after the cycles of garden planting had already been established. It refers to the mysterious way in which Kaali "fertilized" (or spiritualized) the earth with his own body, out of which women get manioc and produce the basic staple of bread.

It may also be said that the first story has to do with shamanic powers that set food cycles in motion. The second is about the agricultural calendar and issues of abundance and scarcity resulting from marital conflict produced by planting. By sacrificing himself, Kaali leaves abundance to his family. An interesting parallel can be drawn here with the story of Kuwai, in the sense that, with Kuwai, a mysterious power of growth is hidden at the bottom of the rivers. Both the powers of Kaali and Kuwai are linked to shamanic transformations, seasonal fertility of the earth and the rains, the growth of children, the maturation of the forest fruits, and the production of gardens.

Chanters are attributed powers over the growth of cultivated plants in the earth, as food-producing knowledge is dispersed throughout the villages of the region. Thus it is both centralized in the figure of the priestly chanter, while dispersed among all communities of the region. This knowledge is the basis of any sort of cultivation throughout the region.

By now it should be fairly clear that in the undifferentiated Before World of the deities and great spirits, one personage can assume the attributes and powers of another. Frequently, narrators will begin a story about Kaali and, in the middle of the narrative, switch to talking about Nhiãperikuli. In the Baniwa pantheon, there are connections among all major spirits/deities that demonstrate the nexus of religious power and knowledge among the principal religious specialists. They share in each other's powers and knowledge in some way, as the form of the bone illustrates. One may become the other without losing an original perspective of who he or she is. As in the Before World, in This World, the different "owners" can accumulate power and knowledge, but only at their own risk, for the sorcerers are there to provoke instability and destruction.

"Place-of-Our-Bones," the Worlds Below

The worlds below are grouped into one general level, *Wapinakwa*, the "place of our bones," for the bones of the deceased remain in the underworld. Along with them, there are places inhabited by seemingly strange beings, each of which has some odd, even exaggerated feature of its body. These worlds seem to have come into being around the time of Kuwai's birth, as Mandu stated, and immediately after the felling of the Tree of Sustenance. The spirits of these underworlds appear to be incomplete, in the sense of having no projection of body in the form of a shadow-soul as occurs with the powers of the Before World.

Goldman (2004) considers all of these beings among the Cubeo to represent a proto-humanity that never fully developed into humans; as one Hohodene told me, they "never were born." Yet at "the next end of the world," half of these beings will emerge to repopulate the earth, and half will remain below. This idea of a replenishable stock of "potential humans" is an integral part of the universal order, which foresees the possibility of a future destruction and regeneration.

Several of these individual spirit beings exhibit threatening behavior; they are enemies of humans, ready to capture and cannibalize human souls should they wander into the underworld and forest realms. Other spirit peoples are good to the pajés and display behavior more in line with correct hospitality, offering food, drink, or tobacco to the pajés who visit them.

In order of appearance, from top to bottom, these peoples are (1) those "with large chins who sleep hanging from poles"—no special relation to humans; (2) people painted with red vegetal dye (*urucu*), whose bodies, like the recently deceased, were painted entirely with red dye; (3) *umari* fruit people—yellowish in color, "good people" with whom the pajé smokes tobacco in his search for lost souls; (4) Inaro, a world exclusively populated by women, evidently "good people" who receive the pajé well; (5) a world of spirits with no bodies who offer food to the pajé, yet when these spirits try to drink coffee, for example, the pajé sees it passing right through (the idea of "incompleteness"); (6) a world of "people with huge mouths"; (7) a people with "lights on their chests," whose bodies are constantly alight; (8) a world with people "whose bodies shine" (*kerapen*) differently from the previous peoples whose bodies have torchlights on their chests. Here we see contrasts with Nhiãperikuli, who is the hyperdevelopment of the light/sun and soul/body relation, that is, where a powerful spirit of light is projected throughout the universe. The spirits with bodies of light do not project themselves anywhere; they are simply spirits with lights on their chests in the dark "netherworld of the dead."

Then there are three worlds (levels 9–11) with peoples painted in black, red, and white—all beautiful and all good; and finally (12) the lowest layer is the only world that has truly "wicked people"—who have two bodies stuck together back to back. Evidently they are dangerous to humans and pajés because they constantly deceive them with their duplicity. Here is a kind of proto-duplicity, more obvious than the hyperdevelopments of the same feature in the Other World.

Summarizing, a panoramic overview of the universe, its spatial and temporal framework, and the spiritual values associated with each world allow us to see the fundamental theme of knowledge in its various modalities, along with the transformative, spiritual powers that flow through connecting bones or tubes and the bodily images/avatars associated with the spiritual beings, which reflect the being's most important corporeal qualities. Asymmetric relations characterize Upper and Lower Worlds, where the first is a hyperdevelopment of qualities that appear in the second in proto-form.

Moral evaluations differentiate the good people and the wicked people of the universe, which appear in both the Other World and the Place-of-our Bones. The "wicked" of the Other World are Kuwai and his "secretary," the sloth Tchitamali, avatars of sickness. Mandu also characterized Mawerikuli as the "evil one," *maatchieneri*, although Kuwaikaniri is reversible "death" as well. The world of humans is evaluated by many pajés to be an evil place (*maatchikwe*), a place of rot (*ekukwe*) and pain (*kaiwikwe*). By its central position among the worlds of good and wicked people, This World would seem to be not one or the other but a mixture.

Humans have made This World a bad place, pajés say, because they use sorcery to kill each other, which has left many rotting bodies in the earth. The quality of deception in both the Other World and This World can be seen as either positive or negative, for pajés and spirits may deceive in order to protect, yet sorcerers deceive in order to harm. There is a never-ending struggle in This World between power and anti-power, as there was in the Before World. It is the moral responsibility of the wise men and women to ensure that humans do not lead themselves to the brink of destruction, which, the sacred stories tell, occurred in the past, when the enemy tribes overcame humans.

How the First Shamans Got Their Knowledge and Powers

Nhiãperikuli's younger brother Eeri (another name for Kuwaikaniri) went to the forest to look for shamans' powers. The first power he looked for was to make the sound of thunder (*eenu*). He first tried to kick a hollow tree, but failed to make the sound of thunder. Nhiãperikuli told him to go back to a certain fruit tree (*ibacaba*) and wait. He waited until midnight and then heard a loud crashing sound of something falling through the trees to the ground. He lit torchwood but saw nothing. So he waited until dawn, and then he climbed up the ibacaba tree. There he saw on a branch an eagle feather, which he picked up and sniffed. Suddenly he felt smitten, and his eyes saw things differently. He looked down and saw on the ground a white eagle, but it was a person (*newiki*). He descended the tree and slowly approached the white eagle. They greeted each other, and the eagle asked, "Were you looking for me?" "Yes," the young man replied. "Ah, good," the eagle person said and approached. He plucked out one of his feathers, giving it to the young man and telling him to sniff it. When the young man did, he was smitten by an even greater force and made the powerful sound of thunder, "*Khuk'kululululululu.*" He went home and greeted his brother. Nhiãperikuli looked around but saw no one, because his younger brother had become invisible. Thus Nhiãperikuli's younger brother first got the powers of pajés.

In this first episode, the younger brother was seeking pajés' power and knowledge, the owner of which was the great harpy eagle Kamathawa. Time (the ripening of the ibacaba fruit) and ecology (hunting in the forest, thunderstorms) are intertwined in his encounter with the spirit world. Climbing up the vertical divide (the tree), the young man finds and sniffs the eagle feather, and his vision is brusquely "opened up" to see the Other World. The eagle feather is the source of the power to "see"; thus he saw the eagle as a person on the ground. He descended to a direct encounter with the eagle person, white in color (indicating the spirit world, the Other World).

The ibacaba ripens in August, a short period of rains, when there are major thunderstorms, before the dry season starts in the Northwest Amazon. So the story relates the acquisition of shamanic power to the sound of thunder, which shamans today say they make to announce their presence in the Other World. To make summer, the pajés say, they sing and wave a harpy feather in the direction of the sky to clear it of clouds, opening the sky and sweeping away the jaguar shaman spirits' tobacco smoke. Thus one of the first powers acquired is to bring the dry season on. The pajés' relation to the dry season sun is another manifestation of their control over fire, as in the light of their cigars (Sullivan 1988), lit at the beginning of every ceremony. The control over fire is the main weapon that the pajés have against the potential destructiveness of the spirits.

Nhiãperikuli's younger brother becomes invisible and returns home having acquired shamans' powers. Note that pariká, the psychoactive powder that opens the shamans' vision today, had not yet been found. The transformative power occurs while sniffing the feather body covering (*iidzu maka*) of the powerful eagle person. Its feathers have a mystical power to alter sensory perceptions—they have to be sniffed just like pariká—and the young man becomes invisible.

The body covering of eagle feathers is evidently related directly to the numerous maka, or "cloaks" or "shirts" that a pajé possesses. It was from the primal eagles that the ancestral pajés obtained these powers. Today the pajés blow the snuff pariká through the eagle bone, known both as "maliapi" (white heron bone, or shaman's bone) and the "bone of Kamathawa," to initiate their soul flight to the Other World.

The second episode revolves around the felling of Kaali ka thadapa, which connected the two levels of the universe still in formation at that time and was the arboreal source of all cultivated plants in the world. The Tree of Sustenance is a theme found throughout the Northwest Amazon. For the Hohodene Baniwa, this enormous tree was located at a place called Uaracapory,[7] on the upper Vaupés River, in what is today Colombian territory. The felling of the tree by the primal shamans was an act that not only separated worlds but also signified the breaking up of a unified source into multiple portions of plant foods, which were distributed to all communities of people in this world. (Depending on who is narrating the story, their group gets more.)

From univocality, a rupture in time and space produces multiplicity, division among the levels of the cosmos, but it was from the fruits of the upper layer of the cosmos that the first pajés obtained their original pariká, which is their food. Each tribe has a piece of the tree. Felling the tree also signaled the breaking up of time units connected to the agricultural calendar, gardening activities, fishing and hunting cycles, and the appearance of constellations (Wright 2009a; Hill 1984). It is significant that the story attributes to shamans all of the powers of setting the seasonal cycles in motion. The primal shamans were responsible for this act of setting the food chain, meteorological succession, and seasonal activities of subsistence into dynamic, temporal motion defining various forms of collective activity in consonance with cosmic cycles.

One of the explicit motives for cutting the tree down was to get shamans' powers, represented by the jaguar tooth collar (*dzaui-e*) and pariká, which at that time were inside a little enclosure midway to the top of the tree in the Other World. Once the tree was felled (the best narrators skillfully heighten the expectancy of the event), Nhiãperikuli tried but could not get the pariká because swarms of bees prevented him from getting near the sweet flowers of pariká. The bees and other ecological indicators (the appearance of leaf-cutter ants, the tapir's catching fish in flooded areas) suggest a link to the time of the Pleiades constellation on the western horizon. The link between the Pleiades and a "swarm of bees" is also found in stories of the Barasana, for example, who were historical neighbors of the Baniwa in the late eighteenth century (S. Hugh-Jones 1989).

Suddenly the tapir plowed his way through the brush and, with his thick hide, was able to get the pariká without being stung by the bees. The tapir is characterized here and elsewhere as a gluttonous and selfish animal (Reichel-Dolmatoff, in Urton, ed. 1985), taking all of the shaman's powers for himself and stealing them from their rightful owner, Nhiãperikuli. The question then becomes centered on ownership of shamanic powers.

Who would retain the shamanic powers: the animals or the true pajés, Nhiãperikuli and his tribe? In possession of the pariká, the tapir calls his companions together to sniff the psychoactive powder. The tapir immediately transforms into a voracious jaguar who growls that he wants "to eat people without stopping," a monstrous, excessive predator. The catastrophe that this could have caused prompts Nhiãperikuli to simply snatch the pariká away from the tapir, giving him a sound tap on his snout and exchanging the pariká for a miriti fruit (blood-red in color) to eat. Nhiãperikuli later takes the miriti fruit away, leaving the tapir totally inoffensive and eating leaves, which is what he does today.

The tapir's companions, one after another, "go crazy" (*napikaka*) on pariká: one falls down drunk, another falls into the river and emerges as an otter, and the last runs into the forest and transforms into a forest spirit. Nhiãperikuli regains ownership of the pariká and gave shamans' powers to all future generations: "pajés [*maliri*] are *doutores*," the narrator said, for "they extract sickness, they revive people well. They help us well. That is the truth" (Keramunhe, elder narrator of Ukuki Cachoeira village, taped in 1977).

In "The Fruit of Knowledge and the Body of the Gods" (Wright 2009a), I interpreted the narrative of the pajés' powers specifically for what it explains about hunting, fishing, and agriculture and the relation of pajés to priestly chanters. Another question arises, though—what differentiates the jaguar shaman who "is a doctor, who helps us well," from the predatory jaguar shaman, or simply a jaguar that kills humans? Narrators explained that the transformation occurred because Nhiãperikuli did not do protective chants over the pariká. The pariká, in other words, had not been protected with powerful spirit names. This power only occurs through the actions of chants (Hill 1993; Wright 1993, 1998).

Jaguar is used in Baniwa stories as an epithet (Journet 1995) for powerful spirit beings and deities. Nhiãperikuli is often referred to as Dzaui Nhiãperikuli, Jaguar Nhiãperikuli, just as Kamathawa can be. There is also a *"Dzaui kumale"*—the tall jaguar-cumare palm tree (the Cumare palm tree from which strong fiber, *Astrocaryum tucuma*, popularly called "tucumã" is obtained) found in the plantation of Kuwai. The term *Dzaui Malinyai* refers to the spirits of the jaguar shamans—of the Other World, multitudes of them, all in the Other World, together with Dzuliferi. We conclude that the term *jaguar* is an epithet of spiritual greatness, like the term *the Great*. The epithet indicates that the person/spirit being has great power and knowledge and is held in high esteem, the opposite of a predatory jaguar that wantonly kills people. Pajés generally use spirit darts (*walama*) in wars among themselves, but pajés from other tribes may appear in the Baniwa area as predatory jaguars.

As in numerous indigenous calendars, the annual cycle is divided into two major and several minor wet and dry seasons. The appearance of the Pleiades marks the beginning of the heavy rains, a critical time of the year, corresponding to the ripening of forest fruits and the scheduling of initiation rites; it is also a time of great sickness associated with Kuwai.

The time of the *dzurunai*, or cicadas singing in the trees, by contrast, marks the early summer, dispersal of family units to their gardens, the felling of trees while extending gardens, and the beginning of the pajés' preparation to transmit their knowledge. The pajés transform into "universe people" and "drink the nectar of the flowers of pariká." Like the cicadas that molt their skin at this time, they become new again. Likewise, the jaguar shamans transform in the early dry season as they transmit their knowledge to the apprentices.

The early rainy season (March and April) is the time when the Hohodene Baniwa have finished burning and planting and begun fishing. By May the heaviest rains have fallen, and it is too wet to work in the gardens. Kuwai is associated with the waters, wetness, rivers, the port, and the rainy season. Dance festivals of the Kwaipan sacred instruments were originally scheduled during the months of the ripening of the first forest fruits, which could cover several months corresponding to the Pleiades, which is also called the "Young Initiates" and the "Fishtrap" constellations. Anytime during the ripening of the first forest fruits, Baniwa communities celebrate the dabukuri with Jurupary, called Kapetheapan, when they whip each other and dance with the instruments without it necessarily being a rite of passage. Sometimes a community will bring its own Kuwai flute or trumpet to join with the others. In the sacred chants called kalidzamai, sung at the initiation rites, the entire first set consists of "spirit names" (sacred names referring to sensory qualities of fish, animal species, or places) for spatial, temporal, and ecological indicators corresponding with the beginning of the rites themselves in the rainy season (Wright 1993).

The following months (May and June) are the cold wintery season in the Northwest Amazon. In June the Kaakodzude (bend of the river) and the Dukume (or Tchipanai) constellations appear on the horizon. These are days of mixed clouds and sun, a time known in the region as *aru*, which was once symbolized by a ceramic paddle said to be owned by shamanic beings, the Tchipanai, who ascend the river at this time, bringing the weather change.

As the story goes, at the time of the cold, they come paddling upriver, wearing headdresses of black and white feathers. The days on which they paddle upstream are thus mixed with black clouds and brilliant sun, followed by drizzly rain and intense cold. The Tchipanai paddle beats the water in the rhythm of ha'pe ha'pe, which means "the cold, the cold." A story tells how an old woman asked them to cure her from huge chiggers in her leg, and the brothers pulled up their canoes and said they would. They got their fishing poles and fished an enormous black chigger from her leg. It was as long as a *muçum* (eel-like fish), and the old lady cried out, but they pulled it out. She thanked them, and they went on their way, saying, "We're going north, grandmother, to where the sun goes out, but we'll be back in a few days." They left the cold, but when they returned, it became warm again.

Then come constellations from July to November, which all appear to have hunting and fishing as main themes, and finally the Makwapidani (cooking pot), Khewidapani (sucuri snake, "serpent of seven heads"), coinciding with the falling and rising of the rivers, abundance followed by scarcity of fish, and cutting new gardens. August and September are the times of Niewinai (otters located in four directions of the sky), when rivers are rising, a time of "dance festivals of the fish"; the Umainai (the piranha fish) and Lidzauithiuna (two hunters), when rivers are stationary. According to the story of malikai, the great harpy gave its knowledge and power to the universe people during this time of thunderstorms.

In the dry months of November and December, the rivers fall to exceedingly low levels. The Maalinai are a dry season constellation (January and February), corresponding to the flocks of herons, pure white birds that most resemble the shamans' souls (*maaliri*) in flight. Then come the cicadas, which appear as Dzurunai (Kaali's children) in the month of February, when pajés prepare to transmit their knowledge as the cicadas drink the nectar of the pariká flowers. These sing in the trees and look for gardens. They are pajés in fact believed to "make the world change, and the forest, too," as one elder explained. The forest does take on a different aspect at the time that they sing.

Following this cycle, the story of Kuwai and the rituals of initiation coincide with the appearance of the Pleiades constellation or *walipere-inuma*, the major rainy season, the ripening of forest fruits, a time of great sickness, celebration of initiation rituals, and the spawning of fish at the headwaters of the rivers. In short, pajés and shamanic beings appear in every part of the seasonal cycle and differentiate their apprenticeship initiation in the dry season from regular initiation rites in the rainy season.[8]

In closing this chapter, my objectives have been to provide a panoramic overview of the spirits and deities, their shadow-souls/animal avatars, their shamanic knowledge and powers, qualities and attributes, and pajés' relations to them. We have seen how the Great Tree provides an all-encompassing image for understanding the form and shape of the universe, which was, in the very beginning, an idea of connection between the universe and its "child" that gradually took shape by accumulating spatial and temporal references as planes or worlds. In its full development, as a blueprint of the universe, the tree image is a unifying symbol that is then divided into worlds, each associated with a deity, shadow-soul/ animal avatar, or spirits with attributes that are appropriate not only to the physical and ecological model but also to behavioral and cultural norms, forms of sociality, and spirituality.

In other words, living beings, such as the animal avatars (harpy eagle, sloths and tree animals, various birds, jaguars) or plants (pariká, tobacco) or celestial bodies (the sun, constellations, and especially cloud formations) and temporal modes (ancient past, today, future) provide the concrete imagery through which various modalities of spiritual knowledge and power (superhumanity, the deities, humanity, and proto-humanity) are all arranged into a unified, complex model of the universe that is home to all.

In their various manifestations (omniscience, tricksters, mystery, experiential, canonical, unthinking), knowledge and power are coupled with qualities of goodness or badness in several key deities and spirits. Various tubelike forms serve as vehicles for the spirit or soul that is transmitted through them and through which souls return to their origin.

The pajé as ecologist is fully integrated with temporal cycles as well as the omnipresent spatial markers and traces of the primordial world in This World. These are basic elements of the Baniwa universe, which it is the pajés' job to understand, explain, and protect by keeping in balance.

The dynamic of shamanic powers and knowledge and their relations to ecology show phases of centralization and dispersion, which are also present in the emergence of the prophetic "wise men and women" (Wright 1998), whose nemeses are the assault sorcerers, enemies constantly at war with them. These "wars," however, can be seen either as a struggle against the accumulation of shamanic power or as a will to destroy the most ancient connections to the sources of that power.

5

Mythscapes as Living Memories of the Ancestors

Ethnographic mapping shows that there is an extensive "sacred geography" in Baniwa-Kuripako-Wakuenai territory along the Northwest Amazon border of Brazil, Venezuela, and Colombia that consists of important locations of northern Arawakan creation traditions. This includes waterfalls with petroglyphs and stone formations, sacred hills where humanity obtained food, the beginning of the universe at the Hipana rapids, first initiation rites at Ehnípan, the first death, and the beginning of shamanism. The ancestors are said to have left traces of their presence at these places as memories for their descendants (*walimanai*) of what they had created.

These sites can be understood as "portals to the sacred," a concept that Vine Deloria used in speaking of Native North American sacred geography:

Such "portals" should not be viewed as limited in size or scale. Some may be large in their geographical extent while others are limited in size. Likewise, use of the portals concept must include the understanding that ... they are not only positioned

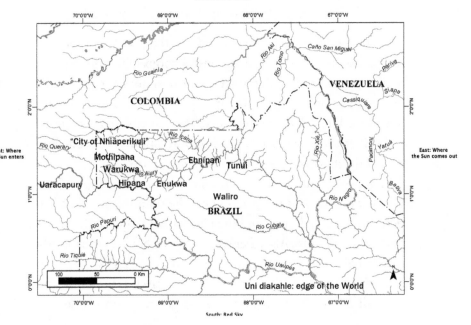

Map 2. Mythscape of the Northwest Amazon (northern Arawak). (R. Wright 2010.)

Uaracapory: Great Tree of Sustenance and source of shamans' power

City of Nhiãperikuli, the creator

Mothipana: Women's fortress; origin of all waters

Warukwa: Island of Nhiãperikuli's house, where the anaconda was killed

Hipana: Center of the universe, celestial umbilical cord, birthplace of Kuwai and the sacred flutes and trumpets

Enukwa: Ancestral emergence of the Walipere-dakenai; Pukweipan, the rapids below

Ehnípan: House of the first initiation ritual

Tunui: Hill of the origin of fish

Waliro: Kaali's great plantation

Uni diakahle: Where the waters no longer run; edge of the world in geography but also positioned in time, such that they become sacred "time/spaces." (Deloria in Taylor, ed. 2005: 1448)

I shall use the term *mythscape* to refer to the large landscape with sites relevant to the creation traditions.[1] A comparable notion might be the "Dreamtime" of the Australian Aborigines, for indeed the Baniwa maintain a living relationship with their sacred sites, for example, asking for the protection of the deities who are believed to dwell at these places or avoiding outcroppings of stone and grass as dwellings of the *yoopinai* sickness spirits.

Map 2 is a preliminary version, since a number of spots have been left out, such as the place where the phratric ancestors had their historic longhouses and the places of the souls of the ancestors (five small hills). Also, there are the stone houses where minor primordial beings lived and animal soul houses (*iaradathita*) everywhere in the underworld, as well as caves, mountains, and lakes, all of which are in some way associated with primordial beings.

Several significant places in the Baniwa universe are plotted in map 2.

1. Hipana is the birthplace of the universe, of humanity, and of Kuwai (as a living being and as a set of trumpets and flutes). Located on the upper Aiary River, it is considered the birthplace of the ancestors of the following northern Arawakan peoples: Piapoco, Hohodene, Dzawinai, Warekena, Kabiyari, Yukuna, Baré, and Tariana.

   The Walipere-dakenai emergence site is Enukwa [also called Pukweipan], a rapids slightly downriver from Hipana.

   The emergence site of the Baniva, a distinct ethno-linguistic group on the upper Guainia River around the town of Maroa, is located on the Cuyari River (Vidal 1987: 139), a totally distinct origin place from the Baniwa and Kuripako of the Içana. It is

17. Reproduction of petroglyphs on boulder of "false Kuwai" at Hipana Rapids, showing "the sound of Kuwai music" and "the pain of the whip."

the responsibility of the pajés who reside at Uapui — since the early twentieth century, the Hohodene — to guard the rapids from any kind of destruction or defilement. They ensure that everyone who visits shows proper respect for the sacredness of the place. The boulders and petroglyphs there illustrate the following elements from the episode of Kuwai's birth:

a) A line of boulders show the place where Amaru "sat" before she gave birth to Kuwai and where girls at their menarche sit today so that their bodies become strong.

b) A boulder with designs of the Pleiades constellation, plant growth, a divided rectangle (perhaps a representation for a star?), and a lizard — all said to be associated with Amaru.

c) A boulder that represents the "false Kuwai," with petroglyphs of a serpent representing the "pain of the whip," a "sieve for

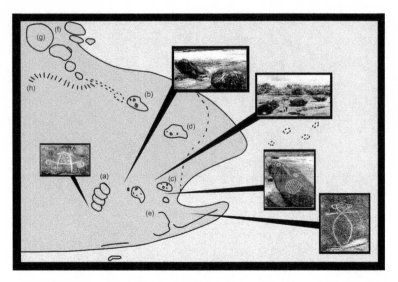

18. Petroglyphs at Hipana: birthplace of Kuwai, illustrating the meaning of the arrangement in boulders. (Adapted by M. C. Wright.)

producing manioc," and spirals that are said to represent the "sounds of the sacred flutes." Nhiãperikuli made these in order to trick Amaru into thinking the music came from her son, but she was not deceived.

d) Another boulder, a short distance away, is said to represent the "true Kuwai" (called "Kurawa," no translation).

e) A stone that has the shape of the placenta of Kuwai after he was born, with the shape of a freshwater stingray.

f–g) Several boulders representing the sacred flutes of Kuwai and hawk feathers that empowered the original flutes to make the "voice of Kuwai." Rubble that represents the "wasting away sickness" of the first young boys to be initiated. The rules and restrictions related to Kuwai were not followed.

h) A place of the ancient village where Nhiãperikuli left the Kuwai flutes.

19. Petroglyph of Kuwai at Pukweipan facing downriver. (Koch-Grünberg 1927.)

Several stones at Hipana and at Pukweipan feature images of Kuwai. At Pukweipan, Kuwai is displayed as a figure with lines connecting the center of his body (the central location of the heart-soul) to his extremities, and the number of fingers on each hand is different (two and three, representing the first pair of male flutes, called Maaliawa, and the three female flutes, called Waliadoa. At the upper rapids, a figure appears as a set of point indentations, forming a triangular torso, with a large pair of eyes in the place of its head and a baton in one hand. This figure could also represent the Pleiades constellation, the time when the Kwaipan are to be held.

2. An island called Warukwa on the Uaraná stream where Nhiãperikuli lived. One of my Hohodene research assistants went to the island and filmed the place where, according to the sacred story, Nhiãperikuli caught the great anaconda, Umawali, having sexual relations with his wife and killed him. There is a beach where several boulders mark the event, but the forest on the

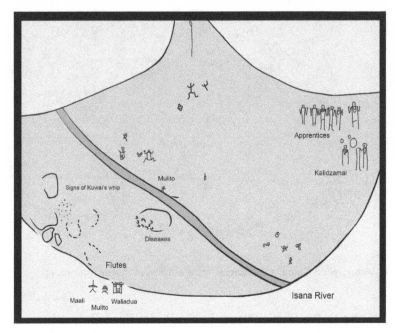

20. Reproduction of petroglyphs at Ehnípan (Jandú Rapids): place of the first initiation rite, illustrating the meanings of petroglyphs. (Adapted by M. C. Wright.) On the bottom left, several parts of Kuwai's body are represented as Maaliawa, "white heron," male flutes; Waliadoa, "young sister," female flutes; Mulito, frog, Kuwai's "penis." On the top right, the drawings show the initiates in seclusion (*itakeri*) and the kalidzamai priestly chanters with their instruments; sicknesses, the remains of Kuwai whips, the "vagina of Amaru," and the mulitu frog. (Adapted from an Etnollanos pamphlet, 2000.)

island is impenetrable, making it impossible to discern any other petroglyphs or stone formations.

3. On the far upper Uaraná stream is a place called Motipana, where large stone formations represent the cave-fortress of the first women, who stole the sacred flutes and trumpets from the men and hid inside. Here the women performed their first initiation rites for their daughter. It is also the place of the Origin of All the Waters of the Rivers in the region. There are

stone formations of Amaru's fortress—the female equivalent of Nhiãperikuli's "city."

4. A cluster of stone formations on the Yawiary stream off the upper Içana is called "the Great City of Nhiaperikoli." (Carlos Xavier Leal's excellent master's dissertation, defended in 2008 at the Museu Nacional in Brazil, presents fascinating material that Kuripako guides showed him.) This site is located about an hour's hike into the forest away from the Yawiary stream. Nothing similar to it has been reported in the literature on the Baniwa (or northern Arawakan peoples for that matter). It is an arrangement of boulders—apparently occurring in a natural manner, yet with an order and meanings attributed to the whole arrangement that the Kuripako called "the city of the creator sun god, Nhiãperikuli." The boulders are aligned along an east/west axis. Since Nhiãperikuli is the sun deity, this alignment may be significant. The site as a whole shows a scene from the story of Mawerikuli, the first person to die, who was buried underneath the house of Nhiãperikuli, following the tradition of burials many generations ago.

Under the huge "stone house of Nhiãperikuli" is a stone slab which appears very much like a stone coffin with a piece of a metal bell placed atop one end, looking very much like the carved wooden masks the Hohodene put on their dead up until a few generations ago (Nimuendaju 1950 [1927]).

Behind the "house" boulder is a "kitchen" boulder, and behind that are several "sentinel posts" where Nhiãperikuli's pet birds, the harpy eagle, and other sentinel birds called Tchitchiro and Madoodo could warn of approaching people. The scene is reminiscent of the moment when death came into the world and Mawerikuli was laid to rest under the House of Nhiãperikuli. On the eastern side of the site are the house and the tomb; to the west are the smaller boulders of the sentinel birds.

If there is a correlation, in the cosmovision of the Kuripako or Baniwa, between the sun's path across the sky and the arrangement of the boulders, this would reinforce an association with the themes of death and rebirth. Like Hipana, the "city" is part of a much larger and more complex site associated with other places, such as the "cavern of women" that Xavier Leal photographed. This complex site contains a large number of petroglyphs, rock formations, and caves. Near it, there is also a place on the Surubim stream, deep in the forest off the upper Içana, where a large flat rock sits atop a hill overlooking the river and a vast expanse of forest—a place where, it is said, "Nhiãperikuli sat and saw how the world would be" (Xavier Leal 2008).

It is possible that this conjunction of several sites in one place means that the site was in itself a sacred center, from which the creator could look out over the vast terrain of rainforest and see clusters of hills or know where important waterfalls were located. From this perspective, the mythscape acquires a view from the center looking outward. This would be totally distinct from a person situated at Hipana, the universe center, looking upriver or downriver, up to the sky or down to the world below. Ehnípan is considered another center, since it is the origin of the most important rite.

5. Uaracapory, on the upper Vaupés, in Colombian territory, is considered to be the emergence place of a Baniwa phratry that later adopted the Tukanoan Cubeo language. It is also the site of the Great Tree of Sustenance, which existed in the First World. When the Great Tree was cut down, all humanity obtained food for their gardens and the pajés gained their powers.

All of these sites are connected not only by the riverways but also by wide trails, such that a complete mythscape would demonstrate the interconnections in themes. Out of all the sacred stories the

Baniwa and Kuripako tell, the most important as a totality of the creation story have to do with (1) the beginning of the universe, (2) the Great Tree of Sustenance and shamans' snuff, (3) the first initiation rites, (4) the battle over possession of the sacred flutes and trumpets, (5) the beginning of death, (6) the beginning of fish, and (7) the first plantation.

The entire complex of sites constitutes a "sacred geography," a meaningful mythscape, for each site consists of the petrification of events from the Before World of the primordial past. Many of these sites are hedged with tabus preventing unblessed (unprotected by shamanic chants) people from approaching or stepping on them. It is said that the sites are full of poison, just as the entire world of the dead ancestors is. Why? The petroglyphs and boulders are believed to be the petrified transformations of what was once living, where the primordial beings—full of their dangerous powers—made things happen which later became petrified and timeless reminders of how life came to be the way it is today.

Kuwai's relationship to the ancestral territories of the phratries is one of the most significant aspects of this entire tradition. Many of the names of the sacred flutes can be found in the mythscape of the great events in the primordial times when Kuwai was alive. Hipana, Ehnípan, Tunui, and Motipana form a subset of the mythscape specifically related to the story of Kuwai.

The Kuwai "mythscape" forms the central core of the priestly kalidzamai chants sung at male and female initiation rites, or Kwaipan. In those chants, there is a great deal of place-naming that traces a virtual map of the "Voyages of Kuwai" (*Kuwai ianhiakakawa*) when the women took away the sacred flutes and trumpets and played them throughout the world. The powerful sounds of the sacred flutes made the world open up (expand) like a balloon from its miniature size to the size it became when the primordials left it.

This mythscape and the content of the priestly kalidzamai chants illustrate how the traces (*hlinapia*) of Kuwai are spread throughout the Northwest Amazon and upper Orinoco (Vidal 1987; Hill 1993; Wright 1993; González-Ñánez 2007; Xavier Leal 2008). Further analysis might be done with satellite mapping of the entire region, possibly detecting ancient roadways and the interconnections among the sites.

The kalidzamai chants contain hundreds of place-names that are actually spirit place-names that sometimes intersect with material places and sometimes don't. It is possible, on a large-scale geographical map, to show how certain geographical places on the rivers in the Northwest Amazon are more densely elaborated with meaningful features than others. From this, in addition to the numerous places mentioned in other sacred stories, the notion of mythscape more fully illustrates the Baniwa's sense of sacred territory.

Each community may have its own Kuwai flute or trumpet hidden at the bottom of a nearby stream. Thus there is a direct connection between community identity, phratric identity, and mythscape. From this we can understand what Baniwa pajés mean when they say This World is the "Kuwai world."

As in other indigenous areas of the world, the presence of the ancestors through petroglyphs, sacred sites, and actual parts of the ancestor's body constitute the evidence of an unbroken link between living people and their local ancestral territory. This link can only change when, for example, a community moves permanently to another place, but then a ceremony guided by the pajés must be performed to ensure that the power of the Kuwai ancestor is safely transferred. A major change such as this is the equivalent of moving the bones of the sib's first ancestor—and the sacred power embodied in them—in one package to a new place.

At this point, it is appropriate to introduce what some ethnologists have called the "religion of Kuwai" (Vidal 2002: 253) expressing the main concerns of the pajés: the existence of sorcery and the prevalence of sickness in the world, how culture is transmitted across generations, how elders teach the children about the laws of living, and what relations hold between the Other World and This World.

THE KUWAI RELIGION OF THE NORTHWEST AMAZON

The sacred traditions of Kuwai at one time were part of a much larger religious tradition in the entire Northwest Amazon, from the middle Solimões up the Rio Negro and to the Orinoco. This corresponds to the culture area of the northern Arawak-speaking peoples, whose history in that area dates back several thousand years (Neves 2001). These traditions have attracted the attention of scholars since 1890, when Ermanno Stradelli published his poetic rendition of the Yurupary traditions based on written manuscripts from the Tariano, Tukano, and other peoples of the Uaupés River region. *Yurupary* is a term from the lingua geral language introduced by early colonial missionaries to refer, erroneously, to a demon of the Indians, in opposition to Tupã, the Tupian god of thunder. Both Yurupary, spirit of the forest, and Tupã are still widely used in the northwest region of the Amazon as *lingua franca* names invented by the Catholic missionaries to substitute for the distinct deities of the twenty-two ethnic groups.

The first serious ethnological studies of the Tukanoan versions of the traditions were published by Reichel-Dolmatoff (1969, 1989) and Christine and Stephen Hugh-Jones (1981, 1989). For the Arawak-speaking Baniwa of the Içana and its tributaries in Brazil, Theodor Koch-Grünberg left field notes on these traditions in the first years of the twentieth century; in the 1950s Eduardo Galvão left sparse field notes on the initiation ceremonies and stories among the

Baniwa (Biblioteca do Museu Emilio Paraense Emilio Goeldi). The Salesian priest Wilhelm Saake published various short articles in German concerning Baniwa sacred stories, including Yurupary and shamanism in the late 1950s.

It has only been in the past twenty-five to thirty years that the results of prolonged field studies on cosmology and shamanism among the Kuripako and Baniwa (specifically the Hohodene, Dzauinai, and Walipere-dakenai phratries) have been published (Journet 1995; Wright, 1992a, 1992b, 1992c, 1992d; Hill 1987, 1993, 2009). Since then, a veritable archive of ethnological, ethnohistoric, ethnomusicological, ecological, and linguistic material has been produced. (In bibliography, see references to Hill, Journet, Garnelo, Wright, Xavier Leal, and González-Ñáñez.)

In his article of 1989, G. Reichel-Dolmatoff argued that the sacred flutes and trumpets can be understood as having to do with the reproduction of all life. The biological reproduction of natural (plant and animal) species serves as a metaphor, in the Dessano Indians' view, for human reproduction. Reproduction in nature is a model through which humans reflect on their own biological and social reproduction. In his 1996 analysis of the Yurupary myth, Reichel-Dolmatoff focuses exclusively on the Tukanoan stories, which are quite different in their emphasis on the rules of exogamy, in contrast with the Arawakan traditions of Kuwai, which cover an entire life story and several generations.

Reichel-Dolmatoff only analyzes Yurupary as sacred flutes and trumpets, relating it to the "law of exogamy," which all Tukanoan-speaking societies observe. For the Arawak-speaking peoples, the equivalent figure is Kuwai, child of the sun, whose body was both music and sickness, which was transformed after his death in a great fire into the sacred instruments and all sickness in the world.

Thinking in the historical manifestation of the Kuwai religion as a kind of institution, Vidal defined it as the "sociopolitical and religious basis for the regional leadership of powerful Arawak-speaking chiefs and groups" (2002: 253). After capably summarizing the research that had been done up until 2000, she highlights the following aspects of the "religion": (1) the central importance of rites and secret societies associated with Kuwai throughout the Northwest Amazon region; (2) the link between Kuwai and biological and sociological aspects of indigenous peoples of the northwest Amazon, and (3) the links between Kuwai and sociopolitical organization that involve the formation of powerful religious leaders in conjunction with war leaders and powerful chiefs.

In other words, according to Vidal's model, social and political organization was originally linked to stratified religio-military macro units and, later, in post-contact times, the formation of multiethnic confederations. The Kuwai religion, she states (and all agree), was the highest expression of religious life of the Arawak- and Tukanoan-speaking peoples. We see many vestiges of its importance on the upper Guainia River in the numerous petroglyphs and sacred sites (González-Ñánez 2007; see also *Etnollanos* 2000), as well as in the names of Kuwai ancestors that populate vast stretches of the upper Guainia River (Hill 1993).

Vidal's historical research and Alberta Zucchi's archaeological work were important for their time. They opened up a regional perspective, tracing Arawak migrations, hypothesizing on macropolitical units, and providing a wealth of data on the Kuwai religion among northern Arawaks, including virtual maps based on the "Voyages of Kuwai" chanted during the initiation rites (Vidal 1987; González-Ñáñez 2007; Hill 1993; Wright 1993).

The idea of looking at the so-called religion of Yurupary regionally was also suggested by Stephen Hugh-Jones (1989). There is documentary evidence from distinct peoples of the Northwest Amazon and Orinoco regions showing the existence of similar religious traditions from the Maypure "cult of the serpents" called

Cueti and the cult of flutes around the Tomo River, which naturalist Alexander von Humboldt visited in the 1780s and about which he wrote: "There are but a small number of these flutes near the confluence of the Tomo and Guainia. . . . Had colonization not destroyed indigenous societies in the early eighteenth century, then the botuto cult [*sic*] could have been of some political importance where the guardians of the trumpets would become a ruling caste of priests, and the oracle of Tomo could gradually form a link between bordering nations" (1907, 362–63, 364).

The "oracle" may refer to one of the Kuwai flutes, called mulitu, which has this function of answering questions posed to it during the rites by the women (Hill 1993, 2009).

Von Humboldt then described the cult in exactly the same terms as the Hohodene did in the 1970s: fertility of palm trees, ripening of forest fruits, central importance of the ancestors, the harvest, jaguar shamans (who held masked dances with jaguar pelt cloaks), and the growth of social groups. Thus we should take seriously von Humboldt's original idea that the Arawakan societies of the upper Guainia had developed a strong religious-political hierarchy and that the rituals of the sacred flutes and trumpets sustained their power.

A key area in the development of the Kuwai religion was, in von Humboldt's estimation, around the confluence of the Tomo and Guainia Rivers, which was the territory of the Guaypunaves, Baniva, and Kuripako. Two hundred years later, Mandu da Silva visited that same area to try to warn the people of an impending disaster if they forgot their traditions, because it was the people's only means of surviving against the whites. At that time, the politicians in the city of Maroa were using shamanic knowledge and power for their own political ends. One of Mandu's most important "cousin-brothers" was Macanilla, the last of the true jaguar shamans around Maroa.

Much fruitful research has yet to be done on the variations in meaning among all of the peoples who have or had something like the Kuwai religion. The brilliant study by Irving Goldman on Hehenewa metaphysics (2004) offers a solid basis on which to construct comparisons among a Tukanized Arawakan sib of the Cubeo, the Hohodene of the upper Aiary, and the Wakuenai of the upper Guainia (Hill 2009).

It was Goldman who first observed that in this region, Tukanoan- and Arawak-speaking peoples are organized into societies based on patrilineal descent, localized patri-sibs, and exogamous phratries. Each phratry consists of a number of sibs ranked according to the birth order of a mythical set of agnatic ancestors. Each sib was traditionally associated with a ceremonial function (chief, shaman, warrior, dancer, servant), important especially for the complex rites of passage in which sacred flutes and trumpets were played. The Hehenewa among whom Goldman worked are the keepers of the religious traditions; in other words, they are generally believed to understand the dynamics of cosmology and the principles of cosmogony in far greater depth than the lower-ranking sibs.

In his 2004 book on Hehenewa metaphysics, Goldman provides a very insightful view of the hybridity that has taken place between Tukanoan and Arawak religious traditions. Cubeo territory lies in the frontier region between the largely Tukanoan-speaking peoples of the upper Vaupès River and the predominantly Arawak-speaking peoples of the nearby Aiary River and upper Guainia. Since the early 1900s, the upper Aiary River region has been predominantly occupied by Baniwa phratries: Hohodene, Maulieni, along with Cubean Dyuremawa villages at the very headwaters of the Aiary.

From the ethnohistory of the upper Rio Negro region, we know that in the mid-eighteenth century, the upper Uaupés around the Cuduiary and Querary Rivers was inhabited by both the Baniwa and the Barasana (or Panenoa, as they were named in the documents;

Wright 1981). The Cubeo are mentioned for the first time in the written documents of 1852, which refer to the Catholic mission Santa Cruz de los Cubbeos at Mitu Falls, further up the Vaupés, which the Cubeo consider to be the place of their origin.

Historical records indicate that, until the end of the nineteenth century, Baniwa and Cubeo sibs (Kapithi-minanai and Dyure-mawa) lived along the Querary River, a short distance away from the Cuduiary where the Cubeo had their principal settlements. Throughout the latter half of the nineteenth century, there were intense movements of Cubeo and Baniwa to escape the violence of the rubber boom. So it is not surprising that Hehenewa and Baniwa religions were hybridized. The Hehenewa in fact were originally an Arawak sib that adopted the Tukano language and forged a hybrid religious tradition.

One of the fascinating aspects of this hybridization process is what happened to the Kuwai religion. A comparison of the stories of the Kuwaiwa, the creator deities of the Hehenewa, and the Hohodene Kuwai reveals that for the Hehenewa, the creator was Kuwai helped by the collective Kuwaiwa, the ancestral people, known to the Barasana and other Tukanoan peoples of the Uaupés as the *he masa* (Hugh-Jones 2004: 410).

Kuwai for the Hohodene is the "owner of sickness," who left all fatal illness in the world upon his "death" in primordial times. He also left his knowledge of healing, and it is to him that pajés travel in their cures of humans suffering from lethal sickness today. The Hohodene shamans also say that Nhiãperikuli has a "tribe of bee-spirit people" called the *Kuwai-inyai*. These are shamanic bees who live in a large city around the lower Isana River and produce powerful honey capable of resuscitating the souls of those who die of serious illnesses.

Another important tradition in this play of identity and differences is the story of Mavichikore, who, for the Hehenewa, like the Hohodene (who call him Mawerikuli), was the "first person to die," that is, he introduced death into the world. But the stories of how each one "died" are very different. And more important, for the Hehenewa, Mavichikore introduces the rituals of the masked dances, about which Goldman wrote extensively in his 1963 monograph. The Hohodene state clearly that Mawerikuli is indeed a Cubeo tradition and that the Maulieni, their younger brother sib, celebrated the masked dances up until the 1940s or so, when evangelicalism was introduced to the Baniwa and Cubeo.

In Hohodene traditions, one of the two brothers of Nhiãperikuli is named Kuwaikaniri (sometimes called Eeri). To many narrators, he is the same as Mawerikuli. Among the Hohodene of the Aiary and the Wakuenai of the upper Guainia River, there are a series of chants and songs related to curing in which Kuwaikaniri appears to be the archetype of reversible death, for he is cured from a sorcerer's poison by the tribe of shamanic bee-spirits (Wright 1998).

Another intriguing contrast and similarity is in Goldman's 2004 ethnography when he cites one of his Hehenewa interlocutors, who wrote: "In the general tradition of the tribes of Amazonia, it is told that there existed at one time an ancient era of the most powerful spirits and knowledgeable beings than those that are of the present era. That era was known as the 'Era of the Kuwaiwa' in the Cubeo language. There existed then two classes of Kuwaiwa: the seniors, authors of all good things, the juniors of all bad things" (195).

Goldman finds it difficult to reconcile this statement with any of the other attributes of the Kuwai. Indeed, he suggests that native scholars have not yet resolved the apparent discrepancies in these traditions.

Something similar occurs among the Hohodene Baniwa, some of whom spoke of a primordial era when there existed only one being, *hekwapi ienipe*, the universe child. The contrast we discussed in the previous chapter—between the world of happiness and the world of sickness—corresponds to the Cubeo notion of the primordial senior era of Kuwaiwa and the present era of juniors. It may be relevant to this question, I think, that both the Cubeo and the Baniwa were evangelized by Sophie Muller around the same time, and she preached to them about a primordial paradise and a present state of evil, the era of the devil.

The Great Tree of Sustenance for the Cubeo is none other than what the Hohodene call Kaali ka thadapa, the Great Tree of the deity Kaali, the source of all food, pariká, and the jaguar tooth necklace.

The first of the Hehenewa pajés is Djuri, "the singing one," who, for the Hohodene, is Dzuliferi, the elder brother of Nhiãperikuli, one of the three main creators. According to Goldman, Dzuliferi is "for the Arawakan Baniwa, a name for their Kuwai who was a leading pajé." This requires a slight revision: in Hohodene cosmology, Dzuli is the primordial healer, the owner of shamans' snuff and tobacco; but Kuwai is primordial sickness, the owner of sickness. They are two distinct spirit persons, socially related as uncle and nephew. Dzuliferi cannot transform into Kuwai, although Kuwai can transform into the shadow-soul of Dzuliferi (not the same as the reverse; see chapter 2 for further explanation).

Another important source of English translations of northern Arawak-speaking peoples' traditions is Hill's collection *Made-from-Bone* (2009). In part 1 of his book, "The Primordial Times," Hill presents several stories of the creator brothers, introduced as tricksters. Unlike the mischief-making trickster figures of North American mythology, who purposefully do things wrong in order to show the correct way, Nhiãperikuli's trickster nature comes from his uncanny ability to know things before they happen and to thus outwit most but not all of his enemies. Through foil, subterfuge, and incredible prescience, Nhiãperikuli—the Hohodene of the

Aiary River say—"knows everything without anybody ever having taught him."

This quality is not the only basis of his trickster nature, but it is connected to the jaguar shaman's ability to divine and prophesy on behalf of, and in service to, his people. It is this shamanic, divinatory quality that is the basis of much of his power and part of a nexus of religious knowledge and power that characterizes contemporary pajés, chanters, dance leaders, and sorcerers. The most striking example of this prescience is in the kind of knowledge that Dzuliferi owns: of the exact moments when people will be born and die. Much like the North American Mohawk traditions of a stick with marks on it representing the number of years a person is destined to live, so it is said that Dzuliferi has a huge book with all of the exact dates when the souls of newborns come into This World and leave it when they die.

Other powerful spirits share some of this quality—Kuwai, for example, knew beforehand that his own father would sacrifice him in a huge fire. Some of Nhiãperikuli's enemies also seem to know what he is up to and escape from his traps, but leave the vestiges of their harmful acts—such as assault sorcery, evil omens—in the world today from which people suffer. The message underlying all of these stories seems to be that in This World, humans must constantly be aware of possible traps set for them by their enemies and try to be one step ahead of them; beyond that, their time in This World is predetermined, without much chance of changing it.

In South American indigenous cosmologies, it has been said that the universe was not created *ex nihilo* but rather as the product of a series of transformations from preexisting conditions (Sullivan 1988). As we've seen in the first creation story above, spatial and temporal differences and processes came into being because of Nhiãperikuli's primordial intention, or will (*liuma*) for a different condition, and that he was a self-generated orphan (*pawaada*), not a transformation from any prior being, thought, or action. *Self-Generated* and *Self-Generating Principle*, he set things in motion by will and intentions.

The power that the universe child possessed to "see how things would come into being" (Mandu's phrase to describe Nhiãperikuli's shamanic power) and the knowledge to do anything "without anyone having taught him" characterize a magnified pajé, or pajés, since he had two brothers, a child, and an aunt all with magnified shamanic powers. His brothers each have the knowledge of healing by chanting (Dzuliferi) and causing death by sorcery (Mawerikuli). Amaru gained shamanic powers when she stole the sacred flutes and trumpets from the men, as well as having a dominion over medicinal plants.

Nhiãperikuli's child, Kuwai, was his own heart-soul shamanically thought into being. Kuwai was an eminently shamanic being of great power, and Nhiãperikuli struggled with the first women over who was going to keep that power. Kuwai was, after all, his child; Nhiãperikuli simply implanted his knowledge and heart-soul into Amaru's body. All narrators with whom I worked agreed that the women "lost the war" for ownership of the sacred flutes and were sent away from their homes. Throughout the story, nevertheless, Amaru wanted her son; if she had retained power over him, society would have turned out very differently.

In Xavier Leal's thesis, he draws attention to the fact that the evangelical Kuripako of the upper Içana believe that Amaru did retain possession of the sacred instruments and that Amaru is their "Mother" deity, not Nhiãperikuli. The Hohodene pajés believe that the ancestral women ultimately were sent to live with the whites, creating a serious problem for the Baniwa, with the sickness they send and the conflicts the whites have historically generated with the Baniwa.

The next three chapters will examine the story of the great spirit called Kuwai. Each chapter corresponds to an episode in his story. Chapter 6, regarding Kuwai's birth, asks what exactly is being born in this extraordinary being? Chapter 7 covers the entire initiation cycle and the creation of new generations, in which sickness and sorcery also came into the world. Chapter 8 relates the struggle between the men and women over the possession of the sacred flutes, which are Kuwai's body and have the power to produce new generations of adults. Kuwai signifies continuity, the transmission of culture, and especially shamanic knowledge between the ancestors and their living descendants. But Kuwai is also the change that his body effects in others during passages of the life cycle. The combination of these principles (continuity of knowledge and heart-soul; change in body qualities) are key themes in the mystery of the Kuwai world.

Continuity of the traditions is constantly threatened by enemy Others. The mission of the jaguar shamans turned prophets is to alert society to threats to this continuity. If the young adults are not initiated, society will be vulnerable to the enemy outsiders who impose the kind of change that breaks the connection with the ancestors, just as if there were no more jaguar shamans, society would become vulnerable to the attacks of sorcerers and new diseases.[2]

Part 3

*Transmission of Shamanic
Knowledge and Power*

6

The Birth of the Child of the Sun, Kuwai

The child Kuwai is an extraordinary being—the child of the sun, who is spirit, animal, and person all in one. Part jaguar, part sloth or other tree-living animal, he can transform into a set of beautiful, melodious songs, or he can transform into a mysterious, monstrous, all-consuming, demonic Other. Kuwai is a complex mixture of aspects of being, many "intentionalities" that don't necessarily all work together but which produce changes in the world and especially in the initiates. The narrative of his life, death, and remaking into sacred flutes and trumpets contains in effect a whole worldview, Weltanschaung, of the Baniwa. It is a foundational myth, one in which the universe and society—meaning every important transformative social process—come into being and are reproduced over time.

NARRATIVE OF THE KUWAI STORY: PERFORMANCE, EXPLANATION, AND METHODOLOGY

The original narrative of the story of Kuwai is approximately twenty-eight pages of single-spaced text, which would make a book in itself if accompanied by images from the landscape or drawings.

Given that the principal objective of this book is to understand the relationship of the jaguar shamans to Kuwai, what is required here is a version that is both acceptable to Baniwa pajé narrators and readable for a wider public. Such a version exists in the collection of Baniwa narratives entitled *Waferinaipe Ianheke* (Cornelio et al. 1999), which is based on a narrative taped in 1977 by the most knowledgeable elder at that time on the upper Aiary River, a Hohodene named Keramunhe (Ricardo Fontes). That version and all other stories in the book were translated into Portuguese with the assistance of several pajés and narrators in 1997.

To perform this story requires great concentration and skill to get across an underlying moral and message that lay listeners will begin to understand and that the pajés understand very well. The narrator was considered by everyone on the Aiary to be outstanding, but many other narrators contributed details to the story that will be useful to consider as exegesis for the interpretations each chapter provides. The narrator was not a maliri pajé, but he was a well-known "chant-owner" with extensive knowledge of the stories and the chants that go along with them. He was a dance leader (*manderokai iminali*), and his singing of dance songs and imitations of the flutes formed an integral part of this narrative. It is as though the narrative, as a whole, uses the sacred language of cosmogony to its fullest extent, which makes it such a demanding performance to observe.

For the purposes of interpreting this foundational myth, the story can be divided into three major episodes, consistent with the way narrators themselves present the entire drama. The three parts are (a) the conception and birth of Kuwai (chapter 6); the first initiation rites (chapter 7); and the struggle between men and women over ownership of the sacred flutes and trumpets, the "body of Kuwai" (chapter 8). It is possible to divide the first initiation rites into two parts corresponding to a complete cycle of exchange festivals, but it would not make any sense to consider them as separate chapters.

Complementary to the narrative, a drawing of the young boy Kuwai was made with the help of a jaguar shaman kin of Mandu and is reproduced in appendix B with permission from Omar González-Ñáñez (2007) from his book on narratives of the upper Guainia. This is an extraordinary drawing accompanied by numerous bits of information, including names of body parts, referring to both the initiation themes of the flutes, the "heart-soul" of Kuwai containing much sickness; the umbilicus containing medicine; and the crown of his head, where sickness and remedies are combined.

This drawing allows us to see clearly how Kuwai's body, as a "boy," is similarly mixed, both as the holes that produce the sound of flutes and the most important forms of sickness in Kuwai's body and heart-soul. As in the pajés' drawings of the universe, it is the arrangement and the relations between the parts that are of greatest importance, for Kuwai's body is totally perforated on its appendages, with holes corresponding to the pairs of flutes and trumpets that eventually were fabricated from that part of his body after its transformation into a paxiúba palm tree. Lethal sicknesses and their remedies are concentrated in the heart-soul and crown of the head. The navel is noted as a place of remedies against a grave sickness called *fiukali*, produced by eating raw or rotten meat.

In order to understand what Kuwai is all about, four methodological guidelines have served as sine qua non in the interpretation of this story: first, the idea of semantic multivocality (V. Turner 1995 [1969]) referring to the multiple layers of meaning that a single image or symbol may have in a given context. Second, to complement the multiplex meanings of images, the notion of shamanic "world-making" (Overing 1990) is of importance here, too. The pajés' explanations for, and exegeses of, the images in this sacred story reveal the world-making power of their knowledge.

The semantic multivocality of Kuwai in itself allows for ample plurality in shamanic world-making. Third, pajés' exegeses show that they understand this story not only as a pedagogical instrument but also as a way of displaying the overwhelmingly powerful and mysterious forces of the cosmos.

My hypothesis here is that the narrative demonstrates to the pajés the means for bringing external cosmic powers into the heart of society and utilizing them for reproducing culture over time. Recalling that the stories provide the explanation that is the basis for the actions of curing, we can expect to find that in each episode, there is a form of shamanic action that occurs, accompanying all phases of the life cycle.

Fourth, the challenge of this interpretation is to be attentive to nuances of meaning that reveal the emotive content of the heart-soul and not be restricted to a set of cognitive oppositions or contrasts that are used in other kinds of interpretation. Also, the meaning of the details relating to symmetries and their properties is repeated in various contexts throughout the story. These lead us to understand processes related to temporality (generational, seasonal) and spatiality (the opening of This World to history). These can best be seen in the chapter on the theme of initiation.

Kuwai is his father's heart-soul, that is, the externalization of the paternal heart-soul, its transmission over time, and the harnessing of ancestral power. The sacred story of Kuwai is about the transmission of heart-souls between patrilineal ancestors and descendants, between elders and new adults, and the relations between men and women. The ancestral heart-soul is creative and inseminating in its transformative power, but it also is extremely dangerous and can destroy society from within, through the devastating power of venom, poison, and assault sorcery.

In this chapter, I shall interpret the first episode and its relationship to birth shamanism. Chapter 7 follows sequentially with an interpretation of all that is implied by the theme of "initiation." Chapter 8 discusses all that is implied in the ownership of ancestral power embodied in the sacred flutes and trumpets, also called Kuwai.

Episode I: Conception and Birth of Kuwai
Translated from Cornelio et al. 1999, narrator:
Ricardo Fontes, Keramunhe, of Ukuki Cachoeira

Kuwai was conceived when Nhiãperikuli sent his thought to Amaru, his aunt (likuiro). Conception did not take place by sexual relations; rather, Nhiãperikuli transmitted his thought (lianheke) into the body of Amaru. In his village at Warukwa, Nhiãperikuli ate coca, "thought toward" where Amaru was, and sent his knowledge, which penetrated her at Hipana. He chanted over his coca, and she became pregnant with Kuwai. But Amaru was not like the women of today. She had no vagina; Kuwai could not be born. Nhiãperikuli then took a patauá log and broke a passage into her. She "died," but Kuwai popped out. Nhiãperikuli revived Amaru, but when she looked for her son, she found that the men had taken him away to be nursed by a sloth of the forest. Nhiãperikuli saw that Kuwai was extraordinary. He was not of this world, for his body began to hum and sing melodious animal song as it urinated and cried. He had the mouth of a jaguar and ripped off his sloth mother's breast. Since there was no way he could remain in this world, Nhiãperikuli sent him away—first to the forest until he was a young man, and then to the sky where Kuwai lived for a long time before he appeared again.

(Kuwai kenyua) Kuwai kenyua
(The beginning of Kuwai, the beginning of Kuwai)
Nhiãperikuli ienipepe tsa!

(Nhiãperikuli's child!)
Kamui lhaneri, Kamui, Kuwai haneri
(The sun is his father, the sun is Kuwai's father)
(Ricardo's narration, 1977)

INTERPRETATION: CONCEPTION AND BIRTH

Powerful knowledge is embedded in the chants with which Jaguar Nhiãperikuli blessed his sacred coca and sent his thought into the body of Amaru. The conception of Kuwai was the result of Nhiãperikuli's intention (*liuma*) and emotional thought (*iapihenta*), but it was his shamanic knowledge (*lianheke*) that penetrated Amaru's body without sexual relations.

The question of whether Amaru was a consanguineal relative is unequivocally denied here, for according to Baniwa usage of *likuiro*, the term refers to a woman who is not of the same biological family (I. Fontes pers. comm., May 17, 2011). Nhiãperikuli is said to have had numerous wives from other primordial tribes (the Thunder-people, the Fish-people, the daughter of Night, to name a few). Nhiãperikuli is an orphan whose paternity is unknown. The word *incest* would make sense only if there was a strong indication that two beings of the same consanguineal group produced a child by sexual relations, but that is not the case here. There is actually spatial distance separating the parental couple (Amaru was at Hipana; Nhiãperikuli was at his house on the island of Warukwa, on the Uaraná River).

Today the Hohodene say a child is conceived through the penetration of the woman's body by Nhiãperikuli's heart-soul, that is to say, the patrilineal, ancestral transmission of life force. The body of the child is produced by sexual relations; the heart-soul is transmitted through *likai*, the sperm of the father. Traditional Baniwa refer to Nhiãperikuli as "Our Father" (Hfaneri). Nhiãperikuli's

"thinking toward" Amaru is accompanied by his blessing (a shamanic prayer) and eating coca, which effectively reproduced in her
body the father's heart-soul. This is a very clear statement of the
sacralization of transmission in the patrilineal line by shamanic
means.

The verb *thinking to, remembering* (*iapihenta*) is also used to refer
to the way chanters travel to other places when they make their
"thought voyages," called *kalidzamai*, accompanying the "pepper
blessings" performed at all passage rites. The coca—made from
dried coca leaves—was used quite often to stay awake when the
men went out to hunt at night or to stimulate their thought when
they were telling stories around the fire. It makes a person more
alert with memories primed, which is ideal for the kalidzamai
chanters who have to "pursue," "remember" the spirit names of
dozens of places and species of fish and animals.

The word for the sacred coca used here is *hlipatukairi*, which
means "the powerful essence of his coca." The suffix -*kai* (essence
of) is of major importance to understanding many religious ideas
in Baniwa culture: *malikai* (shaman's knowledge and power),
mandero-*kai* (dance owner's knowledge and power). Together
with the negative -*me*, the word -*ikaime* refers to the sorcerer's
poison. The word *likai* means "semen," the essence of paternity,
making the sense of "power" something "owned by men."

Patrilineal societies in general privilege the powers of men,
while women have an ambivalent position, beginning their lives
with their natal families and then, after marriage, moving close
to their husband's family. How are gender relations represented
in this story? Amaru is the bearer of Kuwai, the mother of Kuwai,
who nurtures him in her belly until the time of birth. Yet she is
deceived by Nhiãperikuli, who takes her child and hides him.
Amaru does not forget, and in the final episode, she takes the
transformed material body of Kuwai away from the men, only to

have them wage war against the women. As a result, men retained power over the ancestral flutes and trumpets. This can be a political issue because there is an entire tradition of Amaru stories that have to do with representations of the contact with the whites. This is a fertile field for much elaboration by narrators and pajés alike who seek to understand, for example, how it is that Amaru and the white men can bring so much sickness. Amaru, at the same time, is a key person in the beginning and end of the story for the fact that she opened up the entire horizontal world with her blood, which became the waters of all the rivers.

In the final episode, Amaru performs the first girl's initiation ritual (Kwaipan), complete with the priestly pepper-blessing (kalidzamai) and the sacred flute. She later became the mother of the whites, the mother of the most powerful form of alterity surrounding the Baniwa. Hohodene oral histories also attest to the important role that women have had as intermediaries in their phratry's relations with Other (affinal) phratries. Women have considerable power even if it is not as apparent as the men's in daily life.

Returning to Kuwai inside Amaru's belly, the term *Kuwai-wape* can be translated as "the original, collective body parts of Kuwai." In other stories we find uses of the same suffix to refer to "all the bones of the first person to die," "all the original fish-poison plants." Kuwai is thus a collectivity of many beings in one. On the petroglyphs, Kuwai is depicted either as a single entity (at Pukweipan) or as multiple parts of his body, each of which has the form of a flute or trumpet, like a primordial collective "person." At the end of the sacred story, *Kuwai-wape* refers to the "collection of the first" set of sacred flutes and instruments, the "body of Kuwai" reproduced from the plant elements left behind from his sacrificed body. Multiplicity-in-One is a key notion for understanding the universe.

Amaru was "not like those women of today," for she had no vagina. Her body had no orifice through which the child could come out. Her body was closed, so she could not bring forth new generations. This is key to understanding the episode and for understanding who or what Kuwai is. It is the first birth in the cosmos, when women began to give birth to children of Nhiãperikuli. Without the birth canal and opening, Kuwai, the heart-soul of Nhiãperikuli, would not have been born. He would have died trapped inside her belly. Thus this moment is of utmost importance.

But why did Amaru lack a vagina? The Hohodene tell several stories in which one of the predominant themes is the relationship between Mother and Child, but these don't represent the "difficulty" and pain of "giving birth" as much as this one. Numerous prayers and chants exist to assist women in labor. In these orations Kuwai is responsible for the pain, which pajés try to alleviate through their orations called Madzeekata keramu ("they can't make the child"). They try to "break the knots" that tie the woman's abdomen together in order for the child to be born. It is all the pieces of Kuwai's body, the pajés say, that are blocking the way. The fibers of the jaguar cumare (tucumã) tree have tied together the woman's abdomen and have to be loosened. Kuwai is pulling up on the umbilical cord for the child not to leave the intra-uterine state. It is as though Kuwai's umbilical cord tries to keep the child inside the womb.[1] The pajé thus invokes a wooden cigar holder with its sharp, pointed tip to break open the birth canal/passage, then he invokes piranha fish teeth to cut the knots and the sweet juice of forest fruits to sweeten the way for the child to come out of its mother's womb quickly.

From a pajé's point of view, there is considerably more involved here than the birth of one child. José velho, Mandu's uncle and a well-known pajé, said that a series of things came out of Amaru first: the four main elements of sickness and medicine—a thorn (*walama*), a stone (*hipada*), a piece of wood (*haikuita*), and hair (*tchicole*). These four elements are exactly the same as the "sickness medicines" an apprentice has to swallow at the beginning of the apprenticeship. In a sense, embodied shamanic knowledge is born first.

According to Mandu, at the time Kuwai was conceived, Amaru and the other women (*inamanai*) lived at Hipana, at a place called *liwalikwa eenu*, the "lake with no outlet," referring both to the lake that exists today at the rapids and to the fact that there were no flowing rivers at that time in the world. Hipana was then still "the beginning and the end of the world," self-contained (just like Amaru's body), for the world had not "opened up" beyond its miniature size yet. It was in a condition of stasis.

Here we find again the main theme of the story: that in order to get from the condition of "closure" (a closed passageway), the only way to prevent either the child or the mother from dying was by breaking open a passage using a patauá log, or fish with sharp teeth, or other cutting and breaking instruments. The patauá palm tree is important because Kuwai is closely linked to all palm trees. The ripening of the fruit of the palm trees is one important ecological indicator related to the cycle of whipping and initiation rites. Thus breaking into Amaru's body signifies the beginning of ritual time and the changes related to the body.

In the language of the story, Amaru "dies," but the word used here is *maliume*, also meaning she fell unconscious. She could be brought back to life through a pajé's action. The child, however, is whisked away. Why? According to Mandu, when Nhiãperikuli discovered that Amaru was pregnant with Kuwai, he knew that Kuwai would not be like a normal child, because he had a huge mouth with large, sharp teeth like a jaguar's. When Nhiãperikuli gave the baby to another Amaru (a female sloth) to nurse, the child sucked her breast dry in an instant and then violently ripped her breast off. Nhiãperikuli sent this Amaru to the forest, where she became an *awakaruna*, spirit of the forest.

Kuwai was uncontrollably hungry, a wild animal, a monster, a demon, *inyaime*, for "everything that he saw, he wanted to devour." Nhiãperikuli sent Kuwai away to the sky because, as Mandu explains, he knew that Kuwai would "one day be so angry that he would not be normal and he would kill every child that was born with a normal body. The world would not be good." Kuwai's mouth with its jaguar teeth is, in Mandu's imagery, the most salient feature of the newborn child. The image even brings to mind the "baby jaguar" motif found in other Lowland South American societies and as far away as Central America, where we find such themes expressed as the were-jaguar in some Central American cultures (Neil Whitehead, May 2011).

Other images show Kuwai's raw, brute animal power. His placenta is said to be a freshwater stingray, connoting poison and extreme pain, consistent with Kuwai's nature as one who inflicts pain and sickness. Amaru suffers at the birth of the child, whom she never sees because it is dangerous.

In Mandu's exegesis, Nhiãperikuli took the Amaru who bore Kuwai to a place on the Uaraná River, and when he opened Amaru's belly, a little stream of blood flowed out and curved around in circles (*dzukudzukwa*, which is the name of the Uaraná River), forming a "lake with no outlet." A bit of blood, however, over-flowed the boundaries of the lake in the form of water, and thus the rivers began to flow out of the circle. This is a major change from the prior, static condition without flowing river water, to an enlarged world with rivers flowing throughout the world all the way to the *eenu ta'he*, border of sky and earth.

Amaru "died" at the place where the Hohodene have their House of Souls of the Dead, on the Uaraná River, called "*piduinaikwa*

Putupan Iarudathi." This is a place of great importance to them, where the souls of all the phratry's ancestors lie, inside a hill.

Kuwai's body was indeed very strange, "full of holes" emitting musical sounds from the moment he came out of his mother's womb. All of the sounds have multiple referents: (1) they come from different parts of Kuwai's body, (2) they have the names of animals, birds, and fish, and (3) they refer to qualities or aspects of Kuwai's being (ravenous hunger, transformation, fluid, alterity, growth). By following which songs are sung and when, we may arrive at an understanding of the semantic unfolding of Kuwai's shamanic being in the myth, as the heart-soul and life force of the sun father and what changes he induces in initiates.

The first song is a single high-pitched tooting sound, representing the mulitu frog, a short flute corresponding to Kuwai's penis. There is a complex symbolism associated with the mulitu frog flute; it is the only flute played singly during the rites performed today, and there are moments when it communicates with the women, answering their questions. (See Xavier Leal 2008, Hill 1993, and Hill, in Hill and Chaumeil 2011, for further discussion of the mulitu flute.) In some of the oldest documents that refer to the sacred flutes in this area, von Humboldt mentions that the frog flute acted as an oracle, responding to questions that the women asked.

The second song seems to be three short spurts ("*tseytsem tseytsem tsey*"), like the musical sounds of a pajé's rattle; they correspond to the two fingers on Kuwai's right hand, a pair of flutes, and their name, Maaliawa, means "white heron," a bird closely associated with the pajés, *maliri*. The sounds are sung in a high, falsetto voice, the song of the "young male herons." Complementing the male flutes are the songs of the Waliadoa, "young sister," three long flutes, said to be the three fingers of the left hand of Kuwai. The petroglyph of Kuwai on the boulder facing downriver at Pukweipan likewise shows two fingers on one hand and three on the other.

What can be derived from this composite image of the baby Kuwai? A mixture of two distinct animal forms (jaguar and sloth), male and female (gender), predator and prey (the jaguar mouth with its sharp teeth; the principal predator of the sloth is the jaguar), and the singular appearance of the frog flute (also shown on the Pukweipan petroglyph). Finally Kuwai is dislocated in space from center (Hipana) to periphery (the forest) and sent up to the sky—places of alterity beyond humanity.

At the rapids of Hipana, the story of Kuwai's birth is visibly remembered on the boulders nearest to the hole of ancestral emergence. There are boulders of (1) the body of Amaru, where she sat as she gave birth; (2) the shape of a stingray carved out of a boulder, Kuwai's placenta; (3) four boulders lined up, interrelated by primordial images, and the distinguishing criteria of "true" and "false" Kuwai. The false and true distinction is first displayed in the men's act of deceiving Amaru and taking the child away, leaving only the placenta. Nhiãperikuli wished to deceive Amaru because of the dangerous power that Kuwai had. In the hands of the women, what would become of that power? Would it harm them as well? He feared that a catastrophe would occur.

Kuwai's form and growth defy the boundaries of all ontological categories of life in this world; as narrators say, he is totally unlike anything that existed prior to his entrance into the world. Besides this, he embodies processes of dangerous growth, monstrous "openness," and change in physical, material, and spiritual senses. He is the paradoxical mixture of creative and destructive forces through the music and the sickness that form his body.

Since Kuwai embodies liminality, he can only be seen in moderate doses or until the person who is seeing is able to withstand the effects of this revelation. Should there be unmediated "mixing up" of substances or people that cannot be mixed, then the full force of Kuwai's destructive being is unleashed, and deaths annul the element of change.

In all of the above, we have the foundations of a complex metaphysics (Goldman 2004) represented through concrete imagery. The next chapter focuses on the second major part of the story, consisting of the initiation of four children by Kuwai.

7

Death and Regeneration in the First Initiation Rites, Kwaipan

Initiation is a major transformative moment when the children become adults and are taught to live well in society and the world. The children are taught the differences between truth and falsity, the Other World and This World. They see the full force of the cosmic jaguar that Kuwai becomes, as he devours three children and then flies away to his place in the corner of the sky, unbridled shamanic power which then is harnessed at the conclusion of the ritual, transformed into priestly knowledge that makes the world safe for the new generations. This entire episode, I shall show, is about the reproduction and transmission of power and knowledge from grandfather's and father's generations to son's or grandson's generations, containing various parallels with shamanic initiation processes.

The episode is structured in two parts that correspond to two kinds of festivals when the sacred music of Kuwai is played and when there are whipping rites to make children "grow" and make adults be "strong and resistant." The first ritual is called Kapethea-pan (House of Whips), which can be performed whenever there is an abundance of forest fruits. This ritual can be followed by the second, called the coming-out festival, on the occasions of initiation rites for boys or girls.

When the initiates have terminated their month of seclusion and are ready to emerge as new adults, the second ritual begins. This second ritual is highlighted by the priestly chants with pepper, called *kalidzamai*. The purpose of these chants is to "bring Kuwai down" from the Other World, and with his music, "open up" and make This World safe for the initiates. At the end of these chants, the music of Kuwai is sent back up to his place in the sky where he lives eternally, only accessible to the shamans.

The first ritual that brings Kuwai down and into This World is performed in order to separate the initiates and the men from the women and uninitiated so that growth of the boys and girls into adults occurs; separation is complete at the seclusion of the initiates. In the story, seclusion of the boys is dramatized as the symbolic "deaths" of three of four boys (that is, their total removal from society). The second ritual, which is held in exchange for the first, brings Kuwai back down, to end the initiates' transformation into adults and reintegrates them into society, culminating in the dramatic "death" of Kuwai at the end of the rite. His life was sacrificed in exchange for the lives of the initiates who "died" during the seclusion. Kuwai is then sent back to his place in the Other World.

In the entire process, the vertical dimension is of utmost importance. Initially, a connection is opened gradually between the Other World and This World as the spirit of Kuwai reveals his power in the contexts of various transformations that occur in the other-than-human world.

CONTINUING WITH THE NARRATIVE

One day, four children are playing with noise-making instruments, tying up bumblebees and wasps, and putting them inside ceramic pots (*akhe*, used to contain manioc beer for dance festivals). As the wasps and bees drone inside the pots, the children dance. Unknown to them, Kuwai is watching from the sky; he comes down to approach them, and they see a white man (*yalanawi*) with shoes, watch, and hat. They tell him they are making Kuwai music, to which he responds that it is nonsense, for he is the real Kuwai, and that if they wish to hear his music, they must undergo ritual seclusion and not eat pepper or cooked food for three dry seasons. The children accept this condition, and Kuwai sings four melodies from the holes of his body while whipping the boys. Then he gives them a fruit (japurá) to sniff to stave off hunger and promises to return later.

A second time Kuwai appears, stays with the boys a short while, singing the same four songs as before, and then flies away. When Nhiãperikuli finds out the children have seen Kuwai, he immediately makes preparations for the "owner's" (=Kuwai's) return, sending the children's mothers away and waiting for Kuwai's return at the ritual house of Ehnípan (today, Jandu Falls) on the Içana River. Nhiãperikuli instructs the children that when Kuwai comes, they are to take him to the center of the ritual house. They wait in anticipation and whisper. When Kuwai finally comes, the children hide, but Kuwai flies up and inside the house directly to the center. Then Nhiãperikuli, who has stayed behind the door, jumps out and stands face-to-face with Kuwai, demanding that he confirm who he is and what life will be like during the seclusion period. Kuwai confirms the period of fasting but tells the boys it will all be good, for they may eat all types of forest fruits that are ripe during the fast. He sings for them again, but this time all parts of his body sing together in a great roar, and then he leaves them. They thank him, and he announces that he will return at the end of the fast to whip (*likapetan*) them.

When the time of seclusion is drawing to an end, Kuwai's full power and danger are revealed. The children are restricted and cannot eat roasted food. Kuwai takes them to Hipana, where there is a huge uacu tree (*Monopteryx uaucu benth*).[1] He climbs it and sits on top, breaking open and throwing down ripe uacu nuts to the children below. He is like "a big-bellied monkey." The children gather the nuts, and they should return to the ritual house at Ehnípan, where Kuwai will do the necessary chants to end their restrictions. But three of the children cannot withstand their hunger. They roast and eat uacu nuts, breaking their restrictions. The littlest boy does not eat the uacu nuts, but witnesses everything that transpires.

The smoke of the fire rises up to Kuwai and blinds him. He "falls unconscious" in the tree as his orifices open up entirely, and saliva gushes out in streams from the holes. Kuwai's entire body opens up with a tremendous bellowing sound.

As the narrator describes the saliva pouring out, his hand traces a falling motion to the ground. Narrators say that the saliva became a vine that one can see on the uacu tree today (Tsamiale-wape, in Baniwa; Cupi, in lingua geral; hence the alternate name for Hipana is Cupikwam, place of the Cupi vine); this vine flowers at the time of the Pleiades.

José velho told this part as follows:

> Kuwai revives, descends the uacu, and asks the children, "Who ate?"
> "We didn't, we didn't . . ." They quickly take manioc bread and rub it over their mouths to remove the smell.
> Kuwai sniffs the mouths of each and knows who has eaten. The little one who didn't eat, he sends away.
> Then he calls rain •• A Great Rain, Huge Waters!!
> TZZZEEESSSSHHH!!! It fell, the rainwater.
> "Paah, I want our house. Let's go find it," he says like so.

Then he lay his mouth down on the ground, HUGE!! A HUGE rock cave appeared in front of them.

It was Kuwai's mouth, Kuwai's belly.

"Hey, I stay in here! Come in here!" Well, they stay out of the rain! "Come, come!!" [Kuwai calls to them]

Then they enter. Three of them enter Kuwai's mouth.

The youngest brother comes and sees one of Kuwai's eyes blink.

DZUUUUU!!! [Surprise, fright.] "They should know it is Inyaime."

He says, "Only one eye he has. COME OUT!!!!" he says.

"COME OUT of it before he closes his mouth!!" PT' TUKK!!

[Kuwai's mouth closes,] done ... PAUGH!! Kuwai eats them." [my translation]

The three "thoughtless" children were devoured when they entered the mouth of the Great Spirit Monster of the Dead Inyaime, a stone cavern that was the mouth of the "Other Kuwai," a trap. The one child who stayed outside the mouth of Kuwai screamed to them in warning, but what had to be was done. Nhiãperikuli knows immediately what has happened, for blood falls from his hand. He rushes back to the house and hears the sound of Kuwai flying away, with the jaguar song "Heeeee Heeeee." He has eaten three of them; only the littlest one is safe.

INTERPRETING THE EPISODE

It begins with the initiates, referred to as *kanheka-nai*, "children acquiring knowledge," around 6 to 10 years old, an age when they are considered ready for initiation. There are four boys, Malinali ienipe (the Malinali children). The names of the three older brothers refer to the body paint colors and adornments of each: *kerawidzuna*, painted red with *caraiuru* (*Bixa orellana*); black, painted with carbon; and white (*mali-*, the white heron), tufts of heron feathers are stuck on the bodies of the initiates. The colors evoke their ritual meanings of happiness, new blood (red), death (black), and the spirit world (white) — in all, the liminal condition of initiates. The three named children are older than the fourth, unnamed, no identity, "littlest one" (a figure with whom real initiates would identify). He is the one who witnesses, learns, and communicates all that will happen to his elder brothers. Their relationship to Nhiãperikuli is as "younger brother's children" or some say "grandchildren" or "his children." The point is that they are of the generation of children about to be initiated.

The entire story contains all of the principal age and sex groups, all of the kinds of religious specialist functions in Baniwa society. We suggest that Kuwai is at one and the same time the heart-soul of his father (i.e., patrilineality) and the principal forms of alterity, whose powers are eventually to be incorporated into Baniwa society as the means for its own reproduction. The entire plot of the episode revolves around the transformation of the externalized heart-soul of the father into an internalized power that is the source for the reproduction and transmission of culture over time.

Kuwai first appears to them as a white man. The alterity he manifests makes him unrecognizable — fully clothed, covered with hair, a watch on his wrist, shoes on his feet — everything that characterizes a white man's external appearance (a local image of the same, shaped by historical experience: like a Brazilian or Colombian rancher, or miner, or rubber boss). All of these apparent disguises highlight Kuwai's capacity to deceive, precisely in order to show the initiates how to distinguish between the "false" and the "real" worlds. It is not by appearance but by his powerful transformative speech (*likaako*), including musical speech of the flutes and trumpets, that the children would recognize the real Kuwai.

Rites of passage are times when those undergoing change are dangerously vulnerable ("open") to sickness-giving spirits and require protected seclusion. Initiates are referred to as *itakeri*, secluded/closed off. Kuwai says at the beginning of the rite of initiation "so dangerous (kanupa) am I, you must stay secluded for three dry seasons." *Kanupa* refers to the condition of liminality, when categories are dangerously mixed, which requires restrictions, fasting, and seclusion of the initiates. The categories that are mixed in Kuwai are the "open holes of his body" (producing musical speech, but also harmful sickness), the covering of fur/hair (tree-living sloth/monkey; poison), the condition of wetness (saliva, heavy rains), for which reason it is three dry seasons of seclusion that the initiates have to bear (note here, the symmetry of the 2 + 1 sequence repeated throughout this episode, which Hill, following Turner, suggests has to do with generational time: 2 + 1 means grandfather, father, plus initiate; Hill 1993). Also, the categories of open (in the sense of vulnerable) and closed (protected) bodies, invulnerable to attacks by the spirits, are important themes in shamanism as well.

When a person gets severely sick, he undergoes restriction and/or seclusion, along with the shaman's treatment and specific diet. Individuals who have gastrointestinal ailments or who are fasting cannot tolerate the smell of food cooked in fat or oil. Just the strong smell of the food will nauseate the person. In the case of a person who is already sick, the smell exacerbates the sickness, even bringing on death (cf. the story of Mawerikuli, the first person to die).

Initially the boys play their imaginative instruments trying to produce Kuwai song. The earth pot (*akhe* in Baniwa; *camoti* in lingua geral) is generally used as a container for water or beer for a dance festival. One source compared it to "Kuwai's belly" due to its shape, referring to Kuwai's "pot-bellied" feature when he sits atop a uacu fruit tree like a "big-bellied" monkey throwing down nuts for the children to gather.

Some narrators mentioned that this episode begins as Kuwai's urine falls from the sky into the pot, and bumblebees fly around the stream. Large red bumblebees and wasps are flying around, and the children catch them. They tie the bees and wasps together and let them buzz and drone in and out of the pots. Their noise resembles the sound of the transformative "Jaguar Bone" trumpet, which is Kuwai's thorax. The pots make the deep-throated sound "Heee Heee," as the children stomp-dance around the plaza. Most narrators said that "they play-acted Kuwai." The instruments they made are nonsense, not the real voice of Kuwai. It indicates they are ready to be initiated.

Kuwai sings the first four songs identifying his true self: Maa-liawa (White Heron, male), Waliadoa (Young Sister), Halu (White Monkey), and Dzauinapi (Jaguar Bone), each with a distinctive melody of rising and falling notes. The first two are parts of Kuwai's body (two fingers/flutes on one hand, then three fingers/flutes on the other), male and female initiates. In the song of Young Sister, the word *yamatawa* refers to the thumb plus two other fingers.

White Monkey cries a song that alternates, starting with a high note, then descending the scale, and then returning to the high note. Any being with whiteness attached to its body or name is of the spirit world. White Monkey—a tree-living animal of the same "tribe" as the sloth and the big-bellied monkey—is thus associated with Kuwai's identity as a tree-living animal spirit.

The sound of the Jaguar Bone, by contrast, is the deep, resounding roar of a large jaguar. It is called *makaiteri*, the "one who does not speak" (an allusion to its roaring sound) and *mepukutetsa*, which means "the one that does not dance in circles, that stays in one place." It is Kuwai's thorax and the longest of the flutes which stays in one place when it is played. The Jaguar Bone song ("Hee Hee HEE") is, like the song of the jaguar shamans, the transformative sound in the sense of "opening up," growing. In another story, Nhiãperikuli took the Jaguar Bone trumpet and blew it, and each time, according to the narrator, the "world opened up like a balloon to the size it is today."

The Jaguar Bone trumpet emits the "powerful sound that opened up the first world" (Hill 1993). It is considered the most sacred of all parts of Kuwai's body ("el grande tigre Dzawinaapa," according to Luiz Gomez's drawing of Kuwai in appendix 2), I believe, precisely because it is the operative principle of "opening up" the world, the expansiveness of the Kuwai world that is capable of universally incorporating every living being, new and old, into its body.

Kuwai gives the children the Japurá (*Voquisaceas Erisma Japura sp.*) a forest fruit to sniff, to stave off hunger during the fast (the children's "non-food"). Japurá fruit is frequently used in real life to temper fish, and it has a rather pungent smell like slightly rotten cheese. All foods that Kuwai offers are fruits, notable for their aromas/scents/stench, several of which recall the strong scents of sexuality. Kuwai is of the forest, and his fruits are eaten mixed with water and typically not cooked. Again this is a feature of the diet of those undergoing restrictions.

In an emphatic afterthought, the narrator declares that Kuwai's songs are sung together with whipping, as a part of "knowing" Kuwai. The Tarira flute to which the narrator refers is the name of a large freshwater fish. When the narrator says that whips and songs are "Kuwai's fruits," one way of understanding this is the linguistic similarity between the word for "to whip" (*liiyaka*), the word for fruit-shell (*liiya*), the word for tree bark (*haiko-iiya*), and the word for a person's skin (*liiya*). They are homonymous. Kuwai's whipping-with-song is thus like striking shells of ripe fruits, which is like striking the skin of a person. As we've seen in discussing the concept of -*ikai*, word similarities such as these are important to understanding metaphysical principles, in this case the embodied marks left by Kuwai's whips.

Why do the Baniwa elders whip the skin of their children undergoing initiation? "In order to make them grow more quickly," the Baniwa say. Growth and fertility, bear in mind, are two key themes of the entire story. In the ritual of Kwaipan performed today, immediately after the elder whips the initiates or any other young participant in the ritual, he makes the one whom he has just whipped stand facing him, and he lifts the initiate up by the elbows while stepping on the child's feet: a kind of stretching action to make them grow quickly (*natawiya kedzako*).

Summarizing to this point, Kuwai has revealed his music and imposed a three dry season restriction on pepper, that is, since social life is defined by pepper-pot meals, they must withdraw from social life. Then their bodies are "open" to the music of Kuwai. The children are prohibited from eating animals or fish, both of which are normally consumed with pepper-pot. They begin to understand about the potent mixture in Kuwai's body of metaphysical principles such as true/false, identity/alterity, transformation, growth, and gender differentiation. All of these are encoded in the appearance of the first four flutes.

The second appearance of Kuwai is quick: after a formal greeting among them, the same four songs are heard, and one hour later Kuwai leaves. It is basically a confirmation that the boys' identities have already begun to change. Ritual dialogues such as these are indicators of the formal interrelation between the spirit world and those undergoing ritual transformation.

The third appearance of Kuwai is preceded by much anticipation. Nhiãperikuli realizes what is happening and thus introduces ritual order. He intercedes as ritual guardian of the children; he will prepare, explain, and intervene to prevent the danger of unmediated contact with the Other World. He lures the women down to the port, separating them from their children, who nevertheless forget the instructions to take Kuwai to the center of the house when he finally comes.

The entire sequence of Kuwai's appearances follows a gradual withdrawal of the children from the social order and a gradually increasing dosage of "opening their sight to Kuwai" (i.e., the ancestral spirit world) coinciding with the installation of the ritual order of the Kwaipan ceremony. Just as the shaman's apprenticeship is marked by solitude, abstention, and fasting, as his vision is altered by the "blood of Kuwai" he snuffs, so anyone undergoing initiation also fasts, stays in seclusion, and eats only the "flesh of Kuwai," i.e., his "tree fruits," which have ripened at the time of the ceremony.

In the rituals today, the initiates are made to see the "Before World" (*oopi*) in the form of the sacred flutes, the "bodies" of the first phratric ancestors, by their elder "grandfather." The elder stays with the children at the house door and calls out to the sacred instruments to come up from the port and "see their grandchildren." On the third call, the parade of flutes and trumpets marches up to the plaza. After circling the plaza three times, the players stop and put the instruments on the ground, and the elder removes the blindfolds over each child's eyes and says: "This is Kuwai. It is not WE who made this. It was made LONG AGO. *Dakidali tsa noada* (it is of his body). . . . Do Not Speak of It to Anyone! Do Not Speak of It to Women! Or You Will Die by Poison." And then the elder whips each initiate three times.

In the story, Nhiãperikuli waits until Kuwai arrives, instructing the children to take him right to the house center, his sacred ritual place. There at the house center, true identities are established, and the regime under which they will live over the next two dry seasons is fixed. Kuwai defines all forest fruits as "his food," their diet for the period. Then he lets all of the holes of his body "open up," and all of his body sings out in a powerful roar. The sounds reveal a full power, after which he says, "You will be well with me." Thus the ritual seclusion is scheduled to begin.

Kuwai, now the "owner of the ritual," instructs Nhiãperikuli to send the mothers to gather manioc and to make beer in preparation for when Kuwai will return to whip them. All of the following part of this episode refers to this first stage of the ritual, corresponding to the festival called Kapetheapan (House of Whips), beginning the "seclusion" phase of the rite of passage.

Kuwai's coming is preceded by the sky becoming totally dark with rainclouds (indicating the seasonal time immediately before the heavy rains begin). Then, as one narrator put it, "It became like night, very dark. Nhiãperikuli put a shield over the door, for Kuwai made a great inferno in the sky. It was dark, almost like night, when Kuwai descended."

The extraordinary combination of darkening sky and celestial fire [reminiscent of the coming of Dzuliferi, a great ball of fire, actually the light of a tobacco cigar] marks the beginning of "liminality." What follows belongs to "a different time" when Kuwai dances with the initiates. It is sacred time, and there is a sense of trembling in the voices of the children ("How is it going to be?") for a mysterious being had come among them.

The mysterious being is ancestral power combined with the explosive force of unbridled natural powers. The "wild powers" of nature can be seen in other ways in Baniwa chants. For example, when traveling by canoe in isolated streams, a hunter boils water in a pot and the steam spills over into the fire, making a hissing noise that causes the spirits of the forest, air, waters, the world in general to become "wild," blowing their flutes and trumpets with such force that poison darts begin flying. The chant called *tchiakali* has to be spoken to calm the "wild" spirits down.

Nhiãperikuli's relations with Kuwai are noticeably marked by negativity at this point, as though they both have the same magnetic charge and hence repel each other. Until now Nhiã-perikuli has intermediated the relationship between Kuwai, the initiates, and the women. Nhiãperikuli and Kuwai are connected as father and child; they are part of the same universal being. The father is "knowledge, wisdom," and his child is his "heart-soul, emotion"—life force. There is always tension between them, a constant inner struggle between the light of wisdom and the darkness of the heart-soul. As in the beginning, the light of day was forced away by the darkness of night.

Up to this point in this episode, whenever Kuwai appears to the children, Nhiãperikuli is not around. At those moments, the sun—Nhiãperikuli's body—is always at the noonday zenith, that is, it is as though Nhiãperikuli is "watching" when Kuwai meets the children. Three spatial connections are made: the center of the sky/Other World is vertically connected to the center of the universe at Hipana and to the center of the ritual house at Ehní-pan. At those moments the heart-soul–life force of the father is gradually entering the initiates' heart-souls, since they are now open and vulnerable to Kuwai's power. Kuwai is internalized to society when he enters and takes his place in the center of the house. This process, however, is carefully monitored and controlled by the wisdom of the father.

There are many possible interpretations of the dramatic moment at Hipana, when the children were devoured. This critical moment is, I think, best understood as a dramatization of the dangerous and powerful mystery of ancestral fertility in This World. It is this fertility which can kill those who do not follow the rules.

Kuwai sits on the giant uacu treetop with his "bone" (*liyaapi*, cognate with whip, *liiya*), striking the raw uacu nuts, breaking open their shells, and throwing them down to the children. When the children, overcome by hunger, roast and eat the uacu nuts, narrators say that "they eat Kuwai's body," "the flesh of Kuwai," inupa Kuwai. Kuwai knows that they have eaten his body when the smoke of the roasted nuts rises up to him and he smells his burning flesh. Later in the story we learn that only one thing on earth can "kill" Kuwai (i.e., prevent him from remaining in This World), and that is fire.

Kuwai then sings out, "Why have you eaten my roasted flesh?" using the words *kethine kerapokoli* (pacu, a red-and-black freshwater fish).

The kerapokoli is highly reminiscent of the initiates' in-between condition. The red-and-black striped pacu fish make their voyage upstream to their spawning grounds at the time of the ripening of the uacu nuts and the beginning of the heavy rains, when the constellation Walipere-inuma (Pleiades' mouth) is seen on the horizon. Just as this entire story is about sacred moments of transition, it connects human growth to cosmological change in the concrete imagery of the spiritualized animal person that embodies transformation. His song, directed at the children, equates his own "dangerous mixture" (*nunupa*) with the roasted uacu nuts (oily flesh) and roasted pacu fish (which also have oily flesh). Pacu swim upstream at this time of year and presumably eat the uacu nuts as they fall into the river.

Kuwai "dies" from the smoke that rises to the top of the uacu tree, and he becomes totally altered, the "Other Kuwai." His orifices open up entirely, a compelling image of total incontinence and an unleashing of the total life force of the Other World. The smell of roasting uacu nuts is likened by men to the smell of women's sexuality, which provokes the outpouring of Kuwai's saliva (*liahnuma*) from all his orifices, a creative fluid in itself in Baniwa thought (as opposed to being a metaphor for semen, the word for which is *ikai*). It is a joke among the men: "Have you ever smelled roasting uacu?" We see here also a clue for understanding why shamans say women's sexuality, specifically menstrual blood, can "provoke a sickness in the blood of the shaman," and why sexual reproduction is at the core of Kuwai's transformation into a monstrous being. What most threatens initiates at this age is "partaking of the forbidden fruit." Like apprentices, they are secluded and prohibited from having sexual relations.

Kuwai then transforms into Inyaime, spirit of the dead, the "Other Kuwai," making a huge flood of rain come, transforming again, now into an enormous stone cave/mouth, and he summons the initiates into his mouth to escape the rain. The narrator, Keramunhe, said the following:

> Then it is, the smoke rises, Kuwai smells ...
> Then he sings the great song:
> "TSEEYtsemtseytsemtseytsemtseytsemtseytsemtseytsemtseytsem-tseytsem ..."
> Oh, why do you eat my dangerous flesh, the roasted pacu fish Malinaliene, you eat my dangerous flesh, the roasted pacu." He turns around and lies down ...
> THE GREAT SONG COMES OUT: "HIIHIHIHIHIHIHIIHIHIHIHIHI..
> TSULULULULULULULU ..."
> [Kuwai's saliva falls] ALL OF HIS BODY LIKE SO!!!!

The Great Rains in the Baniwa astronomical calendar occur during the months of April and May, coinciding with three constellations that all refer to the period of initiation: "the beginning of the Pleiades," the "fish trap," and the "Pleiades initiate/new adult" (*Walipere-inuma, Opitcina, Walipere-ieni*). The appearance of the three constellations coincides evidently with the transitions the boys must undergo, the beginning of a new phase in life that requires their restrictions (inside the trap). In other words, they "die" to their prior childhood lives upon entering the mouth of Kuwai. The popular lingua geral name for Kuwai is Yurupary, which etymologically means "fish trap mouth" (*iuru-*, mouth; *pari*, fish trap).

The rainy season is the time of trapping fish in large traps called *cacuri*, set up on the river banks. The fish are said to "make their dance festivals" and drink "until they are drunk." The fish trap is also explicitly compared to the image of a menstruating woman (her "openness") attracting fish into her womb (*Pitsiro*, Baniwa e-bulletin, 2008).[2] Three of the initiates blindly walk into the mouth of Kuwai to escape the floods.

Initiates undergoing restriction who disobey the order to abstain from roasted food or who see Kuwai without being under the tutelage of the elder grandfather get a "wasting-away sickness" called *purakali*,[3] in which they vomit and defecate, their skin becomes yellow, they begin to eat dirt, and they salivate uncontrollably. Indeed, at Hipana today, there is a place of rubble at the port that is said to be the purakali, which destroyed the initiates who did not obey ritual restrictions. Wasting away is a sign of total incontinence, the opposite of what the boys should be. The outpouring of Kuwai's saliva marks the loss of his creative fluids. Kuwai loses all the power that has been stored up during the dry seasons that have passed.

It is plausible to interpret the drama as the Fertilization of the Earth by Kuwai's saliva and the rains, although the elements come in exaggerated doses. This heightens the drama of the moment. The overwhelmingly transformational symbolism is apparent in the animal shadow-soul sides of Wamundana, as a tree-living, fruit-eating monkey, and as the sloth that sings before it descends the tree in the early rains. The exaggerated outpouring of life-giving fluids of the "Animal" suddenly transforms him into Inyaime, the one-eyed demonic spirit of the dead, devourer of souls, the sorcerer.

The surviving initiate is shown a powerful moral lesson through the monstrous scene he witnesses. The physical remains of his brothers are taken away to be vomited out into three bread baskets set out on the plaza of the ritual house at Ehnípan, bloody masses without any heart-soul, like the pulp of freshly scraped manioc tubers about to be squeezed to make bread. Kuwai, it is said, had made "holes in the children's chests" (opening them and eating their heart-souls in evident exchange for the three boys eating his flesh). Their heart-souls have been consumed; their bodies have been reduced to bloody masses inside the large sieves used in making manioc bread, which are the types of artwork real initiates make during the seclusion phase today.

Some narrators say that after Kuwai ate them, Nhiãperikuli turned over the palm of his open right hand and let drops of blood fall. "Oooh, already Kuwai ate them," he says sorrowfully. Or, in some versions, Nhiãperikuli sees rain falling and knows what has happened. Both the rain and the falling blood are images in Baniwa myths of death, loss of kin, and sorrow at the loss. Rain is also said to be Kuwai's "tears." Keramunhe makes the dramatic impact of the loss more forceful by the two drawn-out "HEEEEE HEEEEE" songs of the celestial jaguar Kuwai as he flies away. A major transformation has taken place.

Yet there is immediate comic relief, as Nhiãperikuli says, "Aaaahh" [as if to say, "Now it's been done," to which the narrator's son, the listener, chuckles]. The little one tells Nhiãperikuli that Kuwai has eaten his brothers. In Keroaminali's version, this is a very sorrowful speech: "Already Kuwai ate my kin. I told them to keep the restrictions well. I told them, but he ate them."

Why was Nhiãperikuli not present with Kuwai in the forest at Hipana? Implicitly he was there because the sun was high at noon, which is his bodily presence. Everything in the story had to happen the way it did because that is how the remaining initiate was taught to distinguish the "real Kuwai" from the "Other Kuwai," Inyaime, coinciding with the change of the seasons, sickness and death, incontinence and restrictions, all at once.

While the timing of the initiation rites coincides with the rainy season, the timing of shamans' apprenticeship coincides with the dry season. For the shamans, the dry seasons are the times when the cicadas drone, the shamans' bodies transform, the cicadas shed their skins, and the shamans transmit their knowledge to their apprentices.

By transforming in early summer, the pajés are free then to mediate the powers of ancestrality in the rainy season, for there is an intimate connection between the ancestors and the aquatic world, specifically Kuwai, whose tears (*liidza*) are said to be the rains (*iidza*). While the dry season renews the pajés' being in the Other World, transformations, and identification of the pajés with the light of the sun, the rainy season requires the specialized malikai of the kalidzamai priestly chanters in order to "dry the wetness" (a predominant phrase in the kalidzamai chants) from the initiates' bodies and complete the process of their transition from the aquatic world of the ancestors to the post-seclusion world in the sun.

KUWAI CONCLUDES THE RITUALS AND RETURNS TO THE SKY

Nhiãperikuli wishes to end the fast and to lure Kuwai back down to the ritual house. Nhiãperikuli makes wooden statues of the regurgitated children, fully adorned, and sets them up on a log. The statues will trick Kuwai into thinking that the children have been revived, and thus he will return to end the festival. Nhiãperikuli makes headdresses of red and blue macaw feathers and other ornaments, such as knee bands and necklaces of silvery triangles, all in preparation for the coming-out festival that will end the initiation.

Nhiãperikuli sends a little wasp called Kalimatu up to Kuwai bearing a gift of white maggots, which Nhiãperikuli has scraped from the devoured flesh of the children. The white maggots are food for the spirit of the dead, Inyaime. The gift is intended to lure Kuwai down to finish the initiation, for "the children have suffered enough."

INTERPRETATION

Kalimatu is a "small fly or bee" that lives in the roofs of houses. Kalimatu also makes its home in the yellowish earth near Hohodene graves (referring to the old practice of burying the dead underneath the floors of the longhouses). The maggots that Nhiãperikuli sends along with Kalimatu appear in flesh that has rotted, as little whitish specks that consume flesh. Thus we have the predominant theme of the "rotten underworld" in the food gift for Kuwai that—once accepted—will oblige Kuwai to return and finish the festival. In other words, Kuwai has devoured the heart-souls of the three boys; he now eats the maggots of their rotten flesh. He is obliged to return to complete the process by reinstituting sociality in the community. This means, however, that once his functions are completed, he will be sacrificed as he has sacrificed the children.

The little fly, with its tiny belly, is an image of the one initiate who remained, who has passed through hunger and is now ready to complete his initiation. He passes through great difficulties to deliver the message to Kuwai/Inyaime, but it is crucial that he does, to show that he has become a fully cultural being who, by formal ritual dialogue, can persuade the dangerous Other to accept his gift and to return in exchange.

Kuwai gobbles up the maggots, throws the wasp back down, and slams the door to his house. Nhiãperikuli pretends that nothing is wrong and later sends another wasp with the same maggots. It succeeds in squeezing through the door of Kuwai's house and persuades Kuwai to return and end the fast. Kuwai ravenously gobbles up the maggots, declaring that they are his own heart-soul, his liver bile, *lidanhe*, as if from a recently killed animal. (Soon after a game animal is killed, the bile from a gland on its back spoils the meat.) Kuwai thus affirms, in this necrophagous act, that his poisonous liver bile is the source of the maggots from the rotten flesh. This statement refers to a type of sickness that results from eating rotten food.

The formal request for him to return and revive the children comes with the certainty that he will die. Despite knowing this could occur, he promises to return and complete the initiation, having transformed from demonic animal to priestly chanter and dancer.

Kuwai returns to bless the initiates' food at the appointed time, at the end of a day, throughout the entire night, following which the new generation of adults will emerge from seclusion, and the process will be complete. The initiates will have "known Kuwai," the music of which has penetrated their heart-souls to remain, and they will continue to pass down this knowledge and power of the ancestors.

Several narrators said that Nhiãperikuli performed a kind of sorcery (hiuiathi) before Kuwai arrived, which was intended to make Kuwai age quickly, go blind from tobacco smoke, and become drunk at the final festival. A major transformation is about to occur, remembering the last time smoke "blinded Kuwai" and "killed" him, but Kuwai agrees to complete his part. He knows that it has to be this way, according to the exchange that has been established and that governs the relation between himself and Nhiãperikuli.

Preparations are made for the coming-out festival. Kuwai arrives and announces he will chant over the pepper, which will be served to the initiates at dawn. Kuwai teaches Nhiãperikuli and his brothers the priestly chants over pepper in an all-night ceremony with dancing and singing.

When the kalidzamai is done, Nhiãperikuli prepares a huge bonfire, all the while blowing tobacco smoke on Kuwai's eyes to make him become temporarily blind, and then leads him, drunk and old, around the fire. Kuwai has known all along that his father will kill him, that it is time for him to die. As though in defiance of his father's banishing him from the earth, Kuwai declares that "nothing can kill me," that "only the flames of fire" can do away with him. Other narrators have Kuwai listing all other weapons (clubs, shotguns, machetes) in this world that kill: "people kill with clubs, they cut with machetes, they kill with poison arrows," all of which are "his body," so none of these could kill Kuwai. Another included accidental deaths as well—"they fall in the river, they climb trees and fall"—but Kuwai cannot be killed by any of these material weapons and accidental or violent deaths. None of these are the way Kuwai will die.

As Kuwai continues to sing and dance, Nhiãperikuli leads him around a huge fire and suddenly pushes him in, throwing the heaviest logs on top. (The huge fire is likened to an inferno that burned the world.) As Kuwai burns, his body oozes out sickness and venom, his "vengeance," into the ashes of the fire. Then his jaguar spirit again ascends to live in the sky singing the jaguar song *"Heeeee Heeeee."* The moment when they lead Kuwai to the fire is one of the four most dramatic of the whole story, as Keramunhe narrates:

They circle around like so.... They circle around that firewood he brings together.
They heap up the firewood ...
Suddenly Nhiãperikuli pushes Kuwai into the fire: PA!!!
HHHIISSSSHHHHEEEEE-in-the-middle-of-the-fire-of-theirs.
HIIIIIIISHI!!!!
PA! All around it burns! He gets trees ...
Those brazilwood: HIIISHI!

Blackwood: HIIIISHI!!
This, then, Uacaricoara: HIIIISHI!!
TTZZ''T'T'T'T'T'T'T'T ...
He left poison, Pat't't
Kuwai
His fur, Pat't't't, "My vengeance it will be," he says.
Oooooh ... Dead: Baaaaaaaa ...
So it was ... [Narrator's son chuckles.]
"HEEEEEEE HEEEEE." (This one does not die.)
That was the way!! (That's the way!!)
His father's soul!! (yes)
That's truly all!! (The last!!) The last!! (Until today!!) Until today!!
We did not see those people.

As Nhiãperikuli pushes him into the fire, Kuwai tells him to
return later to the burning place at Hipana. Nhiãperikuli knows
that, in return for his killing, Kuwai will leave behind the materials to make the Kuwai flutes and trumpets for all future initiation
rites. When Nhiãperikuli returns, a paxiúba tree shoots up from
the ground with the crack of a rifle shot, connecting earth with
the Other World. Along with the paxiúba palm comes the plant
materials with which the sacred flutes and trumpets are made:
the bark of the tree *Purpurea Iebaru sp.*, used as a covering around
the "bodies" of the flutes, and then a thick ribbing vine that ties
it together. The bark and the vine are considered the paxiúba's
companions because they "always go together."

The challenge then is to break the great paxiúba tree so that
it doesn't fall and kill Nhiãperikuli, that is to say, the process of
reproducing Kuwai in material form is not yet finished, and there
is great risk that Kuwai's spirit will seek an exchange for his death.
The tree is marked by a squirrel (*takairo*; some say a grasshopper)
from bottom to top to coincide with the sizes of the multiple flutes.

Then the woodpecker flies full speed into the middle of the tree, breaking it and causing the marked pieces to split apart and tumble to the ground in a heap, much like the heap of bones that fell to the ground from the body of the first person to die, Mawerikuli. Unlike this "unfortunate one," however, the pieces could remain separate and be joined together again at future festivals, like the original being of Kuwai, in order to initiate new generations of adults.

There are more than twenty pairs of these flutes (only the Waliadoa has three in a set)—one shaman stated that there are thirty-two pairs used in initiation rites today. "Jaguar Bone" is the most sacred, for it is Kuwai's thorax where his heart-soul is.

THE RITE OF KALIDZAMAI

This is the most important blessing, or priestly chanting, with tobacco over manioc bread and pepper. The chants are about the world-opening process when the women blew the sacred instruments throughout the known world, "re-memorizing" (remembering) this foundational event. The chants provide a protective shield for initiates that they will have throughout their lives.

They are a highly complex form of shamanic knowledge and power, the purpose of which is to end the restrictions on food by making cooked animals and fish safe for those undergoing transition (Hill 1993; Wright 1993). Kalidzamai is also done at the conclusion of each stage of the shaman's apprenticeship after the apprentices have caught their shamanic specialties in the form of fish, which will be blessed by the kalidzamai, sanctifying the apprentices' competence as pajé.

In initiation for boys today, three seated elders chant and bless the food with tobacco all night and until noon of the following day. They are the three elders of the story: Nhiãperikuli and his two brothers, Dzuliferi and Eeri, who learned from Kuwai the kalidzamai chants, the knowledge and power to reproduce the world. Following a set of chants, the elders drink cane beer, dance with whips, and sing initiation songs.

The flames of the great fire where Kuwai burned are a powerful symbol of all that it means to live in society. This moment corresponds in the ritual to the moment when sacred pepper is given to real initiates after the chanters have finished their work. A piece of manioc bread—in itself, the body of the deity Kaali, who ordered his son to push him into a great fire—is dipped into the sacred ceramic bowl made by the hands of the first woman, Amaru. This is the moment when the elder explains to the new adult(s) all of the laws of society. The correspondence to the myth is not fortuitous, as we've seen by utilizing the material from myth and ritual together, which is how the Hohodene understand and explain their performance in the initiation rites.

The content of the laws for the Hohodene are pretty much the same as for the Wakuenai and Kuripako: Never reveal what the instruments look like, because that will lead to death; live and work in harmony; treat your family well (meaning the community or several of the same sib) and give them food when they come to visit. When strangers visit, treat them well and give them food. Never fool with manhene; it's bad, and it kills. Obey the elders in whatever they ask of you.

When the elder is done, he takes the "whips of the sun," which he has been "cooking" with the chants and the smoke of the tobacco all night long. Pepper burns like fire, the Hohodene say, and kills all living substances from the food that people eat in normal circumstances. The Baniwa have a saying that "burning sloth hair is a good remedy for pepper," which cryptically states everything that happened in the Great Fire that burned Wamundana, the black sloth shadow-soul, whose pelt is full of sicknesses.

To burn the material form of sickness "cures" and gives strength to pepper, the food of sociality. It makes the "fire" (of pepper) have greater efficacy against harmful spirits or sorcerers. Fire and "commensality" are connected in the form of food that has been blessed and is devoid of danger. Specifically, the danger exists of eating "live" food that has not been cooked well or that is "rotten," which brings on the sickness called *ifiukali*, in which the victim's body becomes emaciated, as though it were being eaten from the inside by the still-living flesh or the rot of the food.

Further along these lines it is plausible to interpret Kuwai's speech from the fire in the following way: animals and humans are hunted and killed with weapons, but none of those weapons can kill Kuwai. He is immortal; all other humans and animals who come later in time will die violently. The only thing that can kill Kuwai is fire. If the fire refers to the sociality marked by the consumption of pepper, then the heavy wood that is thrown on top of the great fire refers to the most durable logs that people use to make their houses, again a material form of their living sociality. Eating pepper, manioc bread, or cooked food in a communal meal inside a house are the ingredients of living well in society, protected from the dangers all other living forms, visible and invisible, could present.

The powerful life force that Kuwai transmitted to society has been internalized; the dangerous power that Kuwai represented could be sent away. The seriousness of the whole process of turning children into adults, apprentices into shamans, is one that involves the entire cosmos, all of the powers of the shamans and chanters, and all of the primordial world as well. Little wonder that very serious prohibitions are enforced against "seeing Kuwai" without intermediation.

The whole event of preparing the fire to kill Kuwai can be seen as the context in which Transmission of Knowledge and Culture is realized. It was not an event of eradicating a being but rather of transforming it from its dangerous and unmanageable univocality into a manageable multiplicity over which the knowledge and power of the shamans can work and against which the new adults are protected. From inside the fire Kuwai, shamans explain, summoned all people and taught them everything he knew about sickness, everything related to sorcery. After he had completed his task, then Kuwai announced that his time on earth had ended, declaring that he would leave This World before them all, and that everyone else would follow him afterwards, that is, all others would die from poison.

Kuwai's entire being then dissipates in the flames, breaks up into sickness-giving spirits, poisonous plants, all forms of sickness splatter about from his heart-soul. Sickness and poison can destroy sociality from within. Kuwai leaves his vengeance (*ipwaminawa*) as poisonous plants in the fire and venom that is his fur.

The fur covers all parts of Kuwai's body, as on the body of a black sloth, *wamu*. When Kuwai's fur left his body in the burning, it entered the fur of the wamu, then a little white sloth (*tchitamali*), and the night monkey (*ipeku*), all Kuwai's shadow-souls or animal avatars today. The appearance of the night monkey on the border of the village at dusk is an omen of impending death.

Kuwai's liver (*lixupana*), however, transformed into a liver-shaped leaf plant, called *hueero*, that is poisonous. Venom takes many forms in the world today.

Kuwai's fur, viscera, and heart-soul — full of sickness and pain — were externalized into the most potent forms of sickness — spirit darts, *yoopinai, hiuiathi, iraidalimi* — that the shamans must know how to cure. Mandu specialized in curing several of these sicknesses. From the ashes where Kuwai burned, there emerged spiders, lizards, biting insects, and all types of yoopinai, spirits of the earth, water, air — in short, all of the world was populated in a chaotic way by these sickness-giving spirits. The yoopinai are still a major force to contend with.

Then Kuwai ascended in a huge cloud of smoke, singing the jaguar song of transformation. Society and the world had transformed. As a spirit Kuwai lives eternally in the sky, "where one does not die," and only a few pajés actually see Kuwai, the owner of sickness. This perhaps is the most important moment of separation between the primordial past; eternal spirits of the world; and the world of the future generations, *walimanai*. Kuwai's body remains as the connection between the eternal spirit world and This World. Kuwai is brought back to life in This World at each initiation rite.

The narrator again injected an expression of comic relief at this point, which translates into something like "Oooh, what a shame, he's dead," and the narrator's son laughed and said, "That one doesn't die." As in the previous episode, this is a revealing reaction which differs from the reaction to the first death in the world, of Mawerikuli, which is more one of disgust at an inexplicable mistake that only brought people sadness.[4]

Kuwai's entire body was then reshaped into numerous domains of the natural and spirit worlds. As a result of this dramatic moment of separation, all of the principal stages of ritual transition that the human body undergoes in life were henceforth defined by what had happened with Kuwai's body. The priestly shamans and chanters became the key intermediaries in the relations between the ancestors, the sacred flutes, Kuwai, and humanity today. Kuwai's extraordinary powers of growth and change represent the nature of the world taught to initiates, and it is the duty of the priestly shamans to ensure that knowledge is passed on in the correct way, since the lives of the entire community are involved. Kuwai's body (skeleton) remains in This World, always "hidden," at the bottom of the rivers (the place of the ancestors) or streams near the villages. In the same way, sorcerers hide their poison at the bottom of the streams near the villages. The paradoxical duality of creativity and destruction materialized into concrete forms at Kuwai's "death," but no one can know or say in public where they are or what they look like. They are secrets supported by an enormous respect, fear, and awe of their power.

With its durability and its numerous aerial roots, the paxiúba was the perfect tree from which to make the sacred flutes, for it grows in wetlands but does not rot in water, and the multiple aerial roots above the water give the impression of multiple umbilical cord souls attached to a single umbilical cord, as in the "celestial umbilical cord," Kuwai's umbilical cord through which the souls of newborns descend from the "great nursery" (José Garcia's expression) in the sky. The paxiúba is a concrete image representing the idea of the elongated tube that branches out at its roots (many heart-souls connected to the one unique tube, that is, the celestial umbilical cord). Some pajés say that the original tree had leaves of gold. In the end the umbilical tubular connection from the spirit source was transformed into the material form of the sacred paxiúba tree.

At Hipana, the great tree was the second major cosmos vertical axis in the history of the Baniwa universe. The first was the Great Tree of Sustenance, Kaali ka thadapa, at Uaracapory, which was the source of human and shamanic sustenance. When this was felled, the second age of humanity began, when Nhiãperikuli made everything in This World. At the conclusion of this period of creation, the paxiúba at Hipana connected the center of the world at Hipana with the center of the sky where Kuwai lives in immortality. Thus the story of Kuwai comes around full circle to the very origin of the cosmos, when Hekwapi ienipe, the child of the universe, floated suspended in a vast expanse of nothingness, only a little ball of stone with a "hole" (from which humanity emerged) at Hipana. The hole of emergence and its invisible celestial umbilical cord had become materialized in the instruments. With Kuwai's death and transformation into the sacred flutes, the process of reproducing generations of new adults is successfully incorporated into society.

It would be most unlikely to have all the many pairs of instruments represented and playing in any one ritual. All of them correspond to different named parts of Kuwai's body—not necessarily only the long bones but his thorax, his penis, and the fingers of his hands, which evidently are related to dexterity for playing the instruments. The melody of each flute or trumpet is distinct. Their music and meaning have everything to do with growth, transformation, gender, alterity, and ancestral phratric identity. Some of the trumpets are the very first ancestors of the phratries, which were zoomorphic beings in the sense that the flutes and trumpets were mixed shapes, with the instrument as the head and body of an animal, insect, or bird.

Kuwai was never a single being but rather a unified collection of primordial shapes and forms (Kuwai-wape), each corresponding to a part of Kuwai's body. After his death and ascension to the Other World, a material form—the paxiúba tree—measured, cut, and made to play, became the original phratric ancestors who emerged from the holes at Hipana. The pieces of paxiúba were transformed into replicas of their original namesakes and had life blown into each of them by Nhiãperikuli.

While this may sound like a contradiction with the story of ancestral emergence cited in chapter 4, we must remember that each narrator makes the Before World of the primordial past according to his or her own understanding of sequentiality. There is no single version of the creation story; there are many "pieces" of the entire story of creation that must appear, but as long as the narrator weaves a coherent pattern, we cannot say that one version is more correct than another. Hohodene standards of narrating are based more on completeness and aesthetic, symmetric beauty in narrative performance, not on a rigid sequence.

8

The Struggle for Power and Knowledge among Men and Women

FINAL EPISODE

Nhiãperikuli initiated his son with the flutes and told him to bathe in the river at dawn and cleanse his penis with a suds-making vine. Before the boy arose, Kuwai's mother, Amaru, and the women secretly stole the flutes from Nhiãperikuli. As he tried to get them back, spirit darts shot from the mouths of the flutes, turning the men back. The women gained shamanic power over the flutes and used them as weapons. They escaped and took the flutes upriver to a fenced settlement on a hill called Motípana (headwaters of the Uaraná River, off the upper Aiary). There, their youngest sister had her first menstrual period, so the women began to chant over her food. Nhiãperikuli followed them and watched in anger; he was their enemy and would make war against them. He went downriver to Tunui to get poison arrows. He called his allies, the birds, to get ready for war. Nhiãperikuli and Kathiwa, the owner of the poisoned arrows, tried out the arrows. One pierced the earth, and the other shot like a lightning bolt to the "door of the sky," zigzagging back to earth to kill. Satisfied, Nhiãperikuli brought all the animals back with him to Motípana. When they arrived, they hid inside a fish trap at the port and sang in chorus like frogs, warning the women of their presence. When the women finished their chanting and began distributing food, Nhiãperikuli and the animals charged into the settlement and grabbed the flutes. There was much pushing and shoving. One woman put a flute into her vagina, but Nhiãperikuli caught and killed her. Another tried to run away with a flute; Nhiãperikuli pursued her and took it back. Then he threw four women in the directions of the four skies, one after another, and the war ended. A long time later, Nhiãperikuli completed the adorning of the flutes and trumpets, attaching hair, feathers, and pelts to each one. They were made into complete "people," living replicas of Kuwai's body, which can be played by people today. "Now people can take these . . . and play them," Nhiãperikuli said. He then looked for the Kuwai ancestors of each phratry, and after a long time, he took his place in the Other World with the spiritual governors of the universe. So ends the story of Kuwai.

INTERPRETATION

Nhiãperikuli was initiating his "son" (another "son," not Kuwai) who was approaching the end of a period of restriction and seclusion with the sacred instruments. This episode is thus about another important phase in the rites of initiation that requires more elaboration. Narrators could, however, leave out this entire episode if they wished and stop the narrative with the conflagration that "killed" Kuwai. The more complete versions, however, include this episode, which ostensibly has to do with the struggle between men and women for power over the reproduction of new generations.

Episode 2 hinges on the relations among fathers, sons, elder "grandfathers," and initiates. In this episode, the women's initiation rite is established as well as the relations of knowledge and power between men and women. Once those issues are settled, the final adornments of the real flutes and trumpets can take place. Then the instruments are transmitted to all future generations. Nhiãperikuli leaves This World (according to the Hohodene version) and ascends to the spiritual governance among the eternal masters of the Other World.

During the boys' initiation, the sudswood *padzuma* and one other *molipi* are used at the end of seclusion periods as a cleanser and purifier for those who have undergone seclusion, leaving their bodies free from sicknesses that may have entered during seclusion. In the past, boys were expected to bathe at dawn or just before dawn every morning. They arose from their hammocks to plunge into the cold river to wash. If an initiate could find a colorless, transparent stone under the water, this meant that he would find a good wife. This practice is part of the behavior expected of initiates, to learn how to withstand the cold and to be alert and wakeful, not sleepy and lazy, in order to become strong, healthy husbands and fathers.

During initiation seclusion, when boys see Kuwai, all of their bodily orifices are "opened." Initiates are expected to vomit every morning when they bathe to "clean the dirt" from their insides. Boys' sexual orifices are also opened when seeing Kuwai. Kewiken, referring to ejaculation, is compared with women's menstruation, especially first menstruation (*kanupakan*), and both occur on nights of the new moon, which is also the time when initiation seclusion is at an end. Kewiken occurs while the boys sleep and the new moon's daughter, Tamo ito, is supposed to descend to sleep with them and have sexual relations with them. This makes the boys listless, and they lie in their hammocks instead of getting up early. During a girl's first period, she receives a visit from Tamo, who leaves her with the blood of menstruation.

Nhiãperikuli's son Kuwai was at the end of seclusion and was expected to get up and bathe at dawn with padzuma. But he overslept, and with this "lack of thought," the women were able to take the sacred flutes and flee before the boy arose. The men were suddenly left without their power, which had disastrous consequences.

Walamas are sickness darts that are stuck in Kuwai's heart-soul. The paxiúba palm tree is covered with these darts. In this episode, they are poison darts that have entered the flutes and now shoot out of the flutes' mouths to turn Nhiãperikuli back as he comes to grab the instruments. Mandu showed by his gestures that the darts shooting from the flutes were like a shower of arrows; there was no way Nhiãperikuli could even get close to the women. Their sound is the noise of the walamas flying chaotically. In general, walamas are spines or thorns on palm trees in This World and the Other World. The strength of the walamas' poison varies. All produce hot, stabbing pain, often with inflammations. They produce the equivalent of arthritis or rheumatism. The kinds of paxiúba out of which the Kuwai flutes are made also have poisonous thorns that "pick, bite, and hurt" those who come in contact with them.

Walamas are part of the arsenal that pajés use to attack other shamans, to put sickness on people, or to extract sickness. They are principally shamanic remedies or weapons. Once the women have the flutes, they regain their shamanic power and use the instruments to ward off the men's attacks. Consequently, not only are gender roles reversed but the women assert their dominance in shamanic power. Narrators say that Nhiãperikuli "could do nothing as he used to" because he "became afraid and fled from the women and the loud noise that they made with the flutes." The men "became like women and could only make manioc beer." Gender role reversal, warrior pajés' defense, and the chaotic noise of the flutes were a catastrophe that befell the men as a result of Nhiãperikuli's son's laziness.

On the sociological level, we can understand this situation as corresponding to the practice of uxorilocality, when the newly married couple lives in the wife's village for a year or more, during which time the young husband does various kinds of service for his father-in-law until the first male child is born. At that point the couple moves to the husband's village. The situation of provisional uxorilocality would certainly be an appropriate moment for representing a strong separation between the men and women of the sib, when the men are deprived of power, as in this episode.

From the time Kuwai was conceived, he was a source of tension between the sexes. The women badly wanted the child as they wanted the instruments, that is to say, the women sought to create a society in which they, not the men, had the power to produce new generations.

The women fled up the Uaraná stream, a major tributary of the upper Aiary River. At the headwaters is a hill, called Motipana. I suspect that the "great city of Nhaperikuli" and the women's fortress on the hill are both part of the same site on the upper Yawiary River. This area more or less corresponds to the area the Hohodene say is "in Colombia," for near the creator's "city" is a large cavern in which, it is said, the women hid (Xavier Leal 2008).

Nhiãperikuli sought the help of his allies, the birds, and the owner of the potent poison arrows on the hill of Tunui. The poison arrows were apparently sufficient to reverse Nhiãperikuli's lack of fire power; they hit the sky door, zigzagged back down to earth, and seared their way through the ground, killing whatever was in their way. The arrows received strength from the Other World. The warriors returned to the fortress of the "enemy" women.

At the port, hidden inside a fish trap, they transformed into winter frogs. They sang in unison to make a third omen letting the women know that they had come in war. The song of the frogs, "Ukwekwe," is a play on the kin term *kwikwi*, meaning "aunt." They found the women deliriously dancing with the Kuwai "with happy hearts" (*huiwa*), "their hearts were full of joy," and "they made a lot of noise" (*kahfainade*); by contrast, Nhiãperikuli's heart burned with anger; "his enemies, he looked on them with rage," for they had taken away Kuwai. The situation had become intolerably volatile.

While the women were in possession of the sacred flutes and trumpets, their youngest sister began to menstruate. Men say of women's menstruation that "it began with Kuwai." The elder women then chanted the priestly kalidzamai for the girl inside their fortress at Mothipan. Elder women do in fact perform the kalidzamai for the initiate girls today. Mandu's wife, Flora, for example, related that the time of young girls' initiation is extremely important for teaching them, among other things, "not to depend on anyone."

Traditionally the elder women blessed fish in one beautifully painted ceramic bowl and meat in another. The girl's hair was cut, in order to "grow back totally new" and "never to become white" (the color of alterity—spirits of the dead).

The war between the men and the women resulted in the men taking back the instruments—at least for the Baniwa of the Aiary River. Nhiãperikuli, it is said, gave the remaining Amaru "shoes" and sent them to four corners of This World where they became mothers of other ethnic groups, and they "made industries" (*fábricas*). One Amaru went to "the city of Portugal" (for the Baniwa, this is equivalent to the city of Rio de Janeiro) and raised the Portuguese; another went to Bogotá, Colombia, and gave birth to the Spaniards; two others went upriver and downriver. All but one became the mothers of potential enemies or allies. The first Amaru to die was Kuwai's mother, from whose body blood flowed that became the rivers of the earth. Below we discuss in more detail the shamanic powers of the women, in alliance with the "knowledge" of the whites.

In initiation rituals done today, the remembering of these events (the men chasing the women throughout the known world) forms the principal content of the pepper chants for blessing food, the all-important priestly kalidzamai chants, which are performed as prescribed in this story (Hill 1993; Wright 1993; Gonzalez-Ñáñez 2007). The kalidzamai chants consist of both preventive shamanism done on the food to be consumed by the new adult, and the remembrance of the world's "opening up," increasing in size, when the women played the flutes in all known places.[1]

With the war over, Nhiãperikuli returns to his village at Hipana to demonstrate how to complete the "personhood" of each flute or trumpet by attaching hair, fur, or skins of various animals as adornments to the bodies of the flutes. A large trumpet covered in fur is named after the paca, a nocturnal rodent and the ancestor of a phratry. The long flutes Tariira and Uaracú are marked to resemble freshwater fish. Hair cut from girls at the time of their first menstrual rite is attached to the Waliadoa flutes, which represent the "younger sister," the only ones to dance in three and not a pair. Each flute or trumpet has a distinctive identity and agency attached to it, as Kuwai's body parts did when he was alive, as well as a name of a specific fish, bird, monkey, sloth, or the largest and most sacred of all, the transformative Jaguar Bone, Kuwai's thorax.

The sacred flutes and trumpets are made to be like "people" (newiki), the elders say today, meaning that the power to make new generations of adults was fully incorporated into society. From its externalized, exceedingly dangerous totality, the knowledge and power of Kuwai has been reproduced in multiple facsimiles of his body parts, which the men see as their domesticated pets (wapira); each phratry has its own ancestral pet. All of the sacred flutes and trumpets together would be the equivalent of society as the whole body of Kuwai and, even more universally inclusive, the whole world.

In the penultimate event of the story, Nhiãperikuli tests Amaru to see if she remembers the music of Kuwai. He has done shamanism on her heart, turning it around to erase her memory, and on her tongue, so she would not talk about the flutes. The animals get together and make Kuwai-like sounds, but she doesn't remember if those sounds were true or not. She blows on her hair and finally flees at the false sounds. These sounds of the animals are engraved on one of the boulders at Hipana.

Finally Nhiãperikuli gives the sacred flutes and trumpets to all future generations. This occurs at Hipana, where the universe began. Each flute or trumpet was at the head of each ancestor that emerged from the hole. Nhiãperikuli and the Primal Sun looked for the Kuwai ancestors of the phratries at Hipana. Each sang its own name as it circled around the mouth of the hole, until it finally jumped out into This World and was sent to its piece of land. At some point, the first man and woman, with bodies like humans today, emerged from Hipana and then were taken to a small waterfall in the forest where they were cleansed. These were the first human ancestors, who left their sacred "names" to the phratries. These names are bestowed on newborn children shortly after birth by an elder chanter of the phratry.

Nhiãperikuli then left This World and ascended to the Other World, to the sound of the *ambauba* (Cecropsia) stomping tubes, to stay with the spiritual governors of the world (Enawi-nai). The Enawi-nai in this story and other creation stories are known as "the good people," the "chiefs," the "true governors," "like the government is for the whites," narrators say. They are of the long ago past but are still the governors of the indigenous peoples' world, the chiefs today, in the sense of eternal spiritual governance, parallel to This World's secular governance, phratric chiefs who existed in the phratries' past. For the Hohodene, the sib whom they call their "chiefs" in This World were the Mule dakenai, their phratric elder brothers, but they no longer live in the region. Nevertheless, the Enawi-nai are still held to be indigenous governance, not the government of the whites.

WOMEN'S SHAMANIC KNOWLEDGE, WOMEN AS AGENTS OF HISTORY

I wish to clarify at the outset that the interpretations in this section are tentative and require further research with Baniwa elder women. There is some ambiguity as to how many times the women made the world open up to its present-day size. This is important because each time this happened, there was a distinct meaning associated with the women's actions.

While the last episode is about the "war," which suggests killing, the Baniwa verb *linua* can also be translated as "to fight with" someone, and here it is with the women because they reclaimed their son. From the men's point of view, the women created discord by "wanting their son," not relinquishing maternal connections. Nhiãperikuli was against their possession because Kuwai was, from the beginning, "his father's heart-soul." The women who took that away from the men deprived them of their heart-soul, meaning all of the knowledge and power it took to think Kuwai (the world) into being and to re-create an eternal image of its "body." The women knew that Nhiãperikuli and the men had taken away their child, and they wanted it back. Their excessive desire somehow had to be annulled or transformed. For the men could do nothing without their heart-soul. Had the men not taken them back, the men believe that today they would only know how to make caxiri beer and nothing else. That is, their ritual powers would be severely restricted.

It was shamanic power and knowledge that the women took away from the men, the essence of Nhiãperikuli's heart-soul. This life force is the basis of society-in-time; that is to say, the entire story can be understood as an explanation for how patrilineal heart-soul, or life force, came to be embodied in material forms and reproduced over time. As long as there have been "people" in This World, the belief in the Kuwai ancestors has been the foundation for their organization into society.

The men sent the women to become "mothers of Others," the most significant of which are the hostile white men. The women are the conduits through which openness to the external world occurs. The flutes represent continuity of the primordium across generations. Identity will never be lost as long as one maintains power over its most potent, primordial symbol.

With the Kuwai, the women blew the flutes and trumpets all over the world, and it opened up for a second time (the first was after the birth of Kuwai). The men chased after the women and made omens to warn them of their pursuit. After the struggle, Nhiãperikuli sent the women on missions to the various ends of the earth. Thus there were conceivably three times that the women opened up the world: after Kuwai's birth, at the end of the boys' initiation, and after the struggle at Motipana.

The women's major role in the process of creation was precisely to introduce change in the midst of continuity. The women's kalidzamai chants begin with the story of how the women's blood, after the birth of Kuwai, opened up riverbeds and made the waters flow. This event was one of the most important sources of change and motion in a new, dynamic universe. Before this happened, the primordial universe was self-contained in a miniature area around Hipana. After the change, the universe expanded to its present size; with the kalidzamai chants, society gained the potential to encompass alterity, shamanizing and neutralizing the danger it represents. In short, the sacred story in no way annuls time, but rather seeks to align change and continuity within the temporal and spatial coordinates of the universe.

The second time the world expanded was when the women

stole the sacred instruments, which set off the chase in which the women opened up the world with the sounds of the flutes (*limalia-iyu*) to the size it is today. The women went in five directions, basically along the same routes that Amaru's blood had opened up the riverbeds and the same routes they followed after the war, when they were sent on missions by Nhiãperikuli to be the mothers of the white people (Portuguese and Spaniards). Women retained the power of creating alterity. Like the men, they are also owners of specific kinds of sorcery, that is, an alterity within society.[2] Finally, in the external world, they became associated with industrial knowledge, technology, and sicknesses that derive from the white man's industries.

Nhiãperikuli thus left the women associated with two aspects of alterity—the "Others inside" of Baniwa society and the "Insiders outside"—other ethnic groups surrounding the Baniwa, some of whom are affinal peoples, which in the past represented the potential for war and alliance among phratries and today signifies attacks by jaguar shamans, sorcery from other peoples, and above all, the sicknesses of the whites.

In becoming the "mother of the whites," interrelations between the Baniwa and the whites had been set in motion, becoming an inextricable part of the Baniwa universe. The women and the whites then created industries that eventually brought white men back to the Upper Rio Negro, some to plague the Indians and some to help them. The notion of factories is a historical trope based on the primordial image of Amaru as having been the source of all rivers flowing from the Aiary to the ends of the world.

In these factories, according to pajés, there are pots of metal—gold, silver, iron, aluminum. Constantly heated by fire, poisonous smoke from the pots spreads over the world, and it is the smell of this poisonous smoke which causes sicknesses associated with the white man: flu, whooping cough, dysentery, measles, malaria—all of which produce high fever and are contagious. A major category of sicknesses related to the white people was created as a result of the women being sent on missions, as Mandu said, to cohabit with the whites.

Influenza is imagined as the cotton from the cloth Amaru wore on her head, an image of indigenous women in the context of the colonial history of Amazonia. Amaru works all the time weaving cotton of various colors, and this cotton metaphorically refers to flu in Baniwa curing orations. The poisonous smoke of her factories spreads from the periphery of the world back to the center, where the Baniwa live. How? Today it is by the planes that bring merchandise, for the motors of the planes are produced in the factories of the women, and it is the smell of diesel fuel and gasoline that brings on sickness. Here again, the principle of mixing what should not be mixed produces sicknesses and disease, with the complementary idea of contagious sicknesses transmitted through the air.

The image of a factory that produces motors and poisonous smoke that arises from pots can also be understood as a radical trope of an image in traditional shamanism which refers to sicknesses of the universe (*hekwapi pwa*) that occur during seasonal transitions: at these times sickness spreads, as though through the air, originating from primordial pots of fruits arranged in a great circle in the Other World. Here again, a novel semantic category has been grafted onto preexisting categories and symbolic processes of sicknesses of the world to elaborate an explanation for the historical reality of contact with the whites and the epidemics this has produced. It is a powerful commentary on the destruction those elements representing alterity can bring to Baniwa society.

The Baniwa say that when a person dreams of a plane, it is a warning of the arrival of a white man's sickness. The fumes from the airplanes and the smell of diesel fuel of the boats are sources of the white man's sicknesses. Boats are painted in various colors; the smell of the paint provokes diarrhea and dysentery. Orations to cure the sicknesses of the whites must thus name all the things associated with Amaru that may produce sicknesses: her factories, planes, boats, cars, and cachaça (fermented sugarcane). The danger represented by each comes as a result of breathing in the fumes of burning oil and combustible fuels.

The stories and chants clearly provide an ample view of how the Baniwa think about the white man. What specifically do they criticize in the white man's culture? The sacred stories are elaborate tropes that provide a critical vision of what could potentially destroy indigenous society if the traditions are lost. This, of course, brings us back to the "warnings of Mandu"—most certainly based on these tropes, but elaborated into a "radical critique of the Western world" (Sullivan 1988).

Having Amaru as the "mother of alterity" places her in a position similar to the pajé, who is likewise intermediary to the Other World and the souls of the dead (all "white"). Amaru, however, is of the horizontal plane exclusively (so the stories say). On this horizontal plane, there are still up and down positions nevertheless. Thus her main fortress is the hill called Motipana—a fortress on the top of a hill at the distant headwaters of the Uaraná stream.

In oral histories, Hohodene women have important intermediary roles in forming alliances between phratric chiefs that result in the reversal of the destructiveness of the whites. Like the pajé who can exercise his role as intermediary by resorting to sorcery, although they prefer to state publicly that they only heal, so the women can be of enormous value in the regeneration of society, although their public image—represented in the myths—may seem otherwise. In the end it was Nhiãperikuli who sent the women in the same direction he sent the whites and gave the whites the knowledge of technology.

The danger of mixing with the whites and their merchandise is a theme repeated in other stories and curing orations that explain the origin of the whites at Hipana.

From the body of the great serpent Umawali, who was slain near the present-day city of São Gabriel da Cachoeira, Nhiãperikuli got two grubs, muxiwa, and transformed one into an Indian and the other into a white man. He gave each one a shotgun and told each to shoot at a target. The Baniwa missed, the white man hit, so the white man became the owner of the shotgun and the knowledge that goes with it, while the Baniwa remained with the blowgun and all the hunting knowledge that went along with the indigenous way of life. (Cf. Hugh-Jones 1989; Ramos and Albert 2002; Hill 1988; Chernela and Leed, in Hill 1988.)

In their commentaries, the shamans elaborated further: Nhiãperikuli didn't want the white man to stay on the lands of the Indians. For that reason, he put them in a boat and sent them away to the east, where they would have stayed until they joined up with one of the Amaru and the women.

Orations spoken to cure the sicknesses resulting from the smoke of the women's factories are done to prevent or neutralize their contaminating effects. The notion here is *linupa*: if a person undergoing restrictions either due to sickness or during periods of ritual passage, consumes or does what he should not, he goes against the rule of non-mixture, and the sickness and pain will worsen. In cases of contagious sicknesses, isolation from the rest of the community has a very practical basis of preventing transmission.

In many of these healing orations and chants, there is the idea of moving back from the periphery toward a protected sanctuary, allowing for the full recovery of a person taken ill by respiratory diseases. Along the way, the heart-soul of the sick person is revived from having been poisoned in the white man's world (see also Hill 1993). These chants then have a structure similar to the revival of Kuwaikaniri in his journey upriver back home (see chapter 4).

The movement toward the sanctuary or sacred center entails purifying the sick person's heart-soul through ingestion of fruit nectar and honey. The image of a sanctuary—a space of regeneration, within the mythscape—strongly marks cosmogony, curing practices, and the ideologies of historical prophetic movements. The notion of a sanctuary represents recovery from a catastrophic loss or, if you will, historical re-empowerment. It offers a haven from the disastrous effects of contact and the possibility of regeneration through purification.

WARS OF HUMANS AND SPIRITS

The yoopinai merit special attention for pajés, as they are constantly at war with these spirits who attack humans with their darts. All yoopinai are sickness-giving spirits that emerged from the ashes of Kuwai's body, it is said. There is an enormous variety of sicknesses attributed to the yoopinai.

The yoopinai consist of all types of insects, plants, animals, and spirits of the forest. They are spirits of the air, earth, waters, and the environment in general.[3] According to the pajés, they are people and do everything that humans do, including blowing strong sorcery against humans if they transgress the boundaries that exist between them. Their material bodies that humans see have an enormous diversity of visible forms: termite nests, the Morpho butterfly, black honey, and some bees and wasps. They all have a chief with the visible body of a lizard called *Kapiferi-inyai*. Among the worst sicknesses they hurl at humans with their arrows and darts are the *hiuiathi* hemorrhages, which particularly affect

21. Two Hohodene chanters in characteristic postures of silent chanting inside closed fists.

women and fetuses. It is sorcery to destroy women's reproductive systems or kill a fetus.

The kinds of shamanic actions that a person can take against these spirits are through the "blowing" of protective spells by an owner of orations, *iyapakethe-iminali*. Iyapakana is a broad category of shamanizing activity that refers to the chanting or speaking of protective orations accompanied by the blowing of the words of the chant with tobacco smoke over the intended subject, items that pertain to him or her, and the materia medica utilized in specific treatments (nettles, resins, rubbing alcohol).

CONCLUSIONS

Over the last three chapters, we have seen how Kuwai is shamanic knowledge and power in all its aspects: sorcerer and demonic spirit, teacher of shamanism and healer, priestly chanter and dance leader. During his apprenticeship, a new pajé is required to meet Kuwai

22. The Sacred Boulder of Dzuliferi, Spirit of Power. (Photo by Isaias Fontes.)

face-to-face and to learn how to cure from Dzuliferi–shadow-soul, a shape that Kuwai assumes.[4] Kuwai is also the dance leader and the elder owner of the chants, especially the kalidzamai, which are, along with the dances, the most esoteric form of spiritual knowledge the Hohodene have and the foundation for the reproduction of society over time.

The entire myth of Kuwai presents a drama of the religious imagination whose central themes and storyline are as follows:

Kuwai was the externalization of his father's heart-soul, the life force of the universe. His father, in his knowledge and wisdom, did this in order to "teach the children," the uninitiated, of the traditions. Kuwai was too dangerous to remain in This World, however, for it was a transformative being that combined growth, reproduction, and change, with their correlates of sickness, destructiveness, discontinuity, and stasis. That combination of powers does not easily mix with This World, not to mention the mix of the parts among themselves. Kuwai is ultimately a protean animal-shaped creature who changes at will, given the nature of the situation. There is much "Wisdom of the Ancients" in these traditions. There is also the dark side of the human heart-soul that can, unless controlled, bring about the ruin of the indigenous peoples and the triumph of the enemy.

Kuwai grew up to be a mysterious outsider whose dangerous powers were desired by the people of that time (including the mothers, the initiate children, women in general, and the group of agnatic, consanguineal kin). To experience the power of Kuwai's music, the children had to fast and abstain from sexual relations for an extended period of time. Three young initiates failed to abide by Kuwai's restrictions and were catastrophically consumed inside the stone mouth of the "Other Kuwai," that is, the spirit of the dead, inyaime.

It was only at Kuwai's "sacrifice by fire" (or consumption by flames) that he transmitted all of his knowledge and power to his kin; only in the fire could his dangerous power finally be internalized into society under the control of the elder men, the pajés, and the chanters. They then sang of Kuwai as "Our Owner." These powers could thus be transmitted continuously, as society was now in possession of the means for its own reproduction. But Kuwai had also taught sorcery to Nhiãperikuli's younger brother, Mawerikuli, who brought death into the world from both his "lack of thought" and from his failure to remain secluded and restricted.

The knowledge about sickness was externalized from Kuwai's body and reproduced for all times. Numerous plant forms of sickness were let loose in a chaotic way into the world after the conflagration. These still represent an enormous threat to the living. From the yoopinai spirits' perspectives, they may only be protecting their boundaries when they attack a human with sickness, and as long as there is respect between humans and the spirits, or "other peoples," there will be no sickness attacks. The problem occurs when fewer and fewer of the younger generation know and respect those laws, and consequently sickness increases.

Men and women fought over the ownership of the flutes. It was a powerful force that divided them; warfare came into being, meaning among other things that the initiation of boys and girls into adulthood is directly associated with marital exchange. (This is evident in initiation rites today and confirmed in the histories of past warfare among affinal phratries.) Sociologically speaking, Amaru's being sent in the four directions can be understood as exogamy, going away from the center, open therefore to historical changes. Amaru became the "traveling outsider." Nhiãperikuli "gave the women shoes" and set them on their journey in the four directions. Amaru is associated with the "white man's sicknesses" (respiratory illnesses, mainly, and feverish states produced by contact).

Finally, I have shown how the conjunction of myth and history has been translated into prophetic messages expressed by wise men several generations ago of an imminent return of the whites to the Aiary, for which the Hohodene should prepare themselves. The message of Mandu is likewise relevant to this counsel regarding living in contact with the whites and not losing the traditions.

Mandu: "So, what is your thought? Why did Nhiãperikuli leave Kuwai with us?"
"To teach the children about the world."

Part 4

*Revitalization Movements in
Traditional and Christianized
Communities*

9

The House of Shamans' Knowledge and Power, the House of Adornment, and the Pamaale School Complex

The pajés' songs, discourses about the Other World, and stories of the prophets refer to a place of eternal happiness, Kathimakwe, at or near the top of the universe but hidden to all but the jaguar shamans. Those pajés are believed to have the power to reveal it through the correct transformations. Their bodies become the handle of the harpy eagle Kamathawa, the handle of their rattle that breaks open a passage to the world of happiness.

Happiness for humans, according to the pajés of the Aiary River, is not to be found in This World but rather in the ancient, hidden world of Nhiãperikuli. The prophet Uetsu said, "You will suffer along our way." Salvation from the sick world itself, considered by many to be the world of evil, is found in Nhiãperikuli's eternal world of bliss free from sickness. This is partially the basis for various prophetic movements that have arisen in Baniwa history. Short of these movements, which in some cases have produced violent reactions on the part of the authorities, one of the most successful options for creating happiness in this world is through the planned and careful construction of an aesthetics of conviviality, which can be translated into concrete projects, planned and administered by the indigenous peoples, which combine traditional knowledge with a careful discussion of the implications of change in terms of the equitable distribution of resources, the sharing of information about projects, and the placing of the health and well-being of the people and the culture as the primary objective.

In this chapter, I shall compare three communities — Ukuki, Uapui, and Pamaale — as illustrations of how community leaders and pajés have attempted to put into practice the ideal of the place of happiness and well-being, specifically through recently implanted projects for the revitalization of their culture or for sustainable development. The first two communities have always been traditional with jaguar shamans. The younger generation abides by the authority of the elders. Pamaale is an NGO-assisted and indigenous association–run community with no pajés. The indigenous association consists entirely of younger leadership and students.

The expression *pakoakatsa*, "they are the same," is often heard in everyday discourse, referring to egalitarian social relations among kinspeople. It is an ideal relation for which everyone ought to strive, which is taught from the time children are initiated into adulthood. Egalitarianism is an ideal that is easily marred under contemporary circumstances by inequalities. Social, political, and economic differences are created among individuals that can be the basis of discontent, potentially leading to sorcery.

"Difference" is translated as *poadzatsa*, and it refers to any sort of differentiation — language being the most obvious — but also differences in kinds of animals, fish, etc. Traditional and hierarchical differences among sibs, as in the ceremonial roles of chiefs, warriors, servants, and dancers, are attenuated as a form of ceremonial distinction today. In daily life, the hierarchical distinctions among sibs of the same phratry are still significant in marital exchanges. The current bone of contention that divides communities, however, has to do with the uneven distribution of material and intangible resources. In large part this problem is related to the differences between evangelical and nonevangelical communities and the rise of a new leadership that was initially perceived as a threat to the authority of the traditional elders and chiefs.

The contemporary religious and political affiliations among the Aiary River population may be characterized as follows. First, there are the two large, traditional communities of predominantly Hohodene and Walipere-dakenai phratries, at Uapui (Hipana) and Ukuki on the Uaraná River (ancestral lands of the Hohodene phratry), which have been nominally Catholic since the 1950s. These communities have defended the old religious traditions against all attacks from evangelical missionaries and pastors. They participate in the political associations ACIRA (Association of the Indigenous Communities of the Aiary River) and UMARI (Indigenous Women's Association). There are evangelical communities from about the mid-Aiary to its mouth, along with a number of religiously unaffiliated (neither Protestant nor Catholic) communities. Between the blocs of communities, relations are stable, although a history of feuding, differences in religious affiliations, and competition for project funds are factors that can fuel conflict.

There are many stories circulating in the region of the evangelical crusades of the 1960s, when native pastors from the middle Içana and lower Aiary dragged the sacred flutes out onto the central plazas of their villages and burned them in public. Given the tremendous sacred power that the instruments represented, it would take a miracle to have them somehow come back to life or have the power they once had. There are stories and documented reports from Catholic missionaries of evangelical pastors burning the Catholic Bible on the beaches in front of the mission post at Carara-poço on the lower Içana (Wright 1998, 2005). Such occurrences left scars on the peoples of the upper Aiary, who also were attacked by those of the middle Içana. To them, the whole revitalization movement of the younger generation at Pamaale today is unlike the ways of the ancestors.

One memory of the Hohodene from Ukuki community demonstrates the depth of the existing split between themselves and the communities of the middle Içana. The crente pastors tried to kill Kudui, the jaguar shaman/wise man, in the 1960s, they say, but he turned them away because he knew beforehand what they were coming to do. He revealed their intentions in public when they got to his house. His village was on the island of Warukwa, where he is now buried and where the Hohodene of Ukuki today have their cemetery. This memory clearly serves as a boundary line between the two blocks of communities based on the religious conflicts.

The middle Içana is the traditional area of the very large phratry of the Walipere-dakenai, especially on the Pamaale stream, the location of their ancestral settlements. This was where the OIBI (Indigenous Organization of the Içana River) emerged in the 1980s, and today it is the location of the Baniwa-Curipaco Indigenous School (EIBC). This school has become the hub of a vigorous new cultural formation supported by the regional indigenous organization, the FOIRN, and its main NGO consultant, the Instituto SocioAmbiental (Socio-Environmental Institute).

The upper Içana is an area of predominantly evangelical communities that have little, if any, desire to rekindle the ancestors' ways of life (Xavier Leal 2008). There are only a few individuals in isolated communities, surrounded by crentes, who staunchly defend the ways of the ancestors.

On the lower Içana, most communities speak the trade language lingua geral and not the Arawakan language; they have had a history of contact since the mid-eighteenth century. Many of the adults there work for the betterment of their children's future, through educational and social projects supported by diverse foundations. They are in favor of changes insofar as they provide their children with a better life. Religious questions are not a source of tension in these communities.

THE PAMAALE COMPLEX

The educational complex at Pamaale is not a permanent village but rather an NGO creation that has received large investments from Norwegian foundations, with the support of the Instituto SocioAmbiental, the largest NGO working today in the Northwest Amazon. The ISA has focused its investments in the Pamaale community as one of its pilot projects for a well-integrated sustainable development program.

Over the past fifteen to twenty years, the ISA has served as principal consultant to the FOIRN, and together they have embarked on complex, regionally integrated programs to promote sustainable development projects in several communities of the Northwest Amazon: aquaculture, agro-forestry, marketing woven products through the fair marketing approach, and what is called differentiated education. The ISA has used a pilot project approach in which, once having selected a community where the greatest potential existed for extensive investments turning out well, all efforts are made to train local leadership in the methods and techniques of managing and administering the projects. Once a base of qualified leadership has been identified, then these leaders serve as intermediaries between local communities and funding agencies.

Typically the leaders are young, male, prestigious, politically astute, entrepreneurial, and fluent in Portuguese. They are facilitators of change, and consequently they run the greatest risk of being delegitimized should they lose their support in their home bases or are directly affected by traditional means of repressing the accumulation of power, that is, sorcery (Cruz Penido 2005; Wright 2009b).

Two young leaders of the Walipere-dakenai stand out as having been most instrumental in mediating change between the communities of the middle Içana and the NGOs and foundations: Bonifacio Fernandes and André Fernandes, both from the same village of Walipere-dakenai, both ex-coordinators of the OIBI. André later became director of the FOIRN and the other vice director, and then one became the vice prefect of the municipal government while the other has started his own NGO in Manaus. However, the vice prefect has demonstrated that his vision of the ideal way of life does not extend much beyond those communities where there is evangelism, the OIBI orbit.

Through Andre's leadership, the communities affiliated with the OIBI participated in several sustainable development projects, all supported by the ISA, including the sale of basketry (Arte Baniwa), certain types of pepper, and the differentiated educational complex for grade school and high school students at Pamaale. In the 2005 film *Baniwa: Uma historia de plantas e curas*, André makes a point of demonstrating how much the Pamaale school has become the hub of an entrepreneurial culture, which is an ideal that he has pursued for decades, even risking his own life (Wright 2009b).

Over the past twenty years, the ISA has invested heavily in the Pamaale community in the following ways: (1) an aquaculture project which was linked to the school as a source of food for the students; (2) the installation of a small hydro-electric at a nearby stream to generate energy for the school; (3) a well-equipped school with computers, projectors—a lot of things that other schools among the Baniwa do not have; (4) telecommunications with a satellite dish (the only one in the region); and in many other ways. The Pamaale community has received more funds from external foundations (mainly Norwegian) than any other

Baniwa or Kuripako community in the entire region; and this has not gone unnoticed by those other communities outside the orbit of the OIBI, who have not received such massive assistance.

Despite the modernity of these projects, the students have shown a strong interest in demonstrating how they know the traditional dances, although it is clear that the dances they present are more symbols of their new identity and autonomy that they seek to resignify than the ancestral way of life.

There are numerous ways in which outside observers can see this reshaping of indigenous identity through the differentiated school at Pamaale. The dance festivals held at Pamaale, for example, as they are performed today, have the young adult men and women adorned with bodypaint, feather headdresses, woven skirts, and necklaces, somewhat like the ancestors' ways. The patterns in the bodypainting and decorations with heron feathers, however, are altogether distinct from the old ways of adornment, as illustrated by photos from the early 1900s, the end of the 1920s, and the 1950s. The men today play the (non-sacred) flutes, the women accompany them, somewhat like the old ways. Their festivals, however, are held to celebrate, for example, the first ten years of the school. This is a reflection of the ISA's image (which also celebrated the first ten years of its existence in 2007) that has been incorporated into the community's self-image.

in 2008 the Pamaale students participated in a festival hosted by the Ukuki community for the inauguration of a newly constructed traditional longhouse that the community of Ukuki called their House of Adornments. Members of the downriver evangelical community of Pamaale were invited to attend the initiation rite, and they apparently saw it as an opportunity to learn how the ancestors' traditional rites were done. Oddly, however, what began as the traditional dances of the Kwaipan ended up as a discussion about the problems of the Pamaale school—in typical indigenist meeting style. "The meeting was interesting," said the chief of Ukuki, but he added: "Their culture [i.e., of the students] referring to the dances was no longer like the dances of old and rather like a remembrance of the dances of our ancestors; the cultural dances took a long time to be presented to other people from other villages. In short, it was a commemorative fest just for the sake of having a fest. The meeting was more to solve problems of the indigenous schools" (L. Fontes, 2010 interview).

The handprint of the NGO projects model is very evident in the Pamaale youths' aspirations. They seek to incorporate the successful role model of the ISA style of life as researchers and administrators, utilizing elements of the old culture in order to show that, while modern and technologically instructed, they still respect some of the traditions. Note, however, that the young adults do not dance to remember the way the jabiru stork danced in ancient times, nor do they use the rattles that accompanied the taking of caapi (*Banisteriopsis caapi*, or *yajé*). Nor do they play the surubim-flutes, considered by the traditional elders to be the hallmark of Baniwa identity.

In other words, the ritual process displayed at Pamaale is characterized by the indigenization of an essentially exogenous model of time and identity in the production of graduating classes of students. In the 1970s, the elders of Uapui would say, "The evangelicals only want to become like whites." At that time, there was no other stable and accepted model of the whites that could be successfully incorporated into the social and ritual process, except for the crente cycle of rituals. Today, however, the dances at Pamaale celebrate the "new Baniwa" entrepreneurial culture (the conjunction of sustainable projects with the differentiated education), added onto the layer of the crente identity. In other words, the ancestral way of life as interpreted by the Pamaale students employs some of its symbols but at the service of the new identity.

This transformation, still in process, can be seen to have its advantages and its problems. The great advantage is that the students demonstrate that there is a certain space for both layers of identity to coexist. The fact that this process has lasted ten years is certainly something that should be celebrated. The problems, however, stem from (1) privileging and favoring one cultural formation economically, politically, and socially, while marginalizing others; (2) ignoring altogether the possibility of regenerating the shamanic worldview in favor of an indigenized evangelical ethic; and (3) stimulating the formation of competing cosmologies and cosmo-praxes. Without addressing these problems, the future is very uncertain; one day, the funding may very well not be renewed. Then what?

Another feature of the new cultural formation at Pamaale has been, I believe, to shift the sources of knowledge about the environment and ecological resources over to well-trained individuals whose perspectives privilege the western technical and administrative know-how and not the knowledge of the original ecologists, the pajés. Since most of the students come from evangelical families, and the leadership of the oibi is evangelical, it comes as no surprise that little credence is given to the pajés' ecological knowledge.

Consistently throughout, this book has drawn attention to the pajé's critical role in securing food resources for the communities under their protection. Phratries went to war because of one shaman's upsetting the cosmic balance in food resources. The pajés have the responsibility of ensuring that no sorcerer penetrates the cosmos and casts a spell to make the fish die.

In one of the first and most important creation stories, the Great Tree of Sustenance, the source of all food for humanity, was also the source of all shamans' powers (Wright 2009a; Cornelio et al. 1999; Hill 1984, 1993). Shamanic knowledge and power is inseparably intertwined with the cycles of food production. This is an important relation that has been largely ignored by outsiders.

The communities of the middle Içana region gained a foothold early on in the national and international markets with the total support of the ISA through the sale of baskets and other artwork and a supposedly Baniwa brand of pepper. The communities of the Aiary did their best to participate in the basket production, but for various reasons they were unsuccessful. So while the middle Içana bloc had its projects funded, headwater communities of the Aiary have waited for years until an opportunity appears.

Thus among the Baniwa of the mid-Içana, the logic of market values — competition, quality management, business administration, rewarding achievements, celebrating commemorative events modeled on the ideas of success stories — has become rooted in forming and reproducing the new entrepreneurial culture among those communities targeted for benefits.

As the Art Project began to lose its strength (due to a variety of reasons, among them, the greater attraction of extractivist labor, which the Baniwa have done since the eighteenth century, than the more demanding and tedious work of weaving baskets of all sizes and shapes), a new Baniwa Pepper project began with the selling of a type of pepper that the Baniwa leaders claimed was specific to their culture. The ISA again supported the project. The initiative, however, caused a great deal of resentment among other ethnic groups of the region who affirm that the pepper is not exclusively the property of the Baniwa. The type of pepper commercialized is common throughout the region; therefore, the Baniwa cannot claim it as exclusively their own.

The communities who are not explicitly included as beneficiaries of the projects that are funded express their historical frustration at exclusion, for this has been the seedbed of envy, humiliation, and jealousy in a society that seeks to be egalitarian.

Often the funding organizations are not even aware of such differences because the community or leaders in power gloss over the existing discontent. How do the marginalized communities perceive this situation?

In 2010 the chief of the Ukuki community told me, "The only thing that affects the region is when pilot projects are elaborated covering the whole region, and communities like ours are not contemplated when the project is approved." The Pamaale school complex stands out in the Northwest Amazon region as a reference point for the relations between the Baniwa and the outside world. A large contingent of people along the Aiary River, however, is not content with this situation. They ask: Why can they not get a piece of the cake? Why is just one place singled out to receive benefits? Furthermore, the local history of relations among communities of affinal phratries on the Aiary and Içana is already marked by stories of treachery and sorcery accusations. The Hohodene consider themselves to be the more traditional communities, in contrast with the Walipere-dakenai of the middle-Içana communities who have traveled much further down the way to becoming a success story modeled on the most visible structure of power and success in the upper Rio Negro region, the ISA.

Consequently, despite appearances, there is great resentment in the area, which has reinforced the longtime division between Catholics and crentes. The communities of the upper backwaters region of the Aiary feel that the favored way of life is the technocratic, bureaucratic, administrative, "scientific" way that they see unfolding in Pamaale. The upper Aiary river communities would also like to have a guaranteed supply of food in their communities. They want a school like Pamaale's with computers and laptops. They believe these innovations can coexist with their traditional cosmologies. Why then have they not been considered when the external resources are distributed? Such marginalization produces resentment among a people which has been disadvantaged for centuries.

Ideally, projects should be relevant to the greater health and well-being of a people, not one community or one association. Health and well-being is defined by Baniwa sacred stories and practices, and not by money or marketability alone. The Baniwa sacred stories of creation tell of various moments when the creator gave the ancestors of each phratry the fruits of the primordial Tree of Sustenance, the first tree of manioc and cultivated plants, the primordial sources of fish, and many other food resources (Cornelio, et al. 1999). While there may have been differences in the quantity of resources that each phratry received, all phratries received a portion. The idea of one phratry being benefited and the others not at all runs against the original ethics of resource distribution.

As the current director of the FOIRN observed in a recent interview:

> The ISA, who supported the development of the pepper project together with the Baniwa, has a very strong presence in the region. I would say that they even compete with the FOIRN on other matters. Their active presence is very great, because they are intellectuals who make up the ISA. They are not indigenous. So they have influence in the region, and things end up being guided by them. . . . The ISA has helped us a great deal, but at certain moments we get concerned. If I am your partner, I think that I have to keep you informed of what I am doing, discussing, and not creating exclusivity in the region—we have to prioritize all the regions. But, in fact, I think that we are losing space in that sense. If there is an action that has to be led by the indigenous people, it is the FOIRN that is the representative. It's the FOIRN that has to discuss it. Now, on the question of assessment

and consultancy, I see another situation. For example, we don't have an indigenous lawyer, we don't have an indigenous doctor. We need these professionals in order to contribute, but on the question of the struggle of the indigenous peoples, I think that it should be headed by the indigenous peoples. (UNESP interview, 2011)

In various similar cases reported in Latin America, this kind of relation has produced either dependence (patron/client), or competition between indigenous and nonindigenous associations. Instead of being partners, as in the beginning, one (the NGO) competes with the indigenous organization for ways to use the natural resources and create an alternative economy, with brand-names, patents, etc.

Evidently greater attention could be given to finding culturally appropriate, nonhierarchical means for distribution of available resources to assist indigenous peoples to make their own decisions, based on their criteria, and not that of marketable projects. Indigenous religious traditions and specialists provide a privileged understanding of "cosmo-praxis" which provides the springboard from which sustainable development projects are formed. It is a question of equitability, the key to opening the door to harmonious conviviality.

THE HOUSE OF ADORNMENT AT UKUKI, 2008

The founding elder of Ukuki, Ricardo Fontes (Keramunhe), always made a point of sustaining a living "aesthetics of conviviality" (Overing and Passes 2000) in the community. His children and grandchildren remember that message, and it is undoubtedly what has made Ukuki a very independent and relatively prosperous community today. As a kalidzamai chanter, *mandero*, and knower of the traditions, Ricardo was a patriarch of the community in the old ways who believed that all must respect the elders and help them in their work. Beyond that, they should treat people with hospitality, even if they are strangers. (The famous ethnologist Curt Nimuendajú noted, when he visited the Aiary River in 1927, that the Hohodene were a very hospitable people and received him well.) Ricardo's son, Laureano, the present-day capitão, follows the way of his father and is considered to be the only true mandero left on the Aiary today. Ukuki is known throughout the region for its regular celebration of the dance festivals.

When I worked with the young adults of Ukuki in 2000 on their knowledge of sicknesses, one of them discussed with me a project to seek funding to support their recording of the dance traditions, which the elders felt was important to the continuation of their culture. The project was specifically focused on the dances of initiation rites, or Kapetheapan.

At the time, I was collaborating with the ISA, which since the 1980s had established its presence in the Northwest Amazon. The ISA was instrumental in the demarcation of the indigenous land in the 1990s. Once that process was completed, the anthropologists who collaborated with the NGO undertook a research project on public health issues. In that context of interviewing pajés and nonspecialists, the young adults presented me with their idea of constructing a House of Adornment, where they could continue to celebrate their ceremonies, especially the initiation rites.

In searching for potential funding sources, I presented their project to the staff of the Rio Negro Project of the ISA, who I imagined would be interested in collaborating. I was surprised, however, by the negative response of the staff, who showed "no interest whatsoever" ("*nem sequer interessado*" was its response) in supporting the project. It seemed to me contradictory to the stated objectives of sustainable projects, for I understood, as the Hohodene did, that the oral traditions and ceremonies are fundamental to the well-being and prosperity of the indigenous communities. To the ISA staff, however, "sustainable projects" meant whatever could be marketed (e.g., baskets, pepper); the ISA had no interest in supporting the continuity of ceremonies, however much they were important to the indigenous peoples.

With admirable autonomy, the community of Ukuki went ahead and built a very large house of rituals, inaugurated in 2008, called Nakuliakarudapani (House of Adorning), with no financing whatsoever but rather only by the community's will (IF-RMW, pers. comm., August 2011). It was an extraordinary demonstration of the community's commitment to the continuity of their traditions; moreover, the first major ceremony celebrated in the House was a ritual of initiation, Kwaipan, with the sacred flutes and instruments.

One young Hohodene man from Ukuki, Isaias Fonte, wrote a short essay about the cultural significance of the dance traditions, which is a valuable reflection on the dances, the instruments, and the festivals celebrated in the community of Ukuki.

Nakuliakarudapani (the House of Adorning)
There are many forms of dances performed, from the songs of the elders, then the group of singers led by the mandero, who dance around the center of each longhouse, and even the *nakamarrataka* songs specific to the women. Nakamarrataka are a fundamental part of the ceremonies in the longhouses. The melodies echo from various types of instruments, like the sets of panpipes (*cariçú*), *japurutu* longflutes, *embauba* flutes, turtle shells, and principally the ceremony with *jurupari* (Kuwai) and the dance of the *kullirrinân* flutes, which are a trademark of the Hohodene, and so many other dances. Each music has its meaning and origin. The ceremony is the occasion for reliving the trajectory of origin in the Nakuliakarudapana, for remembering the first ancestors of each group [i.e., the kalidzamai chants],

of redoing the blessings (chants with pepper-pot) that protect the community in this world. Culture, in its different forms, both helps in the concentration and the animation of the ritual. The mandero and other singers use carajuru (red dye) for body painting and festival adornments, made of feathers and animal fur, which only some groups have.

Over the years, due to continued external pressures, ritual practices, especially the ceremonies with dances and the consumption of caapi in the longhouses, were forgotten, mainly on the Baniwa side. The longhouses were substituted by villages with individual family houses and a community center. The knowledge of the ceremonies was only kept alive in the memories of the elders.

To restore value to this cultural movement revitalized by us indigenous peoples, the community of Ukuki has ceremonial activities when it is time to show the jurupari, to the boys and at times of a lot of harvesting of forest fruits, and when the young girl completes her fertility cycle, the ceremony of Kuwai, a tradition which is highly valued, is done.

Today, the agnatic group of siblings descended from the founding family of Ukuki gives the appearance of being very united, with a radiophone in their village (which they use to stay in contact with everyone who goes to São Gabriel), and a group of young adults who are keen on making the traditions work. In this, they have the full support of the elder generation. They filmed as much of the initiation rite as permitted, and they are seeking to do further research about their traditions with a new video camera donated to the community.

The power and knowledge of the mandero, is especially exemplified by the chief of Ukuki, Laureano Fontes, and his wife. Dance owners complement the chanters and the pajés in their knowledge

23. Chief and dance leader Laureano, leading the young men with whips (*kapethe*) in a 2008 Ukuki initiation ceremony. (Photo by Isaias Fontes.)

of dances appropriate to each rite of passage and seasonality. The knowledge of the dance leaders in initiation rites was given to humans by Kaali, the owner of gardens, and by Kuwai, the owner of initiation rites, including the kalidzamai chants.

The owner of dance leaders' knowledge puts into practice the ideals of fabricating beautiful instruments and adornments, displaying symmetry in the forms of the dances, leading the music of aerophones and other instruments appropriate for each festival, and transmitting extensive knowledge of the stories of dance festivals and the songs that are appropriate to each. The mandero organizes the dance line in such a way as to be admired but also to create a milieu of enjoyment, happiness, and good company, in the sense that ethnologist Peter Riviére (in Overing and Passes, 2000) discusses among the Trio (Indians of Surinam).

Costa (2009) found in her research on the Aiary that the elders know of twenty-four kinds of dances with instruments such as flutes, panpipes, stomping tubes, and a kind of whistle (*mawaku*). The mandero are specialists in the old dance forms, some of which are said to have been taught to a person by an animal or bird who then transmits that knowledge to other humans. The story of Mamiyule in the collection *Waferinaipe Ianheke* (ACIRA/FOIRN, Cornelio et al. 1999) is a specifically Hohodene story about a dance festival of the fish. This story is told at Hohodene Pudali (exchange festivals) and is considered highly entertaining, making people happy to hear how the fish danced, made their ornaments, and were content.

Laughter, dancing in well-cadenced rhythms, and a good caxiri are the ingredients of a good Pudali, and the good dance leaders should know the songs, steps, orchestration, and the making of the instruments from beginning to end. Some of the dance leaders, besides knowing how to handle the Kuwai flutes and instruments, know how to fabricate the most important flute icon of Baniwa identity, the long surubim flutes, called *kulirrinam*, which are made with a complex wickerwork covering, painted in white zigzag patterns, and decorated with white heron feathers. Its song imitates the deep humming noise of the large surubim catfish swimming in groups underwater.

The dance leader takes care of the feather headdresses and the instruments when they are not in use. The dance leader collects and distributes them at appropriate moments of the festival. He has a distinguishing feather headdress, *acangatara* in lingua geral, with a long tail of white heron feathers. In organizing the community for a festival, he and his wife manage all matters relating to the production of sufficient quantities of caxiri or other kinds of fermented beverages. The dance owner also gives the order for when to gather forest fruits or to hunt game for the upcoming festival. (See Mandu's description of the initiation rite at Uapui in chapter 1.) Just as importantly, they are responsible for managing the relations among visiting affinal communities as the dance festival progresses. The Hohodene have now filmed various dances over the past several years, including the initiation rite in 2008 that inaugurated their new House of Adorning.

THE HOUSE OF SHAMANS' KNOWLEDGE AND POWER, MALIKAI DAPANA, AT UAPUI

In 2009, the community of Uapui also realized a major project of constructing a House of Shamans' Knowledge and Power, funded by the Foundation for Shamanic Studies, through my intermediation.

In Uapui, Mandu worked hard for many years to maintain an orderly and clean village when he was chief, for he believed this was conducive to people living well together in an atmosphere of prosperity and harmony. Mandu's frequent exhortations in the community longhouse emphasized that villagers should work for the community, and he sought to adapt to the presence of the Catholic missionaries who would regularly send work orders for the community to accomplish. Mandu and his wife managed the village of Uapui to the content of most dwellers, despite Mandu's lifelong enmity with Emi and his allies. That seemed to be one of the forces that held the community back. What prevented it from getting worse was the fact that the wives of Mandu and his two brothers and Emi's wife were all sisters, and the men were all sib-brothers; otherwise, tension would have broken out into more violent action.

Hipana and the upper Aiary are an area where traditions still work, although their relations to other Baniwa communities and to the nonindigenous agents of contact and change (missionaries in the 1970s, the Brazilian Air Force in the 1980s, and frequent visits to São Gabriel) have produced situations of mixed blessings—perhaps as much assistance as undesirable change. Incentive for the Aiary Baniwa in their struggles to revitalize their traditions, however, requires a determination that the traditional knowledge and nonindigenous knowledge can work together—in fundamental ways—to confront the real problems of food, transportation, health, and communication. This was in essence why the community of Uapui created the House of Shamans' Knowledge and Power.

Around 2001, inspired by some of the Traditional Medicine projects that the indigenous peoples of the Uaupés had initiated, Mandu's son Alberto and daughter Ercilia formulated a project for the revitalization of Baniwa culture of the Aiary River.

> For many years we have lived under the integrationist policy of the Brazilian government, which has led those populations to, little by little, lose their cultural values. Although the official policy brings with it new directions in development, they do not meet the needs of the indigenous peoples, who demonstrate the need to preserve their cultural traditions....
>
> Contact with the national society and the introduction of foreign values to the local indigenous culture has provoked significant changes in the indigenous communities with health problems, loss of traditions, problems related to migration, and decrease in the indigenous population leading these communities to become more dependent. This situation must be changed in such a way that the local indigenous tradition can be valorized, providing space for a greater harmony with nature, and those who live by utilizing their traditional knowledge can provide sustainable responses to their forms of life in the region of the Aiary River. (CECIBRA project statement, 2002, my translation)

Alberto has been seeking for many years to attain leadership in local politics but without much success. Nevertheless, the project emphasized that the people of the Aiary sought to recover their traditions through their own research agenda:

This proposal responds to the need to organize the cultural productions of the region, since the indigenous people of the Aiary believe that these productions can be researched and developed by the members of the indigenous communities of the Aiary River themselves. What is necessary at the moment are financial resources so that the activities programmed can become a reality. Towards this end, this project represents an initiative, still small, that could result in the strengthening of the traditions of the indigenous peoples throughout the region.

The resources requested were to be employed in specific activities such as the following:

To organize meetings and discussions on Cultural Revitalization and Traditional Medicine of the Baniwa among various indigenous groups of the Aiary;

To gather, systematize, and publish the stories, geographies, and other aspects of traditional knowledge for use in the indigenous schools of the region;

To build a center in the style of the traditional longhouse which will serve as a cultural center where activities and meetings will be held, as well as a center for indigenous cultural activities;

To organize and prepare medicinal gardens for general use among the ethnic groups of the region; and

To set up a library with a collection of materials on the indigenous culture of the Aiary River.

Concluding the project, the author emphasized:

"The most important results expected are (1) that the traditions of shamanism and initiation rituals (with their specialized chants), as well as the use of plant medicines will be conserved and revitalized; (2) that a greater part of the Baniwa population will become more aware of the value of revitalizing their traditional culture, as well as the value of the books that will be produced collectively for use in schools and courses; and (3) that a traditional longhouse will be built which will serve as a cultural center that will contain an organized library of books, tapes, and other audio-visual material that will serve the needs of the schools of the region of the Aiary River." (Project proposal, 2002, my translation)

PROJECT REALIZATION

One of the initial objectives of the project was to promote traditional medicine, but not in the sense of training indigenous health agents and planting herbal gardens, as was being done by communities of the Içana River in collaboration with the Federal University of Amazonas. Rather, the project focused on the metaphysics of the true shamans, few of whom were left in the late 1990s and all of them very advanced in age. Few peoples at that time seemed to be acutely aware that, with the loss of the true jaguar shamans' knowledge, traditional medicine among the Baniwa would be moving in a direction that had little basis in the cosmology and metaphysics of their shamans. The principal Baniwa political leaders of the Içana supported the home gardens and health agents approach, but not the metaphysical jaguar shamans. It was only among the Aiary River communities that such a project to support the transmission of jaguar shamans' knowledge had any hope of becoming a reality.

After years of fruitless searching for support for the shamans' school project, we learned of the important work of the Foundation for Shamanic Studies, founded by Michael Harner, which

supported communities that were seeking to keep their traditional shamans' practice alive and to revitalize interest among the
younger generation to pursue the arduous training of becoming
a true shaman.

The Foundation immediately approved the project to construct
a shamans' school—that is, a place where Mandu and his brother
Mário could train new apprentices, where a library of films and
tapes of pajés could be maintained, and where research would
be done on Baniwa jaguar shamans. The Foundation went much
further by recognizing Manuel da Silva through its Living Treasure award, including a certificate and a small annual pension.
By Living Treasure, the Foundation referred to the extraordinary
knowledge that Manuel has and the use to which he has put this
knowledge over the past sixty years to guide his people according
to the ways of the ancestors.

Manuel and his brother became the headmasters of a school of
apprentices. Some had already begun their training prior to the
creation of the school, but the majority were new. The original
project for Cultural Revitalization, or CECIBRA, as it was initially
called, then acquired a new and vital function of transmitting
shamanic knowledge, which was in great peril of being dispersed
if not lost. Alberto and Mandu thus renamed it Malikai Dapana,
House of Shamanic Knowledge and Power.

INAUGURATION OF THE HOUSE

The inauguration of the Malikai Dapana took place on November 30 and December 1, 2009. I had invited a former student,
Marcio Meira, then president of the National Indian Agency (or
FUNAI), to join us in the inauguration. He accepted. Without his
support in authorizing plane transportation directly to the village—where there is an airstrip, reactivated for the event, I doubt
there would have been any inauguration at all. Members of all

Aiary River villages came to meet the president and to participate in the ceremonies. The administrator of the regional FUNAI offices, Benedito Machado, was also present. My son, Michael, filmed the entire ceremony and created several short videos, which may be seen on the Foundation's website (www.shamanism.org) and on my webpage.

We were greeted by José Felipe, who wore the dance headdress of a "dance owner" as he pointed the tiny Cessna in which we flew to a safe landing on the old airstrip. Many people whom I knew as children came to greet us and eventually take us into the new House of Shamans' Knowledge, which was strikingly beautiful in its decorations of sprigs of sweet-smelling branches, strips of bark woven into birdlike shapes hanging from the ceiling, and the incredibly intricate architecture of the very high ceiling of palm thatch, open at each end of the house, allowing refreshing drafts of air to blow through.

The initial presentations were conducted by the grade school teachers, one of whom, Plinio, was the son of a pajé I had worked with in the 1970s. He coordinated the dance presentations by the students of the grade school in Uapui—all of them executed with excellent coordination and a lively spirit—dances of the acará fish, the saúva ants, and others. I was impressed and told the audience that in the 1970s I'd seen none of those dances. Manuel da Silva himself had told me back then that those dances were already coming to an end, as though he wished to assure the non-Indians of that time that they were already becoming civilized, following the orders of the missionaries. Thirty-five years later, I was delighted to see that, much to the contrary, the dances were more lively than ever before. There was a new pride in the dance attire and the beautiful gifts of necklaces and woven baskets given by young men and women to the authorities who were visiting.

The vigor and enthusiasm of the afternoon dances by the younger

24. Young women waiting to greet guests at the 2009 inauguration ceremony for the Malikai Dapana.

generations seemed like a light taste of the evening performances, when an array of dances in the style of the Baniwa Pudali was performed by the adults. Two dance leaders led the dances. Caxiri, the lightly fermented brew of manioc, açai fruit, and sweet potato, was served in endless rounds as the dances continued. It was an extremely pleasant feeling to be sitting in the huge, dimly lit longhouse—the product of our labors together—with the buzz of conversation, laughter, and good feelings among hosts and guests, as the caxiri continued to go around, and special performances were done "for the guests, for the authorities."

As one elderly lady gave the caxiri to us, she sang a traditional drinking song when offering beer. "A song sung from the heart," the schoolteacher and pajé's apprentice Plinio translated, of how she was just a poor, sad, and lonely widow. She enjoined us to be happy as we remembered our wives and girlfriends back home. The style of these traditional *pakamaratakan* songs is to sing of themselves, their identity, and their sentiments. At a break in the performance, Alberto spoke the traditional offering of the humble dances to the illustrious authorities and presented us with special gifts of placards woven with our names and beautifully strung necklaces. Whether as a gesture of thanks for the help or as a gesture of a refined culture with very appropriate ways of expressing sentiments, the organization of the inauguration was a memorable expression of how traditional cultural life is the greatest valuable that the Baniwa have.

But the highlight came with the pajés' dance or blessing, which was saved for last, clearly as the performance moved from the social dances to bringing into the House the sacred reality of the Other World. Reconstructing the scene: Mandu entered the longhouse with his brother Mário and the twelve apprentices. The two pajés squatted in the center of the line, as the main instructors in Malikai Dapana. The apprentices sat in an arc around Mandu. Three of the more advanced apprentices sat as a group to one side of the arc. José Felipe, as the most senior of the new generation of pajés, directed the seating patterns; Plinio purposefully held up a rock that had been handed down from his father and his father's father, which he evidently was showing as a credential of his shamanic knowledge and power.

The two master shamans removed their instruments from their bags and placed them carefully on the ground in front of them. Mandu untangled his jaguar tooth collar—the highly prestigious symbol of the powerful jaguar shaman. At Manuel's instructions, Mário blew pariká snuff into the nostrils of all the apprentices seated in order of rank and power, ending with the authorities, each of whom was given a light sniff. After blowing protective tobacco smoke over the group of apprentices, Mandu and Mário began to chant between themselves, which was soon followed by all the apprentices chanting together in soft unison, to the accompaniment of the two rattles of Mário and Mandu in cadenced rhythms. All the while, the laughter of children playing outside provided a lyric counterpoint to the shamanic spirit and power, the "reality of the universe," being sung inside the house.

The two schoolteachers interpreted for the authorities the meaning of the songs. One stated that the pajés were reconnecting to the ancient, sacred reality of the Other World of the divinities, of the great jaguar divinity. Plinio explained that the work of the pajé is a tradition of curing sickness: "Today there is the science and surgery of biomedicine, but we cannot forget our tradition. There is need for exchange between western biomedicine and the pajés, for the pajés know how to cure sicknesses that western medicine is incapable of curing." The ceremony concluded in a spirit of unity of purpose that consecrated the entire project of the House of Shamans' Knowledge, Malikai Dapana, a foundational experience that has to be nurtured in order to continue.

On the morning of the following day, the Living Treasure award was presented to Mandu; the new Shamans' House also received an album of photos of all Baniwa pajés of the Northwest Amazon; a photo taken in 1959 of a dabukuri held between the villages of Uapui and Seringa Rupitá (which, in 1977, moved downriver to the old settlement of Ukuki where they built what is now the largest settlement in the region); and an album of reproductions of ancient maps, drawings, early photos of Baniwa villages and families (from the 1920s to the present), and various individuals important to their history. The last was intended not only as a pedagogical tool but also as a way of "bringing the ancestors closer to us," as one Baniwa schoolteacher—who requested the album long before the inauguration ceremony—stated.

Following these presentations, I asked Mandu to reflect on how life had changed from the times of the malocas, when the elders would bless everything at every moment possible: "I speak to you, my people, we don't see these things anymore," he said, "but it is good that the dances and ceremonies continue to be performed, to remember that people still live by the traditions of the ancestors, so that those ways of life, while changed, will not be forgotten. Today there is a great danger of using the traditions incorrectly and even losing those traditions, but people should not be sad. It is through such projects as the School of Shamans' Knowledge that people will have a new space, in which to hold the dance-festivals, the Kwaipan, and other events."

It is my and the Foundation's hope that the coordinators of the House will now create new projects related to shamanic art and healing, exploring ways in which western biomedical knowledge and the metaphysics of jaguar shamanism can mutually benefit from each other. A film recently produced in 2010 by Mandu's daughter on the making of pariká, showed the entire school of apprentices, consisting of Mandu's sons and grandsons, along with Plinio and José Felipe engaged in the making of the sacred snuff, with each of the principal pajés expressing his thoughts on the necessity for continuing the traditions of the pajés. This is the kind of cultural commentary that is crucial for the objective of keeping the traditions alive.

By honoring the place of the creation of the universe for all Baniwa, we have drawn attention to the profound importance of shamanic knowledge and power, which, after all, had its beginning there. Whether the various cultural centers that have emerged in Baniwa territory over the past decade will eventually form a single body, only time will tell.

Conclusion

In August 2010, when this book was in its early stages, an historic advance in favor of the protection of indigenous knowledge—in particular, shamanism and the sacred traditions related to "Yurupary"—was announced by the Colombian government. This measure was acclaimed by one unidentified anthropologist as "quite an enlightened way to deal with issues of bio-cultural diversity in Amazonia and of safeguarding Jaguar Shamanism for all the right reasons." According to the Resolution "Lista Representativa de Patrimonio Cultural Inmaterial del ámbito Nacional" (Bogotá, DC),

Hee Yaia ~Kubua Baseri Keti Oka, the *Curing-Knowledge Words of the Jaguar Knowers of Yurupari*, condenses sacred knowledge that was given to us from the beginning to take care of our territory and life, and is manifest through rituals, dances and chants, management of sacred places, elements and sacred plants. This is the cultural manifestation that is being strengthened internally and that this decree intends to protect.

[*Hee Yaia ~Kubua Baseri Keti Oka, el* Conocimiento-Palabra Curativo de los Sabedores Jaguares de Yurupari, *condensa el conocimiento sagrado que desde el origen nos fue dado para cuidar el territorio y la vida, y se manifiesta por medio de rituales, danzas y oratorias, el manejo de lugares sagrados, de elementos y plantas sagradas. Esta es la manifestación cultural que se está fortaleciendo internamente y que se pretende proteger.*]

In the same spirit, this book has sought to document the jaguar shaman traditions among the Baniwa of the Aiary River but in such a way that it supports the case for the declaration of the Baniwa "Yurupary" tradition as "cultural patrimony" that can likewise be protected by international law on indigenous knowledge. (See also *Traditional Knowledge of the Jaguar Shamans of Yuruparí* on YouTube.com.)

In the chapters of this book, I have presented the principal religious functions in Baniwa culture, summarized in Table 1. These functions are complementary yet distinct in their "knowledge and power," interconnected as a "nexus," each taught or given by the creator deities and great spirits to humans through which humans would be able to sustain the cosmos throughout time. These functions are cumulative such that it is possible for a single person to exercise the roles of priestly chanter, jaguar shaman, and dance leader. The sorcerer, by definition, is always an enemy Other, an outsider who, paradoxically, may be or become an "insider" from an Other group. Exchanging wives provides the basis for making alliances among families of different phratries, but it also has the potential for prolonging serious disputes among affines (*nalimathana*).

In the literature on Amazonian shamans, the duo of healing shaman and sorcerer has most often been studied from the point of view that they are a single person characterized as a morally "ambiguous" figure, the *pajé*. Among the Baniwa, as among other peoples such as the Patamuna and Warao (Whitehead and Wilbert, in Whitehead and Wright 2004), however, the two functions are embodied in distinct figures, mortal enemies forever at odds with each other, until one is eliminated. The differences in knowledge and power between the two are expressed by an inversion: what one seeks to construct, the other seeks to destroy by taking away the other's life force. The pajé's main stated objective is to heal, to restore wholeness, health, and well-being to a sick person's heart-soul and thus return the person to the community. Pajés certainly can learn the "advanced knowledge" for killing and be hired to do so, although they prefer to rely on external sorcerers to perform this task. Also, the pajé's knowledge of killing seems to be directed exclusively at pajés of other phratries, and not at enemies within their own phratry.

The sorcerer's objective, however, is perceived as retribution for the loss of a kinsperson by sorcery or for a felt imbalance in ideally "egalitarian" relations, killing someone who is seen as having an excess of power (social status, prestige, material wealth, political recognition).

The healing shaman and priestly chanter duo complement each other in all respects and in many cases they are the same person. There is no clear sense among northern Arawak-speaking peoples of how one is "vertical" and the other "horizontal" as has been argued for the Tukanoan shamans (Hugh-Jones 1996; Viveiros de Castro 2002), neither in the sacred stories nor in practice. A jaguar shaman can accumulate the powers and knowledge of healing and protection along with the priestly chants, for both are forms of protective shamanism for transitions that society must undergo. Both are considered malikai, shamanic power and knowledge.

The Baniwa jaguar shamans consider themselves to be healers and warriors whose bodies have accumulated malikai from the "Other World" and manifested the most complete transformation into a "jaguar shaman spirit." Their office is to restore the well-being of those who seek their services and, beyond that, the entire cosmos. They attack other pajés as part of their constant struggle to defend their peoples' territory and resources. They are deeply engaged in conflicts among affinal phratries or between "enemy Others" (distantly related Arawak-speaking peoples, most Tukanoan-speaking peoples, Makuan peoples).

The priestly chanters are learned "savants" who have acquired malikai in the form of encyclopedic, canonical knowledge of the spirit world that is necessary in rites of passage for the reproduction of the entire universe and the transmission of the ancestral ways of life to new generations. They are generally senior elders. Given the nature of their function, they are less likely to be engaged in the power struggles that characterize the relations among jaguar shamans of different phratries or distantly related peoples.

Between the jaguar shamans and the priestly chanters, the differences in knowledge and power are based on two ways of world-making: the chanters bring the ancestral powers of the Other World into This World of the living, remembering in their "thought-voyages" how This World "opened up" to its present size through the transformative power of the jaguar song. The jaguar shamans, for their part, become jaguar shaman spirit others in order to recover souls in the Other World, bringing them back into This World, and reintegrating them with the bodies of patients. Both functions require the transformative jaguar function. The jaguar shamans' vision of the Other World all depends on the "opening up" of the Other World, knowledge of the shape-shifting characteristics of the "sicknesses" the pajé takes from the Other World during cures, and the constant interrelation between the conditions of This World and the powers of the Other World.

It is through the jaguar shamans' powers—of being warrior shamans—that This World is protected from harm. Through thought-journeys and powerful naming processes, the priestly chanter does what the jaguar shaman, armed with a complex system of defense, does through his journeying to the Other World and directly meeting the eternal spirits. Both are "guardians of the cosmos" and of This World, ensuring their followers that they and the world will return to health, that they will be immune from the dangers the world presents, and that society will continue to be reproduced and transmitted over time. The most knowledge-able of the "savants" consult with "Dio"; as true *kanhenkedali*, the "wise people" are by far the strongest of the protectors.

The kanhenkedali accumulate the functions of the healer sha-man, the priestly shaman, and dance leader, but they add another dimension of moral leadership and direction in times of conflict and disorder. Their ideologies are aimed at strengthening and "animating" (*kathimana*) the community and its traditions, for without these, society will be destroyed by "the enemy" other. The enemy is often the white man, but can also be internal, the affine or the sorcerer, which sacred stories confirm have existed since primordial times.

The Baniwa must, I think, consider it a gift from "Dio" that such "wise people" exist, because there are so many concerns they have over the changes that have befallen them, from the time of their ancestors until today. In the film *Las Advertencias de Mandu*, it was clear that the society of Maroa had gone very far along the way to transforming into what anthropologist Omar Gonzalez-Ñáñez called "this surreal condition of the indigenous cultures of Latin America." In the film there was hardly anything left of "traditional culture." All had transformed into a rural Latin American way of life. Mandu da Silva had a great respect for the culture of the alto Guainia, because some of their closest phratric kin live in that region and that is where he obtained his most advanced power and knowledge. That is why he went to warn the people of the danger of losing everything in their tradition because of "the enemy" (in this case, the corruptive influences of local Latin American cul-ture). Mandu had a special relationship with the jaguar shaman Macanilla. "They were like blood relatives." Macanilla was the last living jaguar shaman among the Kuripako-Baniva cultures traditionally from that region.

In his late 1980s, Macanilla was a highly respected pajé; only he had managed to avoid all corrupting influences coming from the whites, who had bought off other pajés to do their political dirty work. Macanilla has since left This World and perhaps only one follower will continue the tradition.

Among the villages of the upper Aiary, we see that the traditions continue to be well known and practiced: the Kwaipan and pudali celebrated according to the ritual calendars. There is pride in shamanic treatments: it is widely believed that only the shamans of the upper Aiary can extract "poison" and cure other serious sicknesses; western medicine has its limitations in that region.

While their culture and society have transformed greatly over the past thirty years, I believe that those communities continue to represent a stronghold against the deterioration of cultural conditions. When the senior elders of today have gone, they will have left a strong enough legacy for the younger elders to remember and carry on. For the Baniwa, the old ways of living have found new expressions in festival dancing, training of pajés, and the most sacred rites. In this, they differ in fundamental ways from the evangelical communities of the middle Içana, many of whom are staunch followers of fundamentalist evangelicalism or the new entrepreneurial culture that has arisen over the past fifteen years.

RECAPPING WHAT WE HAVE DONE IN THIS BOOK

Chapter 1 introduced Mandu da Silva, jaguar-shaman of the Aiary River, one of a handful of these religious specialists (if not the only one) left among all the Arawak-speaking peoples of the Northwest Amazon. His biography, recorded and translated by his daughter, demonstrates the strength of his perseverance in becoming a pajé and resisting outside challenges. Mandu's experiences in receiving shamanic malikai were of deliberate spiritual encounter and acquisition of power, of great suffering that marked his life and career. He was respected as a great chief in the 1970s. Today he is passing on his extensive knowledge to his sons, daughter, and grandsons. He is transmitting the knowledge of all his experiences of the Other World, "giving the songs," showing to the apprentices the "map" that he has made of the Other World.

Much of the whole situation involving actual sorcery accusations is explained in the stories of the constant struggles between Nhiãperikuli and the "animal" tribes of sorcerers. If someone today asks, "How did sorcery come into the world? Has it always been with us?" the immediate answer would be the sacred story of Kuwai. "So what can be done about it? Will we always have it?" The answer is more often than not affirmative, which means that the sacred story and shamanism have great legitimacy among the Baniwa of the Aiary.

The knowledge of Kuwai is at the very foundation of Baniwa cosmology, society, and shamanism. It is marked everywhere in their territory with petroglyphs, reminding the living about the deeds of the ancestors, which should never be forgotten. The universe and the "unseen" spiritual connections among all "worlds" are known through the sacred stories, the pajés' songs, the patterned stories of their voyages to the Other World, and the experiential knowledge pajés communicate every time they undertake a cure. Each level has its inhabitants, with distinct powers and features, which altogether constitute an order of knowledge and power. The occult nature of Kuwai is a constant reminder that the Other World is eternally "there, " but access to it is controlled by the pajés because of its dangerous power to "make holes," i.e., open excessively those who see it.

Shamanic knowledge and power and its hierarchy are manifest in the order of the upper worlds, beginning with the light that reveals and the vision that creates (Nhiãperikuli), the great "Spirit of Power" of the pajés' substances (Dzuliferi), the spirit of "misfortune" who brought death into the world, and the creator father's heart-soul, composed of sicknesses as well as the voices and sounds that are responsible for the growth of This World.

On the plane of This World, the women left the mark of their powers bathing the world with the rivers; they became the mothers of "Other peoples" (indigenous and nonindigenous) who surround the Baniwa—both necessary to the reproduction of Baniwa society, yet potential enemies who can do harm. According to the men, the women's shamanic powers became allied to the white man's powerful "industrial" knowledge, thus producing the Baniwas' most treacherous enemy but also whites who are some of their staunchest allies.

Three key notions stand out in the stories the Hohodene Baniwa tell of their ancestors. (1) The "wise men and women" were "powerful in knowledge" (*kanhenkedali tapame, kanhenkedali*); that is, they were not only jaguar shamans and not only "savants" but also moral counselors for all of society who warned of impending dangers. (2) The "enemies" include "affinal" tribes, the "whites," and a host of spirits that attack humans all the time, giving them sickness and misfortune. These "enemies" are usually characterized as cunning, dangerous, and destructive. They can be outwitted by "trickery" but also by the "sábios' knowledge," which derives from the primordial light of revelation, while the enemy's power derives from darkness and secrecy. (3) The state of "happiness" or a "world of happiness" (*kathimakwe*) is a much-desired place in which people celebrate their dance festivals, with all of its "harmony" and "liveliness" (*katimanadali, katimanã*) and live well together.

In the stories of the primordial times, the miniature universe consisted of the self-generated "child of the universe" and the "celestial umbilical cord" in a vast expanse of Nothingness. Then, alone, or with his "brothers," the orphan child brought the first ancestors of humanity into being, bringing them out of the hole at Hipana and giving them places in the world that was still in formation.

Suddenly the affinal tribes appear in the stories as villains, yet, by the same token, the affines were the source of change, making the universe a dynamic place in motion. The differences persisted between "Identity" and "Alterity," Us and Them, for the original "universe-child" had a wife whose father gave him the basket of Night. Differences between kin and affines coincide with the beginning of temporal differences between night and day. The stasis at the birth of the world ("the sun did not move") is now engaged in change (which came into being as the result of a radical break from the initial condition). The First Long Night was, in the pajés' point of view, the first catastrophe (the first "end of the world"), that Nhiãperikuli himself brought about, purposefully, intentionally, as it was he who saved his people from the disaster.

Stories abound concerning Nhiãperikuli's struggles to create an orderly world in which there is at least a balance between the affinal tribes and all kinspeople. Yet balance remained an unresolved issue, for there were just as many losses of kinspeople as there were among the affines, enemy others. It is not surprising then that the key relations between "Us" and "Them," "This World" and the "Other World" are the domain of the jaguar shamans. At stake in these relations is the question of continuity; the "enemy other" brings change that can disrupt the sacred bonds of ancestral continuity. The only way to live with that dilemma is if the dangerous and "wild" powers of the "other" to change could somehow be transformed and embodied into the bonds of ancestral continuity, as the sacred instruments.

The two principles had to be mixed in some way; Kuwai was the embodiment of this mixture (*linupa*): a totally "liminal being," in between "open" and "closed," constantly transforming into Other beings (or becoming his own "shadow-soul"): Inyaime, a demonic predator that can assume any form; a celestial jaguar whose abode is in the Other World but whose material "body" lies in pieces hidden at the bottom of the rivers in This World; a tree animal (sloth or monkey), signifying continence and gluttony whose music embodies the most fundamental powers to make things grow; a mysterious ancestral power that is treated with much awe, deep respect, and even fear.

One jaguar shaman drew the body of Kuwai as a totally perforated young boy (see appendix B), whose appendages are open with holes corresponding to the sounds of each pair of the sacred flutes.

The great spirit owner of sickness, Kuwai, "makes holes" in the initiates, which is to say, they become filled with the life force of their ancestors, which penetrates the pores of their bodies through the music of the sacred flutes and trumpets as well as the whips that "make them grow more quickly."

In the great fire that burned Kuwai, much shamanic knowledge and power was incorporated into society to be transmitted to all future generations. Those generations now have the responsibility of continuing to transmit that wisdom.

The traces of the extraordinary knowledge and power of the before times are seen today in the mythscape, heard in the sacred stories and music of the flutes and trumpets and sung in the music specific to initiation rites. The extensive litany of initiation chants remembers the voyages of Kuwai in which the men pursued the women who played the instruments throughout the world, opening it up to its present size.

The Kuwai traditions in their entirety and the guardians of the sacred instruments—the jaguar shamans, ceremonial leaders, and priestly chanters—reveal a complexity of religious knowledge and power that von Humboldt and others long after him, including Claude Lévi-Strauss, admired and considered to be of an extraordinary and unusually dense expression. At the time von Humboldt wrote, the knowledge and power of the jaguar shamans could very well have formed a complex metaphysics associated with a political, religious, and social organization, the likes of which are comparable only to chiefly/priestly societies such as the now-extinct Manao of the middle Rio Negro, the Achagua of the llanos in Venezuela, or even theocratic chiefdoms of the Orinoco.

The key question of the transmission of the jaguar shaman tradition is connected to the vitality of the other sources of "power and knowledge," the priestly chanters, the dance leaders, and the sorcerers. At the time of this writing, the dance owners' tradition has for many years been going through a strong comeback in several communities of the Aiary. The knowledge of the priestly chanters can only be found among the communities of the upper Aiary where the whole jaguar shaman tradition still has the possibility of continuing.

Outside of Mandu, who has had a great deal of his knowledge taped and filmed, at least one of the remaining pajés —who has been trained by both his stepfather and Mandu, has demonstrated his capacity to overcome sorcery and his determination to keep the House of Shamans' Knowledge going. Ercilia, Mandu's daughter, is likewise committed to the future of this project. Thus it is likely that Hipana and the upper Aiary communities will continue to be the center for shamanic traditions as they have been for many generations. Sorcery, as we've seen, can appear anywhere and is complicated by new forms introduced from the urban area.

As the histories of the "wise men and women" have shown, there is still a hope that another "sábio" will appear in their midst. One whose powers and knowledge prove to be greater than the enemy/sorcerers, combining the wisdom of the ancestors with the stamina, perseverance, courage, and capacity of the warrior in outwitting the enemy. A defender of the traditions and a sentinel of forthcoming dangers, whose knowledge of the dance festivals and the all-important Kwaipan chants will lead Baniwa communities through the uncertainties of change.

Appendix 1

LETTER AUTHORIZING REPRODUCTIONS OF
KUWAI-KA WAMUNDANA AND OF PETROGLYPHS
AND MAPS OF UPPER GUAINIA, VENEZUELA

AUTORIZACIÓN

Mérida, 14 de mayo de 2004
Por medio de la presente autorizo al profesor **Robin M. Wright,**
docente e investigador del Department of Religion, University
of Florida, Gainesville, Estado de Florida, USA para que haga las
transcripciones y traducciones que considere necesarias de mi libro
las cuales serán usadas en su libro *Mysteries of the Jaguar Shamans
of the Northwest Amazon* próximo a publicarse.
   Profesor Omar González-Ñáñez
   Doctorado en Antropología
   Universidad de Los Andes
   Mérida, Venezuela

[Editor's Translation:
By way of this letter, I authorize Professor Robin M. Wright, professor and researcher of the Department of Religion, University
of Florida, Gainesville, State of Florida, USA, to make transcrip-
tions and translations of whatever he considers necessary from
my book, *Las literaturas indígenas Maipure-arawakas de los pueblos
Kurripako, Warekena y Baniva del estado Amazonas*, which will be
used in his book to be published, *Mysteries of the Jaguar Shamans
of the Northwest Amazon.*

Appendix 2

The Mysterious Body of Kuwai, a drawing originally made by a Baniwa shaman, formerly of the Aiary River, is reproduced below with enlargements of sections and English translations of the shaman's exegesis in Spanish (with permission of the anthropologist Omar González-Ñáñez, who assisted him in the drawing in appendix 1). As can be seen, Kuwai's body is full of holes out of which come flutes or trumpets, organized into pairs (except for Waliadoa, "Young Sister," which has three flutes, and the Mulito, "Frog," which is just one short flute). The music that comes from these holes—his "speech"—is that of ancestral animal songs (birds, fish, monkeys, and two land animals), which these ancestral beings sang as they emerged from the holes of the world center.

The creative and transformative breath blown through the bones (the flutes and trumpets) of the Kuwai flutes and trumpets is consistent with the idea of heart-soul and the bones of Nhiãperi-kuli. Kuwai Hekwapi (Kuwai world) is the heart-soul of the sun, his father—a powerful expression of the dynamic principles that reproduce the world and all life within it with every generation.

KUWAI-KA WAMUNDANA: WHERE THE SKY
ENDS, ONLY HE LIVES THERE, THIS KUWAI

The following are translations of all texts in boxes or otherwise connected to this drawing, which the artist and anthropologist added as exegesis for the drawing.

25. Drawing of Kuwai-ka Wamundana, "Black sloth–shadow-soul Kuwai," by jaguar shaman Luiz Gomez. (Reprinted from González-Ñáñez 2007, with permission of the author.)

"Kuwai's Heart-Soul. From there the
pajés suck out:
(1) *walama*, palm tree thorns
(2) *haikuita*, pointed stick of bow
wood
(3) *iraidalimi*, hemorrhage
(4) *Yúpinai*: *Umawali* (water spirits)
to suck out *mawari* pains in the
legs and arms."
"Our navel, *hwaipule* ... umbilicus /
from here you take out medicine to
cure those who have eaten raw fish.
The remedy is called *fiukali*."

LEFT SIDE OF KUWAI'S BODY

Aini (wasp) false name for *Dzawi-
napa* (Jaguar Bone) trumpet
2 *Dzawinapa-ka Kuwai* Great Jaguar
Trumpet
2 *Dápa* (*paca*) trumpets of Kuwai-ka
dápa
2 *Kawawirri-ka Kuwai* hawk
2 *Kuwai-ka Idzadapa* hawk
2 *Ipeku-ka Kuwai* night monkey
2 *chichi-ka Kuwai* black uacari
monkey
2 *Maaliawa or Maali-ka Kuwai*
white heron, young male initiate
3 *Waliadoa* daughters of Amaru,
young sister
2 *Dzáte—ka Kuwai* piapoco or
toucan

2 *Búbuli-ka Kuwai* guardian owl
1 *Mulitu-ka Kuwai* short flute, frog

AT THE CROWN OF KUWAI'S HEAD

Fur or hair of Kuwai, *Kuwai chikule*
(a kind of moriche fibre hair
(Tucum)
Jipada haleduli, white stone that
brings on headaches and pain in
the rest of the body
Hiuiathe, a snake with which sor-
cerers ruin the vision
Liwedaliku Kuwai, Kuwai's throat
These are the holes of Wamundana:

RIGHT SIDE OF KUWAI'S
BODY: FLUTE-NAMES

2 *Tuwiri-ka Kuwai* japú bird
2 *Túwa-ka Kuwai* woodpecker
2 *Kupjelá kúwai ka Taali-jwerri*
"bocachica" fish Kuwai
2 *Jáalu-ka Kúwai* white monkey
2 *Atine-ka* Kúwai trumpeter bird,
"grulla" (sp.) or jacamim
2 *Mámi-Ka* (or) *mámihwerri* grandfather wild partridge
Tuwiri Is the Kuwai of the
Hohodene and of All Other Kur-
ripakos. These Are the Trumpets
of Those Who Lead the Group
or Band of the Thirty-two Sacred
Flutes
(*Tuwiri* is the *japu* bird ...)

Notes

INTRODUCTION

1. The societies of the Northwest Amazon are known for their ceremonial hierarchies, especially among the Tukanoan-speaking peoples (see Goldman 1963; C. Hugh-Jones 1989; S. Hugh-Jones 1989; Chernela 1993). Given the long history of physical displacement in the region, there is little in-depth ethnography on the Arawak-speaking people's ceremonial hierarchies (except Journet 1995; Hill 1987). Vidal (1993, 1997, 2002) has proposed historical models of federations in early colonial history. Evangelicalism and the labor market were two factors that led to the disruption of regional phratric organizations.

2. Among the Tukanoan-speaking peoples, the *Yurupary* complex has been studied by G. Reichel-Dolmatoff (1989, 1996); Christine Jones (1989), and Stephen Hugh-Jones (1989), which are still classic studies on the Barasana version of the traditions, as are Irving Goldman's monographs on the Cubeo (1963, 2004).

1. "YOU ARE GOING TO SAVE MANY LIVES"

1. For the shaman, each kind of fish has an equivalent in the types of sicknesses that he will be able to cure. A swordfish, for example, with its needle-like jaws, is the equivalent of the *walama* darts that the shaman will use both to cure and to throw sickness against enemy shamans. If the apprentice doesn't catch anything, obviously he will not be a good pajé.

2. Bundles of leaves that have been blessed by the shaman are placed in a large pan of water. The shaman pours the water and leaves over the patient. Then, in the bundles of leaves that have fallen to the ground, he will look for the material form of the sickness: stone, thorn, hair, or a piece of wood. This is repeated several times to get rid of all trace of the sickness.

3. "Finalmente pude contactar a un amigo kurripaco de Victorino, en el Alto Guainía de venezuela. Nukitsinda kurripako se llama Alirio Tomás Yusuino quien ha trabajado antes conmigo. Yusuino me informó que en realidad el sitio se llama 'Guapa Sucia' y era una aldea que se localiza muy cerca del San Fernando de Atabapo, a 4 vueltas remontando el río Atabapo. Yusuino conoció el importante lugar pero afirma que ya está abandonado. Trataré de indagar más con él acerca de 'Guapa Sucia'. Seguramente Mandú y el payé 'Macanilla' estuvieron juntos en ese lugar. El payé 'Macanilla' o Laureano Gómez murió hace un año en Maroa. Era un kurripako-baniva que lamentablemente ya desaparecierón. Mandú también tuvo contacto con otro chamán kurripako que vívía en Maroa llamado 'Makana-dérri', Luis Gómez, quien también murió en Puerto Ayacucho hace dos años. Makana-dérri era nativo de Shibarú en el Isana" (pers. comm., Oscar González-Ñáñez, February 2010).

4. The Yoopinai (sometimes spelled Yúpinai) are spirits of the air, water, earth, and forest. They are plants, insects, and animals whose chief is the lizard, *dopo*, who is said to be a dwarf shaman with long and loose black hair, a gold necklace, and a huge cigar. Some shamans have actually seen the yoopinai chief in his proto-human form. Dzauinaipoa are three of the most important "sickness" things that pajés first learn to extract—stones, pieces of wood, and darts.

5. This sickness marked the beginning of a long struggle against what physicians diagnosed as hepatitis. Mandu diagnosed the sickness as *Inyaime mepékam*, a kind of *hiuiathi* (sorcery). An enemy sorcerer is responsible for this sickness by blowing the words of the spell onto the victim or his belongings. It produces weakness in the bones, pains in the chest, in the body, and weakness to the point of being just skin and bones. Mandu said there had been an ailment in Uapui several years earlier that affected many people with severe pain and swelling of the legs. It began *assim mesmo* ("just like that," the usual diagnosis when no one really knows), "it was a sorcerer who gave it" (the other main explanation), and "it seemed like the bones were broken." Mandu was hospitalized several times but never seemed to improve. As a result he lost a great deal of his mobility and could only walk with much difficulty and with help, especially of his daughter Ercilia,

who returned to Uapui after many years, working as a domestic maid in Manaus in order to take care of her parents.

6. Mandu's great difficulty coincided with mine: I was hospitalized during the same period for seven surgeries, the last two being caused by a hospital infection on my right leg. The surgeries involved revisions on a bilateral hip replacement that were done in 1977, shortly after I had returned to the United States from my doctoral field research. Both of us temporarily lost our ability to walk.

7. Lately Ercilia has expressed her worries about what she will do when her parents die. She is now in her forties, and she has never married. Over the past decade, she has been my principal intermediary. With the project to create a House of Shamans' Knowledge, she decided to try to become an apprentice to her own father. It is perfectly possible for a woman to become a pajé, although she has to observe restrictions during her menstrual period. Beyond that, she now has reached a point in her training in which the apprentice has to ingest "medicine"—small stones, pieces of wood, and thorns—that will grow in the body, transforming into a shaman's body. She is uncertain whether she will continue because she says this is the most difficult part of the apprentice's training. Following the ingestion of the remedies, she must then learn how to extract them from the bodies of patients. It is at this point that the apprentice acquires the "mouth of Kuwai"—like the mouth of a jaguar.

2. MANDU'S APPRENTICESHIP

1. Several ways of inhaling exist: a bifurcated bird bone can be used to snuff the pariká from the pajé's own hand; if the shamans work as a group, one blows the pariká into the nostrils of the other, and during training, the pajé may take a pinch between his fingers and snuff it directly into his nostril.

2. These songs appear to be like the *icaros* of the Ecuadorian shamans. The psychoactive DMT here again brings the spirit world into contact with the shamans.

3. How the image of the giant sloth, which actually did exist in Western Amazonia thousands of years ago, came to be the avatar for Kuwai is partly explained by its animal habits, yet it must be recognized as an image

appropriate to other dimensions of Baniwa religious symbolism, which will be explored in detail in chapters 6–8.

4. Here is another link between the shamans of the upper Aiary and the Piaroa shamans. Mandu says the Piaroa have a greater knowledge of "how to kill from a distance," so those Piaroa are sometimes called upon when a family wishes to avenge the loss of someone whom they believe was killed intentionally by sorcery.

5. Similar to the way, perhaps, many Native North Americans express their pride as war veterans, an adaptation of warrior traditions.

3. "YOU WILL SUFFER ALONG OUR WAY"

1. The Universidade Federal de Pernambuco has a collection of photos by the famed ethnologist Curt Nimuendajú, some of which had been previously housed at the Göteborg Museum, showing villages of the Aiary River in 1928, including those at the mouth of the Miriti River, the upper Aiary River settlements of Djuremawa, and the old settlement of the Waliperedakenai chief Mandu at Cururuquara.

2. The title of "master" or "chief," *thayri*, in this world refers to phratric chiefs, that is, the eldest brother of the highest-ranking community in a given phratry. In the past, these chiefs had the power of war leaders who could organize war parties involving the communities of a phratry against an enemy group. Today the power of the peacetime chiefs or *capitáos* of the communities does not extend much beyond their communities. Issues of resource use and land use of another phratry's territory, however, must be negotiated with the phratry chief. Failure to do so, in the past, meant war; today, it results in sorcery assaults. The phratry is understood to have collective "ownership" of a river, which includes the river banks where settlements are made and the immediate surroundings with garden land. Each community is also the "owner" of a part of the phratry's territory, and the "capitáo" represents the community in any intercommunity event, affair, or dispute.

3. The inevitable result of all his extravagances are foreseen in many of the Baniwa myths. Characters who have not undergone the proper shamanic blessing of food before resuming normal activities related to eating meals will most certainly get sick, lose control, and die.

4. They have been compared to the *kanaima* sorcerers among the Carib-speaking peoples of the Guyanas (about whom see Whitehead 2002), although I believe there are important differences between the two practices.

5. In the 1950s, most of the Baniwa and Kuripako of Brazil, Colombia, and Venezuela converted to Protestant evangelicalism, introduced by a North American fundamentalist missionary named Sophie Muller. Baniwa shamans had prophesied that someone would appear in their midst who was powerful enough to resist the attacks of sorcerers. She appeared and was put to the test; she was poisoned but did not die, and for years she was seen by her followers as being like their own prophets of the past. (Baniwa women can be shamans and prophetesses.) (André Baniwa, in *Uma História de Plantas e Curas*, 2005 film.) The shamans of the upper Aiary River, however, resisted her demand that they abandon the ways of their ancestors and urged their communities also to resist. In their eyes, she was not the fulfillment of their hopes and did not have the power to say the world would come to an end — only true jaguar shamans have that power to consult with the deities in order to know that.

6. The evangelicals say that, since there is no story of how Nhiãperikuli abandoned humanity (that they know of, at least), then it is highly likely that he is still here, in This World, and may appear at any moment to save them (Xavier Leal, 2008).

4. CREATION, COSMOLOGY, AND ECOLOGICAL TIME

1. In Reichel-Dolmatoff's 1976 article, "Cosmology as Ecological Analysis," the importance of shamanic cosmologies to sustainable development was demonstrated clearly and concisely. This book provides numerous instances in which the shamans' ecological knowledge could be of enormous use to sustainable development projects.

2. The order in which the phratric ancestors emerged — according to the jaguar shaman Matteo, narrator of this episode — begins with a people called Dayzo-dakenai, whom Silvia Vidal (1987) identified as one of the main phratries of the Arawak-speaking Piapoco who today live in the region of the Vichada River in Venezuela and Colombia. According to Hohodene traditions, the Dayzo-dakenai migrated many centuries ago from the Içana/Aiary drainage north to their present homelands. Following

the Dayzo-dakenai, the Hohodene emerged along with their "servant" sib, the Hipatanene (people of the river foam). Following the Hohodene, the Walipere-dakenai of the Içana River emerged with all of their nine sibs; the Kadapolithana, a prominent Dzauinai sib; the Cubeo (Puwewaya) of the Querary River and upper Aiary with four sibs; and finally the Dethana (or Dessano), who today live in the Uaupés River drainage among Tukanoan-speaking peoples. Both the Cubeo and the Dessano today speak Tukanoan languages, although their religious traditions appear more similar in some ways to Arawak-speaking peoples or a hybridized version of the two cultures (see Goldman 2004; Wright 2009e).

3. The phrases spoken today for the cardinal directions of sunrise and sunset are "where the sun enters" and "where the sun goes out."

4. Journet (1995) mentions that one way the Kuripako of Colombia represent the "orphan father Nhiãperikuli" is as a five-fingered manioc plant, which is consistent with the fact that manioc is a self-regenerating plant that can be found growing wild in the forest but is equally domesticable. He also suggests that Nhiãperikuli's vengeance against the animals can be thought of as the retribution of the plant world (agriculture over hunting as ways of life?) against the predatory animals that dominated the universe until his reappearance.

5. When the sloth descends to evacuate, it digs a hole in which to defecate and then buries it. By covering its waste, there is no smell to give away its position to a jaguar (Mendel 1985). Here we recall the story of the beginning of the universe, as told by Luis, that the first earth was Kuwai's feces deposited by him as a child that became a rock (Wright 2009d, 1998). The sloth is an excellent swimmer, and during the major rainy season it descends the trees to the ground; thus the sloth, like Kuwai, is a being capable of living in several worlds at different moments of the seasonal cycles. His actions of ascending and descending the trees to the ground recall perfectly the actions of the spirit of initiation, Kuwai.

6. The plants gain shelter and sunlight in a forest that is normally kept dark by the vast canopies, while the sloth gains camouflage, which helps protect it from many of its predators (Mendel 1985).

7. Ca. 1° 12'30" N; 70° 04'20" W, just below Mitu Rapids. Today, this place is called Santa Cruz de Waracapuri or Santa Cruz de los Cubeos. It

is claimed by the Cubeo people as their origin place, although today those higher-ranking Cubeo who once inhabited the area around it have moved upstream to a place called Mandi, above Mitu Rapids. (Penha Marques, pers. comm., June 2010.) All of the area around Uaracapory was Arawak until the Tukanoan-speaking Cubeo migrated into it and began intermarrying with the Arawak there.

8. The corpus of Baniwa stories refers to other important beings which are too numerous to mention and perhaps not directly related to the topics of shamans that occupy this book. Many have to do with certain kinds of sicknesses and their prevention. More than explaining their "origin," these stories provide orientations of how people should live in this world in the present and the obstacles they must face in realizing their ideals.

5. MYTHSCAPES AS LIVING MEMORIES

1. This notion of "mythscape" is similar to E. Reichel's notion of "cosmoscape," referring to her work in the Columbian Northwest Amazon, which she explains in her 2009 paper, "The Landscape in the Cosmoscape": "The landscape is part of the cosmoscape where the position of each tribe is negotiated through material and spiritual dynamics to periodically maintain the ethno-eco-cosmic linkages." To analyze all of the issues she raises goes beyond the scope of this book; the chapters where we make major reference to cosmology do present the landscape as a cosmoscape and mythscape. Regarding the impact of globalization and regional development on shamanism, the evidence we present does allow us to examine the relation of shamanic cosmologies and issues of "socio-environmental sustainability" in chapter 9. This will become clear in contrasting the sustainable development complexes introduced by the region's NGOs and shamanic cosmology. Santos-Granero has published instigating work (1998, 2004) about the "sacred landscapes" of southern Arawakan peoples (Yanesha, Amuesha). Thanks to the work of González-Ñáñez and the NGO Etnollanos and the traditional knowledge of the Baniwa and Kuripako themselves, we now have a better mapping of sacred sites for the Northwest Amazon region.

2. In a way, this idea of a "warning" of breakdown or imminent disorder and chaos recalls the idea of "entropy" or "energy loss" that Reichel-Dolmatoff discussed in "Cosmology as Ecological Analysis" (1976).

6. THE BIRTH OF KUWAI

1. In shamanic voyages to the Other World, recall that Mandu stated it was Kuwai who sent down his umbilical cord for Mandu in order for him to traverse the "mouth of the Other World" right into Kuwai's village.

7. DEATH AND REGENERATION IN KWAIPAN

1. This species is found in the Venezuelan and Brazilian Amazon, growing to heights of 125 m, and the nuts are used for cooking oil or butter.

2. Also relevant to this image is that, in Baniwa belief, Inyaime is a demon spirit that traps the souls of the deceased by calling them to its house. During their journeys to the houses of the dead in the Other World, the souls guide their canoe through a rapids where there is a trap, Inyaime Kurara, that can trick the soul into following another path down to its village. There the souls of Baniwa who have done some "wrong" (i.e., sorcery, envy, jealousy, disobeyed restrictions) in this world will go. It is a place where there is no water, and the souls are constantly begging for it. When the soul reaches the point of the trip, the pajé guides it on to the houses of the dead.

3. There is a story about the "purakali children," the children of Kaali, who—disobeying orders-ate *raw* fish and began to waste away. Their body parts transformed into fruits, then fish, then a japu bird, (which happens to be the animal ancestor of the Hohodene of the Uaraná River) until one last drop of saliva falls from his mouth. According to the story:

> he began hearing a loud buzzing in his ears; he saw the "white Kuwai" (Kuwai haaledzuli) and its alter, the white surubím catfish. He thought he was dying, and he called out: "Father, I am dying. I have wasted away (*nupurakawaaa*)." He called and called, as the cicadas today call: "Fa-a-a-ather, I have wasted away." He transformed into a red japu bird and then a black japu, and as they sang, their saliva fell to the ground.

The "wasting-away" sickness exists, it seems, as a startling warning to people undergoing transition to obey the norms of fasting.

4. At the risk of overinterpreting, the "death" of Kuwai is a "false death" in one sense because his spirit remains alive forever in the Other World for the shamans to consult, while his body remains in This World, as the sacred flutes and trumpets, hidden in a stream near the village. If humanity lost its

immortality due to the error of Mawerikuli (the first person to die), then the story of Kuwai can be said to be humanity's regaining of immortality through the ancestral flutes. At his death, Mawerikuli's heart-soul separated from his bones, which fell in a heap with *exactly* the same onomatopoeic sound of falling pieces as when Kuwai's paxiúba fell to the ground. It is this clue which makes it possible to link the two stories and to see how Kuwai is the "solution" to the loss of the connection to the heart-soul occasioned by Mawerikuli's death.

8. STRUGGLE FOR POWER AND KNOWLEDGE

1. Women know a great deal about the shamanic traditions, as I discovered through conversations with Ercilia, who translated information from her mother, Dona Flora, and her sister, who made a point of participating in discussion sessions I would have with the shamans during the summer of the year 2000. These were exciting moments because both the "true pajés" and elder women engaged in these discussions. Elder women perform the kalidzamai chanting, and they make the sacred ceramic plates in which the pepper and salt are blessed. A separate painted plate was traditionally made to hold fish and the manioc bread for the initiate's first meal after the fast. These sacred plates of Amaru are invoked in the opening lines of the kalidzamai chants.

2. Amaru's shamanic powers are known also for two important kinds of sickness and medicines. She has several kinds of sorcery that only women "own" or manipulate.

3. Those of the earth are called *kewakamalinai* and can enter the body of the father of a newborn and suck out the insides of his bones if the father fails to observe those boundaries. They include various kinds of worms (called *majuba* in the local lingua geral). The Yoopinai of the waters are called *umaualinai*, sucuriu (pl.), who also are dangerous to families passing through periods of seclusion, because they enter the body, causing swelling and weakness in the bones.

4. This is not to say that Kuwai is Dzuliferi, who is always described as an "ancient, ancient being" from the distant past, while Kuwai is represented as a "wild being of the forest" in drawings made by the Hohodene. It does show that—in this story—among the ancestral, agnatic group of divine

consanguineal kin, one brother can transform into the other's "shadow-soul" or even transform into the other kin at will. Narrators equated Kaali with Nhiãperikuli, for example; however, the main difference between these two is that while Kaali is Master of the Earth symbolized by his ceremonial dance rattle, Nhiãperikuli cannot be represented as one single being. He is, as Mandu said, in all places at once and appears at the rituals, which is what makes them so sacred.

Bibliography

Arhem, Kaj. 1998. "Powers of Place: Landscape, Territory, and Local Belonging in Northwest Amazonia." In *Local Belonging*, ed. N. Lovell, 78–102. London: Routledge.

———. 2001. *Makuna: Portrait of an Amazonian People*. Washington DC: Smithsonian Institution Press.

Atkinson, Jane M. 1992. "Shamanisms Today." *Annual Review of Anthropology*, 307–30. Palo Alto: Annual Reviews.

Barabas, Alicia M. 1987. *Utopias Indias*. México: Enlace-Grijalbo.

Benson, E. P. 1998. "The Lord, the Ruler: Jaguar Symbolism in the Americas." In *Icons of Power: Feline Symbolism in the Americas*, ed. N. J. Saunders, 53–76. London: Routledge.

Berkes, Fikret. 1999. *Sacred Ecology: Traditional Ecological Knowledge and Resource Management*. Philadelphia: Taylor and Francis.

Boyer, Veronique. 1999. "Les Baniwa Évangelique Parlent des Missionaires Protestants: Sofia et ses Successeurs." Toulouse: Atéliers de Caravelle, no. 18, Pp. 83–99.

Bruzzi Alves da Silva, Alcionilio A. 1977. *Civilizáçáo Indígena do Uaupés*. Roma Librerio Ateneo Salesiano.

Buchillet, Dominique. 2004. "Sorcery Beliefs, Transmission of Shamanic Knowledge, and Therapeutic Practice among the Desana of the Upper Rio Negro." In *In Darkness and Secrecy*, ed. N. Whitehead and R. Wright, 109–31. Durham: Duke University Press.

Carrasco, David. 1990. *Religions of Mesoamerica: Cosmovision and Ceremonial Centers*. San Francisco: Harper and Row.

Centro de Comunidades Indigenas da Bacia do Rio Aiary (CECIBRA). N.d. "Proposta para a Revitalização Cultural entre os Baniwa do Rio Aiary." Ms.

Chaumeil, Jean-Pierre, et al. 2005. *Chamanismo y Sacrificio: Perspectivas arqueologicas y etnologicas en sociedades indigenas de America del Sur.* Bogotá: Banco de la Republica/FIAN.

Chaumeil, Jean-Pierre, and J. D. Hill. 2011. *Burst-of-Breath: Indigenous Ritual Wind Instruments in Lowland South America.* Lincoln: University of Nebraska Press.

Chernela, Janet. 1988. "Righting History in the Northwest Amazon: Myth, Structure, and History in Arapaço Narrative." In *Rethinking History and Myth: Indigenous South American Perspectives on the Past*, ed. Jonathan D. Hill, 35–49 Urbana: University of Illinois Press.

———. 1993. *The Wanano Indians of the Brazilian Amazon: A Sense of Space.* Austin: University of Texas Press.

Chernela, Janet, and Eric Leed. 2002. "As perdas da história: Identidade e violência num mito Arapaço do alto Rio Negro." In *Pacificando o Branco: Cosmologias do contato no Norte-Amazônico*, ed. Bruce Albert and Alcida Ramos, 469–86. São Paulo: UNESP.

Cornelio, J., et al. 1999. *Waferinaipe Ianheke: A Sabedoria dos Nossos Antepassados.* Serie Narradores do Alto Rio Negro. São Gabriel da Cachoeira: ACIRA/FOIRN.

Costa, Yara. 2009. "Análise das Danças Baniwa: uma reflexão sobre a dinâmica identitária e cultural dos povos indígenas da Amazônia." M.A. thesis in Artistic Dance Performance, Universidade Técnica de Lisboa.

Cunha, Manuela Carneiro da. 1998. "Pontos de vista sobre a floresta amazônica: xamanismo e tradução." Mana 4 (1): 7–22.

Cruz Penido, Stella Oswaldo. 2005. *Koame wemakaa pandza kome watapetaka kaawa (Baniwa, uma historia de plantas e curas).* Documentary film. Fundação Oswaldo Cruz.

Davis, Wade. 1997. "Photosynthetic Sloths of Amazonia." *One River: Explorations and Discoveries in the Amazon Rain Forest.* New York: Simon & Schuster.

Deloria, Vine. 2005. "The Sacred and the Modern World." In *Encyclopedia of Religion and Nature*, ed. Bron Taylor, 2:1446–48. New York: Continuum.

Dufour, D. L. and J. L. Zarucchi. 1979. "Monopteryx angustifolia and Erisma japura: Their Use by Indigenous People in the Northwestern Amazon." *Bot. Mus. Leafl.* 27 (3–4): 69–91.

Enimini. Mission bulletin. 1974. Jauareté, Brazil.

Etnollano, 2000. *Rocas y Petroglifas del Guainia: Escritura de los grupos Arawak-Maipure.* Museu Arqueologico de Tunja. UPTC. Fundación Etnollano. Bogata, Columbia.

Fausto, Carlos. 2002. "Banquéte de gente: comensalidade e canibalismo na Amazônia." *Mana: Estudos de Antropologia Social* 8(2): 7–44.

———. 2008. "Donos demais: Maestria e dominio na Amazonia." Ms. Rio de Janeiro.

Fausto, Carlos, and M. Heckenberger, eds. 2007. *Time and Memory in Indigenous Amazonia.* Gainesville: University Press of Florida.

Galvão, Eduardo. 1951–54. Field notes. Biblioteca do Museu Paraense Emílio Goeldi, Belém do Pará.

Garnelo, L. 2003. *Poder, Hierarquia e reciprocidade: saude e harmonia entre os Baniwa do Alto Rio Negro.* Rio de Janeiro: Ed. Fiocruz.

Garnelo, L., and Sully Sampaio. 2005. "Globalization and Environmentalism: Polyphonic Ethnicities in the Amazon." *História, Ciências, Saúde——— Manguinhos* 12(3).

Garnelo, L., and R. Wright. 2001. "Doença, cura e serviços de saúde. Representações, práticas e demandas Baniwa." *Cadernos de Saúde Pública* (Rio e Janeiro) 17(2): 273–84.

Goldman, Irving. 1963. *The Cubeo: Indians of the Northwest Amazon.* Urbana: University of Illinois Press.

———. 2004. *Cubeo Hehenawa Religious Thought: Metaphysics of a Northwestern Amazonian People.* Edited by Peter J. Wilson. Afterword by Stephen Hugh-Jones. New York: Columbia University Press.

Gomés de la Espriella, Carlos. 2008. "Las advertencies de Mandu." 50 min. Selected for funding by the National Competition for Documentary Films, "Yulimar Reyes," 2009. Caracas, Venezuela.

González-Ñáñez, Omar. 2007. *Las literaturas indígenas Maipure-arawakas de los pueblos Kurripako, Warekena y Baniva del estado Amazonas.* Caracas: Fundación editorial el perro y la rana.

———. 2010. "Petroglyphs of Upper Rio Negro-Guainia and Casiquiare Basin and the Maipuran-Arawakan Religions." Unpublished manuscript.

Hamayon, Roberte. 1990. "La chasse à l'âme." *Esquisse d'une théorie du chamanisme sibérien.* Nanterre, Société d'ethnologie.

Hill, Jonathan D. 1984. "Social Equality and Ritual Hierarchy: The Arawakan Wakuenai of Venezuela." *American Ethnologist* 11: 528–44.

———. 1987. "Wakuenai Ceremonial Exchange in the Venezuelan Northwest Amazon." *Journal of Latin American Lore* 13: 183–224.

———, ed. 1988. *Rethinking History and Myth: Indigenous South American Perspectives on the Past.* Urbana: University of Illinois Press.

———. 1993. *Keepers of the Sacred Chants: The Poetics of Ritual Power in an Amazonian Society.* Tucson: University of Arizona Press.

———. 2009. *Made-from-Bone.* Urbana: University of Illinois Press.

———. 2011. "Soundscaping the World: The Cultural Poetics of Power and Meaning in Wakuenai Flute Music." In *Burst of Breath: Indigenous Ritual Wind Instruments in Lowland South America,* ed. Jonathan D. Hill and Jean Pierre Chaumeil, 93–122. Lincoln: University of Nebraska Press.

Hill, Jonathan D., and Fernando Santos-Granero. 2002. *Comparative Arawakan Histories.* Urbana: University of Illinois Press.

Hill, Jonathan D., and Robin M. Wright. 1988. "Historical Interpretation in an Amazonian Society." In *Rethinking History and Myth: Indigenous South American Perspectives on the Past,* ed. Jonathan D. Hill, 78–114. Urbana: University of Illinois.

Hugh-Jones, Christine. 1989. *From the Milk Rainbow: Spatial and Temporal Processes in Northwest Amazonia.* Cambridge: Cambridge University Press.

Hugh-Jones, Stephen. 1981. "Historia del Vaupés." Maguari 1:29–51. Bogota.

———. 1989. *The Palm and the Pleiades.* Cambridge: Cambridge University Press.

———. 1996. "Shamans, Prophets, Priests, and Pastors." In *Shamanism, History, and the State,* ed. Nicholas Thomas and Caroline Humphrey, 32–56. Ann Arbor: University of Michigan Press.

———. 2004. Afterword. In Irving Goldman, *Cubeo Hehenewa Religious Thought,* ed. Peter J. Wilson, 405–12. New York: Columbia University Press.

Humboldt, Alexander von., and Aimé Bonpland. 1907. *Personal Narrative of Travels to the Equinoctial Regions of America during the Years 1799–1804.* 3 vols. Translated and edited by Thomasina Ross. London: G. Bell.

Jackson, Jean. 1995. "Preserving Indian Culture: Shaman Schools and Ethno-Education in the Vaupés, Colombia." *Cultural Anthropology* 10(3): 302–29.

Journet, Nicolas. 1995. *La Paix des Jardins: Structures Sociales des Indiens Curripaco du Haut Rio Negro (Colombie).* Paris: Institut d'ethnologie, Musée de l'homme.

Kapfhammer, Wolfgang. 1997. *Grosse Schlange und Fliegender Jaguar: Zur mythologischen Grundlage des rituellen Konsums halluzinogener Schnupfdrogen in Südamerika.* Völkerkundliche Arbeiten Band 6. Bonn: Holos-Verlag.

Koch-Grünberg, Theodor. 1906a. "Die Maskentanze der Indianer des oberen Rio Negro und Yapurá." *Archiv für Anthropologie,* n.s. 4: 293–98.

———. 1906b. "Die indianerstamme am oberen Rio Negro und Yapurá und ihre sprachliche zugenörigkeit." *Zeitschrifte für Ethnologie* 28: 166–205.

———. 1907. *Südamerikanische Felszeichnungen.* Berlin: E. Wasmuth A.-G.

———. 1911. "Aruak-sprachen Nordwestbrasiliens und der angrenzenden Gebiete." *Mitteilungen der Anthropologischen Gesellschaften in Wien* 41: 33–267.

———. 1967 [1909]. *Zwei Jahre unter den Indianern: Reisen in Nordwest Brasilien, 1903–05.* Stuttgart: Strecher und Shröder.

Langdon, E. Jean, ed. 1992. *Portals of Power: South American Shamanism.* Albuquerque: University of New Mexico Press.

Langdon, E. Jean, and G. Baer, eds. 1996. *Xamanismo no Brasil: Novas Perspectivas.* Florianópolis: UFSC.

Maia, Paulo. 2009. "Desequilibrando o convencional: estética e ritual com os Baré do Alto rio Negro." PhD thesis, PPGAS/MN/RJ.

Meira, Marcio. 1993. "O Tempo dos Patrões: Extrativismo de Piaçava entre os Índios do rio Xié (Alto Rio Negro)." Dissertação de Mestrado, Departamento de Antropologia, Universidade Estadual de Campinas.

Mendel, Frank C. 1985. "Use of Hands and Feet of Three-Toed Sloths (*Bradypus variegatus*) during Climbing and Terrestrial Locomotion." *Journal of Mammalogy* 66(2): 359–66.

Montgomery, Gene G., ed. 1985. *The Evolution and Ecology of Armadillos, Sloths, and Vermilinguas.* Washington: Smithsonian Institution Press.

Morey, R. V., and Donald Metzger. 1974. "The Guahibo: People of the Savanna." *Acta Etnologica et Linguistica*, no. 31, Vienna.

Neves, Eduardo Góes. 1988. "Paths in the Dark Waters: Archaeology as Indigenous History in the Upper Rio Negro Basin, Northwest Amazon." PhD diss., Department of Anthropology, Indiana University.

———. 2001. "Indigenous Historical Trajectories in the Upper Rio Negro Basin." In *Unknown Amazon*, ed. Colin McEwan, Cristiana Barreto, and Eduardo Neves, 266–86. London: British Museum Press.

Nimuendajú, Curt. 1950 [1927]. "Reconhecimento dos rios Içana, Ayari e Uaupés." *Journal de la Société des Américanistes de Paris* 39: 125–83 and 44:149–78.

Oakdale, Suzanne. 2005. *I Foresee My Life: The Ritual Performance of Autobiography in an Amazonian Community*. Lincoln: University of Nebraska Press.

Overing, Joanna. 1990. "The Shaman as a Maker of Worlds: Nelson Goodman in the Amazon." *Man*, n.s., 25: 602–19.

———. 2006. "The Stench of Death and the Aromas of Life: The Poetics of Ways of Knowing and Sensory Process among Piaroa of the Orinoco Basin." *Tipití* 4(1): 9–32.

Overing, Joanna, and Alan Passes, eds. 2000. *The Anthropology of Love and Anger: The Aesthetics of Conviviality in Native Amazonia*. London: Routledge.

Panlon Kumu, U., and T. Kenhíri. 1980. *Antes o mundo não existia*. São Paulo: HRM Editores.

Penido, Stella Oswaldo Cruz. 2007. "Koame weemaka pandza kome watapetaka kawa (Baniwa, uma historia de plantes e curas): caminhos para um roteiro." *História, Ciências, Saúde*——— Manguinhos 14: 305–16.

Ramirez, Henri. 2001. *Linguas Arawak da Amazonia Setentrional*. Manaus: EDUA.

Ramos, Alcida, and Bruce Albert, eds., 2002. *Pacificando o Branco: Cosmologias do contato no Norte-Amazônico*. São Paulo: UNESP.

Reichel, Elizabeth. 1999. "Cosmology, Worldview, and Gender-based Knowledge Systems among the Tanimuka and Yukuna (Northwest Amazon." *Worldviews: Environment, Culture, Religion* 3(3): 213–42.

———. 2009. "The Landscape in the Cosmoscape: Cosmology, Ethnoastronomy, and Socio-environmental Sustainability among the Tanimuka and Yukuna, Northwest Amazon." Ms.

Reichel-Dolmatoff, Gerardo. 1951. *The Kogi: A Tribe of the Sierra Nevada de Santa Marta, Colombia*. Vol. 2. Bogotá: Editorial Iqueima.

———. 1969. *Desana: Simbolos de los tukano del Vaupés*. Bogotá: Universidad de los Andes.

———. 1975. *The Shaman and the Jaguar*. Philadelphia: Temple University Press.

———. 1976. "Cosmology as Ecological Analysis." *Man*, n.s., 11(3): 307–18.

———. 1985. "Tapir Avoidance in the Colombian Northwest Amazon." In *Animal Myths and Metaphors in South America*, ed. Gary Urton, 107–43. Salt Lake City: University of Utah Press.

———. 1987. "The Great Mother and the Kogi Universe: A Concise Overview." *Journal of Latin American Lore* 13(1): 73–113.

———. 1989. "Biological and Social Aspects of the Yurupari Complex of the Vaupés Territory." *Journal of Latin American Lore* 15(1): 95–135.

———. 1996. *Yurupari: Studies of an Amazonian Foundation Myth*. Cambridge: Harvard University Press.

———. 1999. "A View from the Headwaters: A Colombian Anthropologist Looks at the Amazon and Beyond." In *Ethnobiology: Implications and Applications*, ed. Darrell A. Posey. Belém: Museu Paraense Emílio Goeldi.

Rojas, Filintro Antonio. 1997. *Ciencias Naturales en la mitologia Curripaco*. Colombia: Programa Fondo Amazonico.

Saake, Wilhelm. 1958. "Die Juruparilegende bei den Baniwa des Rio Issana." *Proceedings of the 32nd International Congress of Americanists*, Copenhagen.

———. 1958. "Aus der Uberlieferungen der Baniwa." *Staden-Jahrbuch* 6: 83–91.

———. 1958. "Mythen uber Inapirikuli, des Kulturheros der Baniwa." *Zeitschrift für Ethnologie* 93: 260–73.

———. 1959–60a. "Iniciação de um pajé entre os Baniwa e a Cura de Marecaimbara." *Sociologia* (São Paulo) 6: 424–42.

———. 1959–60b. "Kari, der Kulturheros, feiert mit den Baniwa-Indianern das erste Dabukurifest." *Staden-Jahrbuch* 7–8: 193–201.

———. 1964. "Erziehungsformen bei den Baniwa." In *Völkerkundliche Abhandlungen*, vol. 1: *Beiträge zur Völkerkunde Südamerikas: Festgabe für Herbert Baldus zum 65 Geburtstag*. Hannover.

Santos, Antônio Maria de Souza, and Margarida Elizabeth de Mendonça Lima. 1991. "Medicina tradicional e ocidental no Alto Rio Negro: O papel dos rezadores em São Gabriel da Cachoeira." In *Medicinas Tradicionais e Medicina Ocidental na Amazônia*, ed. Dominique Buchillet, 229–40. Belém: Museu Paraense Emílio Goeldi.

Santos-Granero, Fernando. 1991. *The Power of Love*. London: Athlone Press.

———. 1998. "Writing History into the Landscape: Space, Myth, and Ritual in Contemporary Amazonia." *American Ethnologist* 25(2): 128–48.

———. 2000. "The Sisyphus Syndrome, or the Struggle for Conviviality in Native Amazonia." In *The Anthropology of Love and Anger*, ed. Joanna Overing and Alan Passes, 268–87. New York: Routledge.

———. 2003. "Pedro Casanto's Nightmares: Lucid Dreaming in Amazonia and the New Age Movement." *Tipití* 1(2): 179–210.

———. 2004. "Arawakan Sacred Landscapes: Emplaced Myths, Place Rituals, and the Production of Locality in Amazonia." In *Kultur, Raum, Landschaft: Zur Bedeutung des Raumes in Zeiten der Globalität*, ed. Ernst Halbmayer and Elke Mader, 93–122. Frankfurt am Main: Brandes & Apsel.

Santos-Granero, Fernando, ed. 2009. *The Occult Life of Things: Native Amazonian Theories of Materiality and Personhood*. Tucson: University of Arizona Press.

Santos-Granero, Fernando, and George Mentore, eds. 2006. "In the World and about the World: Amerindian Modes of Knowledge: Special Issue in Honour of Joanna Overing." *Tipití* 4(1–2): 57–80.

Stradelli, Ermanno. 1890. "Leggenda dell'Jurupary." *Bollettino della Società Geografica Italiana* 3: 659–89, 798–835.

———. 1890. "L'Uaupés e gli Uaupés." *Bollettino della Società Geografica Italiana* 3: 425–53.

———. 1896. "Leggende del Taria." *Memorie della Società Geografica Italiana* 6: 141–48.

———. 1900. Iscrizione Indigene della Regione dell'Uaupés. *Bollettino della Società Geografica Italiana* 4: 457–83.

Strassman, Rick. 2001. DMT: *The Spirit Molecule*. Rochester, VT: Park Street Press.

Sullivan, Lawrence. 1988. *Icanchu's Drum: An Orientation to Meaning in South American Religions*. New York: Macmillan.

————, ed. 2002. *Native Religions and Cultures of Central and South America*. New York: Continuum.

Taylor, Gerald. 1991. *Introdução à Língua Baniwa do Içana*. Campinas: Editora UNICAMP.

Tedlock, Dennis. 1996. *Popol Vuh: The Mayan Book of the Dawn of Life*. New York: Simon & Schuster.

Turner, Terence. 2010. "The Crisis of Late Structuralism, Perspectivism, and Animism: Rethinking Culture, Nature, Bodilessness, and Spirit." *Tipití* 7(1–2): 3–42.

Turner, Victor. 1988. *The Anthropology of Performance*. Baltimore: Johns Hopkins University Press.

————. 1995 [1969]. *The Ritual Process: Structure and Anti-Structure*. New York: Aldine de Gruyter.

Vidal, Silvia M. 1987. "El Modelo del Proceso Migratorio Prehispánico de los Piapoco: Hipótesis y Evidencias." Master's thesis, Instituto Venezolano de Investigaciones Científicas, Caracas.

————. 1993. "Reconstrucción de los Procesos de Etnogenesis y de Reproducción social entre los Baré de Rio Negro, siglos XVI–XVIII." PhD diss., Centro de Estudios Avançados, Instituto Venezolano de Investigaciones Científicas, Caracas.

————. 1997. "Liderazco y confederaciones multiétnicas amerindias en la amazonia luso-hispana del Siglo XVIII." *Antropologica* 87: 19–46.

————. 1999. "Amerindian Groups of Northwest Amazonia: Their Regional System of Political-Religious Hierarchies." *Anthropos* 94: 515–28.

————. 2002. "Secret Religious Cults and Political Leadership: Multiethnic Confederacies from Northwestern Amazonia." In *Comparative Arawakan Histories: Rethinking Language Family and Culture Area in Amazonia*, ed. Jonathan D. Hill and Fernando Santos-Granero, 248–68. Urbana: University of Illinois Press.

Vidal, Silvia M., and Alberta Zucchi. 1996. "Impacto de la colonización hispanolusitana en las organizaciones sociopolíticas y económicas de los maipures-arawakos del alto Orinoco-rio Negro (siglos XVII–XVIII)." *America Negra*, no. 11: 107–29.

———. 1999. "Efectos de las expansiones coloniales en las poblaciones indígenas del Noroeste Amazónico (1798–1830)." *Colonial Latin American Review* 8(1): 113–32.

Vilaça, Aparecida, and Robin M. Wright, eds. 2009. *Native Christians: Modes and Effects of Christianity among Indigenous Peoples of the Americas*. Burlington, VT: Ashgate.

Viveiros de Castro, Eduardo B. 2002. *A Inconstância da Alma Selvagem e Outros Ensaios de Antropologia*. São Paulo: Cosac & Naify.

———. 2003. "Chamanismo y sacrificio: un comentario amazônico." In *Chamanismo y sacrificio*, ed. R. Chaumeil, 335–39. Bogotá: Banco de la Republica.

Viveiros de Castro, E. B., and M. Carneiro da Cunha. 1985. "Vingança e Temporalidade: Os Tupinambá." *Journal de la Société des Américanistes* 71: 191–208.

Whitehead, Neil. 2002. *Dark Shamans*. Durham: Duke University Press.

Whitehead, Neil, and Robin M. Wright, eds. 2004. *In Darkness and Secrecy: The Anthropology of Assault Sorcery in Amazonia*. Durham: Duke University Press.

Wilbert, Johannes. 1993 [1987]. *Tobacco and Shamanism*. New Haven: Yale University Press.

Wright, Robin M. "The History and Religion of the Baniwa Peoples of the Upper Rio Negro Valley of Brazil." PhD diss., University Microfilms, Ann Arbor.

———. 1983. "Lucha y supervivencia en el Noroeste de la Amazonia." *América Indígena* 43(3): 537–54.

———. 1990. "Guerras e Alianças nas Histórias dos Baniwa do Alto Rio Negro." *Ciências Sociais Hoje*, 217–36. São Paulo: ANPOCS.

———. 1992a. "Guardians of the Cosmos: Baniwa Shamans and Prophets, Part I." *History of Religions* 32(1): 32–58.

———. 1992b. "Guardians of the Cosmos: Baniwa Shamans and Prophets, Part II." *History of Religions* 32(2): 126–45.

———. 1992c. "Uma Conspiração contra os Civilisados: História, Política e Ideologias dos Movimentos Milenaristas dos Arawak e Tukano do Noroeste da Amazonia." *Anuário Antropológico* 89: 191–234.

———. 1992d. "História Indígena do Noroeste da Amazônia: Questões, Hipóteses e Perspectivas [Indigenous History of the Northwest Amazon: Questions, Hypotheses and Perspectives]." In *História Dos Índios No Brasil*, ed. Manuela Carneiro da Cunha São Paulo: Companhia das Letras.

———. 1993. "Pursuing the Spirit: Semantic Construction in Hohodene Kalidzamai Chants for Initiation." *Amerindia* 18: 1–40.

———. 1993–94. "Umawali: Hohodene Father of the Fish." *Société Suisse des Américanistes Bulletin Génébre* 57–58: 37–48.

———. 1998. *Cosmos, Self, and History in Baniwa Religion: For Those Unborn.* Austin: University of Texas Press.

———. 2002a. "Prophetic traditions among the Baniwa." In *Comparative Arawakan Histories: Rethinking Language Family and Culture Area in Amazonia*, ed. Jonathan D. Hill and Fernando Santos-Granero. Urbana: University of Illinois Press.

———. 2002b. "Ialanawinai: O branco na história e mito baniwa." In *Pacificando o branco: Cosmologias do contato no Norte-Amazônico*, ed. Alcida Ramos and Bruce Albert, 421–68. São Paulo: Editora UNESP.

———. 2004a. "The Wicked and the Wise Men: Witches and Prophets in the History of the Baniwa." In *In Darkness and Secrecy: The Anthropology of Assault Sorcery in Amazonia*, ed. Neil Whitehead and Robin M. Wright, 82–108. Durham: Duke University Press.

———. 2004b. "As Tradições Proféticas e Cosmologias 'Cristãs' entre os Baniwa." In *Transformando os Deuses*, ed. Wright, 2: 341–76. Campinas: Editora da UNICAMP.

———. 2005. *Historia Indigena e do Indigenismo no Alto Rio Negro.* Campinas: Mercado de Letras.

———. 2009a. "The Fruit of Knowledge and the Bodies of the Gods: Religious Meanings of Plants among the Baniwa." *Journal for the Study of Religion, Nature and Culture* 3(1): 126–53.

———. 2009b. "The Art of Being Crente: The Baniwa Protestant Ethic and the Spirit of Sustainable Development." *Identities* 16(2): 202–26.

———. 2009c. Review of *Made-from-Bone: Trickster Myths, Music, and History from the Amazon*, by Jonathan D. Hill. University of Illinois, Champaign." *Journal of Latin American Studies* 42(1): 205–207.

———. 2009d. "Review of *Cubeo Hehenawa Religious Thought: Metaphysics of a Northwestern Amazonian People*, by Irving Goldman. Edited by Peter J. Wilson. Afterword by Stephen Hugh-Jones. New York: Columbia University Press, 2004." In *Tipití* 6(1–2): 123–28.

———. 2009e. "The Snuff-Jaguar 'Mandu' Manuel da Silva." *Shamanism Annual: Journal of the Foundation for Shamanic Studies* 22: 20–22.

———. 2010. "Review of Graham Harvey, *Animism: Respecting the Living World*. New York: Columbia University Press, 2006." *Journal for the Study of Religion, Nature and Culture* 4(1): 93–94.

———. 2010a. "Ethnology and Indigenism in the Brazilian Northwest Amazon." *Tipití* 7(1): 107–18.

———. 2011. "Arawaken Flute Cults of Lowland South America." In *Burst of Breath: Indigenous Ritual Wind Instruments in Lowland South America*, 325–56. Lincoln: University of Nebraska Press.

———, ed. 2009. "The Religious Lives of Amazonian Plants." Special issue of the *Journal for the Study of Religion, Nature and Culture* 3(1).

Wright, Robin M., and Jonathan D. Hill. 1986. "History, Ritual, and Myth: Nineteenth-Century Millenarian Movements in the Northwest Amazon." *Ethnohistory* 33(1): 31–54.

Wright, Robin M., and Ismaelillo. 1982. *Native Peoples in Struggle: Cases from the Fourth Russell Tribunal and Other International Forums*. Bombay, NY: E.R.I.N.

Xavier Leal, Carlos Cesar. 2008. "A Cidade Grande de Napirikoli e os Petroglifos do Içana——— Uma Etnografia de Signos Baniwa." Master's thesis, PPGAS/MN, Rio de Janeiro.

Zucchi, Alberta. 2002. "A New Model of the Northern Arawakan Expansion." In *Comparative Arawakan Histories: Rethinking Language Family and Culture Area in Amazonia*, ed. Jonathan D. Hill and Fernando Santos-Granero, 199–222. Urbana: University of Illinois Press.

Index

animals (*itchirinai*): anacondas as, 68, 209M, 213; ants as, 17, 160; avatars as, 171–72, 187, 206–7, 345n3; bees as, 202, 224, 248–49, 254; crayfish as, 182, 183; frogs as, *214*, 244–45, 277, 280; lizards as, 154–55, 211, 290, 344n4; monkeys as, 155–56, 250, 253, 254, 272; music and songs of, 276, 280, 339–41, *340*; shadow-souls as, 154–56; souls of, 141–42, 150, 172; stingrays as, 212, 243; tapirs as, 63, 202; tribes of, 124, 125, 182, 186, 331; wasps as, 248–49, 254, 264–65. *See also* fish; sloths

ants, 17, 160

apprenticeships: advanced knowledge and specializations during, 42–46, 89–91, 93–94, 102–3; calling of, 36, 61–62; of Ercilia da Silva, 345n7; first and second stages of, 37, 38–42, 62–72, 81–86; pride and respect for, 103–4, *104*; songs during, 79–81; time for, 62, 204, 206, 264

arrows: pepper as, 68, 177; in wars, 276, 279, 280, 290. *See also* darts

assault sorcery. *See* sorcery

attacks: by Emí, 119; by jaguar shamans, 75–76, 98–99, 327; by sorcerers, 88, 99–101; by spirits, 73, 87. *See also* killings

avatars, 171–72, *174*, 187, 345n3

Baniwa: ancestors and phratries of, 3–4, 76, 178–79, 347–48n2; calendar for, 204–6, 261; community identities of, 193, 218, 303–4; enemies of, 75–76; ethnography of, 1, 2–3, 3M; evangelicalism and, 4–5, 19, 96, 347n5; Pamaale complex and, 300, 301–7; regarding retribution, 98, 100, 132; sacred sites for, 21, 165–66, 208–19, 209M, *211*, *212*, *214*; regarding sorcery, 120–27, 131–32; specialists within culture of, 6–7, 7–11T, 11–14, 121, 196, 252, 326–29; warnings for, 2, 18, 133; white people and, 103, 181, 286–89. *See also* cosmologies; traditions

Baniwa, a Story of Plants and Cures. See Baniwa: Uma historia de plantas e curas (Cruz)

Baniwa: Uma historia de plantas e curas (Cruz, 2005), 130, 302

baskets, 17, 153, 158–59, *163*, 163–64, 306

baths, 276, 278–79

bees, 202, 224, 248–49, 254, 265

Before World (*Oopidali Apakwa Hekwapi*), 77, 80, 149–50, 166–67, 170–71, 196

Berkes, Fikret, 150

biomedicine. *See* medicines

birds (*khepiren*): during creation of universe, 153, 161; as

daughters of Dzuliferi, 190; as
harpy eagles, 174–75, 199–200;
marriages with, 39, 86, 97, 191;
of Nhiãperikuli, 215, 276, 280
births, 211–12, 212, 237–43, 283
blessings (*kalidzamai*), 37, 63–64,
239, 266, 269, 346n3
blood (*irana*): as image of death,
263; of Kuwai, 64, 66, 175; from
menstruation, 65–66, 190, 191,
260–61, 278; water from, 191, 243
bodies (*idaki*): and acts of
opening and closing, 87–89,
237, 241, 242; of Dzuliferi,
177; holes in, 66, 122, 263; of
Nhiãperikuli, 173, 259, 263;
protection of, 57, 59, 71, 87, 176;
rattle handles as, 91, 93–94;
shadow-souls and, 154–55; of
sorcerers, 124–25; of spirit
people, 197. *See also* Kuwai,
body of; Kuwai, holes of
bones (*iyapi*): of Kuwai, 254–55,
269, 275, 339–41, 340; of pajés
and shamans, 90, 126, 184,
185, 200–201, 345n1; poisons
in, 125–26, 185; as tubes, 151,
183–85; universe people from,
157, 181–82, 183. *See also* Place of
Our Bones
boulders: at City of Nhiãperikuli,
215–16, 217; of Dzuliferi, 177,
292; regarding Kuwai, 211,
211–13, 212, 213, 245. *See also*
stones

boys: as first initiates, 212,
214, 248–69; initiation and
kalidzamai for, 34–35, 190,
217, 269–75, 277–79. *See also*
children
BP (British Petroleum), 141, 142
bread, 170, 194, 195, 269–71
British Petroleum, 141, 142
bumblebees. *See* bees

Caapi (*Banisteriopsis caapi*), 26, 91,
190
calendars, 204–6, 261
Carrasco, David, 54
Catholicism. *See* religion; Salesian
Missionary Order
celibacy. *See* restrictions, regarding
celibacy and sexual relations
centers: for initiation, 249, 257,
259; of universe, 20, 162–65, 169,
177, 274–75
ceremonies: chiefs of, 194,
309–10, 311–15, 313; hierarchies
and organization for, 179,
223–24, 298, 343n1; at House of
Adorning, 303–4, 310–15, 313; for
initiation and Kwaipan, 34–35,
257, 313; at Shamans' House of
Power and Knowledge, 319–24,
321. *See also* rites; rituals
chanters. *See* Cornelio, José;
elders; priestly chanters
chants: for acts of world-making,
56; blessings as, 63–64, 239; for
healings, 180, 181; power from,

chants (*continued*)
203; of priestly chanters,
291, *291*. See also *kalidzamai*;
orations
chiefs (*nathalikana*): of animals,
182; of ceremonies, 194, 309–10,
311–15, *313*; deities as, 194;
Enawi-nai as, 283–84; power of,
346n2; of Uapui, 31, 32, 48–50,
112, 117–18, 138; of Ukuki, 135–36,
304, 307, 312, *313*; of yoopinai,
154–55, 290, 344n4
children (*ienipethe*). *See* boys;
girls; stories, about children
Christianity. *See* evangelicalism;
missionaries
Cicadas (*dzurunai*), 36, 62, 204,
206, 264
cigars, 41, 176
City of Nhiãperikuli, 209M,
215–16, 280
cloaks, 75, 200. *See also* mantles
clouds, 55, 81, 174, 175, 200, 273
coca, 237, 238, 239
collars, 96, 201
communication, 77–81, 345n2
communities: of Aiary River, 3M,
3–5, 13, 105–8, *108*, 178, 346n1;
enemies of, 329; of Içana
River, 3M, 3–4, 13, 50, 134–35;
identities of, 193, 218, 303–4;
involvement by Emí in, 111–12,
117, 118–19; protection from
poisonings in, 128–29; sorcery
as danger to, 18–19, 128, 335. *See*

also revitalization movements;
villages
conception, 211–12, *212*, 237–43
Cornelio, José, xi, 48–50, *49*
cosmologies: of Aiary River and
Northwest Amazon, 20, 151,
223–28; regarding body and
soul connection, 154–55; and
destruction of world, 133–34,
141–42; ecology as foundation
for, 20–24, 148, 150–51; and
evangelicalism, 96, 347n5–6; of
jaguar shamans, 147–61; layers
and hierarchies of, 161, 172–73,
331–32; regarding sorcery, 132;
regarding truth, 69. *See also*
universe, layers and levels of
cosmos (*Hekwapi*). *See*
cosmologies; universe
cosmoscapes, 349n1
cotton, 287
crayfish, 182, 183
creation: stories about, 17, 130,
152–61, 168, 170, 224, 227–28; of
time, 17, 158–61, 333; of universe,
147–54, 156–61
crente, 5, 20, 300
Cubeo: killings by, 100–101;
origin of, 196, 348–49n7, 348n2;
religion and traditions of,
85–86, 140T, 223–26, 348n2
cults, 21–22, 221–22
Cunha, Manuela Carneiro da, 80
cures: chants and orations for, 57,
287, 288, 289–90; fur as, 41, 71,

83, 121–22, 270–71; honey as,
224, 290; medicines for, 19–20,
57, 68–69; payments for, 70–71,
83, 192–93; for poisons, 124;
sanctuaries as, 289–90; songs
for, 79–81; stages for, 56–61; time
for, 56, 60, 93, 154, 166; tobacco
usage during, 47, 71, 176. *See also*
healings; treatments
Cururuquara, 107, 109, 346n1
cycles: for food, 20, 150, 195, 201;
for gardens and planting,
170, 182, 194, 195, 204;
interconnections among, 162,
167, 190; knowledge regarding
seasons and, 62, 150, 170, 189,
204–7; power regarding, 200,
201; and seasons of rain, 261–
62, 264; for transformations, 74,
204, 206; for water, 162, 167, 169

dance-leaders, 10–11T, 12, 194,
312–15, *313*, 335
dances, 6, 303–4, 309–15, *313*,
320–21, 322
darkness, 159–60, 162, 258–59
darts (*walama*): for killings and
sicknesses, 67, 124, 203, 279,
343n1; from trees, 84, 123, 203.
See also arrows
da Silva, Alberto, xii, 316, 322
da Silva, Ercilia, xii, 51–52, 95–96,
316, 324, 345n7
da Silva, Flora, xi, 48, 52, 95, 281,
351n1

da Silva, Mandu: awards of, 138, 319;
as chief, 31, 32, 48, 112, 117–18, 138;
childhood and family of, 34–37,
47–52, *52*; dreams and visions
of, 36, 46–47, 61–62, 173; films
and, 2, 18, 76, 132–33, 329; as
jaguar shaman and "true pajé,"
1, 2, 25, *44*, 60, 94, 138; Kuwai
experience of, 40–41, 82–85,
350n1; leadership of, 2, 103,
142–43, 315; marriages of, 39, 48,
110; pajé training of, 37–48, *44*,
47, 61–63, 66–81, 89–91, 102–3;
rattles and stones of, 43, 93–94,
95–96; and Shamans' House
of Power and Knowledge, 319,
320, 322, 323–24; sicknesses of,
36, 51, 61, 344n5; sufferings of,
105, 110–15, 117–19; regarding
traditions, 103–4, *104*, 132–33,
183, 222, 324, 329; regarding
universe, 164–68, 173
da Silva, Mário, 34, 50, 58, 319, 322
dawai. See payments
Day, 17, 158–59, 160–61
Dayzo-dakenai, 347–48n2
deaths: of Amaru, 237, 242, 243;
blood as image of, 263; of Emí,
116, 119–20; heart-souls and,
180–81, 184–85; knowledge
and power through, 24, 82;
of Kuwai, 271, 350–51n4;
through Kuwaikaniri, 187; and
Mawerikuli, 130, 180, 215, 225,
351n4; of pajés, 64–65, 74, 75,

deaths (*continued*)
81–83, 88; by poisonings, 107,
111, 113; of prophets, 33, 135–37;
and rebirth of initiates, 81–83;
by smoke, 250, 260, 266. *See also*
sacrifices
decrees. *See* laws
deities, 15, 179, 192–96, 207
depositions, 111, 112, 117
destruction, 21, 24–25, 133–34,
141–42
development projects. *See*
revitalization movements
displacements, 77–78, 103, 181
Djuremawa, *108*, 346n1
DMT. *See* dymethyltriptamine
(DMT)
doors: to Other World and sky, 40,
60, 65, 82–83, 166; as portals, 54,
70, 208, 210
dreams. *See* visions
dymethyltriptamine (DMT), 26, 91,
345n2
Dzauinai, 3, 4
dzauinaipwa, 45, 69, 344n4
Dzuliferi: birds as daughters of,
190; body of, 177; Boulder of,
177, 292; as chief and Eternal
Master, 85, 194; knowledge of,
186–87; as owner of tobacco
and universe, 176–77, 192; as
pajé and primal shaman, 40,
226; shadow-soul of, 41, 71, 83,
226, 351–52n4; songs as voice
of, 77–81, 177; stories about, 65,

175–77; and tricksters, 179–80,
227. *See also* universe people

eagles. *See* harpy eagles
ecology: as foundation for
cosmologies, 20–24, 148, 150–51;
knowledge of, 150–51, 207, 305,
347n1; time and, 199–202
Eeri. *See* Kuwaikaniri; Mawerikuli
egalitarianism, 173, 298
Ehnípan, 209M, *214*, 249, 259
elders, 12, 269–70, 281, 330, 351n1
Emí (kin to Mandu da Silva),
110–20, 125
Enawi-nai (spiritual governors),
283–84
enemies: affines as, 110–20, 186,
329, 332; of communities and
This World, 227, 329, 332; fish
as, 68; of pajés, 45, 75–76, 87–89,
131–32, 326; protection from, 88,
179–80; spirit people as, 197–98
engravings, 91–92, 92
entrapment. *See* traps
Enukwa, 4, 178, 209M, 210. *See also*
Pukweipan
envy, 107–8, 110, 115, 117, 126–27,
129–31
Eternal Master. *See* Dzuliferi;
Nhiãperikuli
Euzebio, Marcellino, 48, 105, 109.
See also Kaaparo
evangelicalism: abuses and crimes
of, 49, 137, 299–300; effects
of, 4–5, 96, 343n1, 347nn5–6;

and sorcery, 19–20. *See also* missionaries

exogamy, 220, 294

extractions, 39, 56–57, 58, *58*, 59, 68, 121–22

Fabricio (specialist pajé), 45–46, 48, 90

factories. *See* industries

fasting, 37, 38–39, 67–70, 249, 253, 350n3

Fausto, Carlos, 172–73, 193

feathers, 92–93, 174, 199–200

Federação das Organizações Indígenas do Rio Negro (FOIRN), 301, 308

Felipe, José, xi, 50, 58, 320, 324

Fernandes, Andre, 130, 302

festivals. *See* ceremonies; rites; rituals

films: *Las Advertencias de Mandu*, 2, 18, 119, 132–33, 329; *Baniwa: Uma historia de plantas e curas*, 130, 302; about Hipana, 76; of inauguration ceremony, 320; about pariká, 324

fingers, 182, 213, 244

fires: deaths and sacrifices through, 194, 195, 267–68, 271, 293; destruction of world by, 134; pepper as arrows of, 68, 177; purification by, 83

fish: curses and spells upon, 76; as flesh of Kuwai, 260; meanings of, 37, 46, 67–68, 343n1; origin of, 209M; transformations into, 174–75; traps for, 261–62, 277, 280

flesh, 259–60

floods, 134

flu, 287

flutes: adornments of, 277, 282; as ancestors, 170–71, 193, 257, 275, 282–83; birth and rebirth through, 184, 185, 283; cults of, 22, 222; in dances, 311, 314; exogamy and, 220; of Kuwai, 92, *92*, 184, 212–13, *213*, *214*, 268–69; songs from, 244; stories about, 276–77, 279, 281–83, 285–86

FOIRN. *See* Federação das Organizações Indígenas do Rio Negro (FOIRN)

Fontes, Laureano, 135–36, 310, 312, *313*

Fontes, Ricardo, xi, 234, 237–38, 261, 267–68, 309–10

foods: blessings for, 37, 266, 269, 346n3; cycles for, 20, 150, 195, 201; guardians of, 20, 74–75, 305; of Kuwai, 255, 257, 265; restrictions for, 66–67, 68, 250, 253, 262, 269, 289; of shamans, 168, 170, 195, 201; sicknesses from, 121–22, 253, 262, 266, 271, 346n3, 350n3

fortresses, 209M, 214–15, 280, 281

Foundation for Shamanic Studies, xii–xiii, 6, 318–19

frogs, *214*, 244–45, 277, 280
fruits, 199–200, 202, 204, 206, 249, 255, 257
fur: as cure, 41, 71, 83, 121–22, 270–71; poisons and sicknesses from, 156, 187, 272; of sloth, 187–89, *188*

Garcia, Guilherme. *See* Kudui
Garcia, José: during cures, *47*, *57*, 58, *58*, 88, 89; entrapment of, 88–89; regarding light, 153–54; as prophet and wise man, xi, 136; regarding tricksters, 180; regarding universe, 162–64, *169*
gardens. *See* planting
girls: attacks and deaths of by enemy pajé, 75–76, 113–14; initiation and *kalidzamai* for, 217, 240, 248, 281, 294; menarche and menstruation of, 66, 190, 211, 278, 281, 282; seclusion from, 38, 72. *See also* women
Goldman, Irving, 148, 196, 223, 225, 226, 343n2
González-Ñáñez, Omar, 2, 18, 119, 132–33, 235, 329
Goodman, Nelson, 54
gourds, 91–92, 94–95
graves. *See* tombs
Great Tree of Sustenance. *See* Tree of Sustenance
Guahibo. *See* Wanhiwa
guardians: of food, 20, 74–76, 305;

jaguar shamans as, 74–75, 150, 328, 334; and owners of plants, 177, 187; phratries as, 193, 211

hallucinogens. See *caapi*; pariká
handles, 43, 91, 93–94
happiness (*kathima*), 7, 297–98, 332
harpy eagles, 174–75, 199–200
healings (*pamatchiatsa*): chants and songs for, 80–81, 180, 181; for heart-souls, 59–60, 68–69, 71, 72, 83, 176; of sicknesses, 41; time for, 60, 93, 154. *See also* cures; treatments
health programs, 19–20
heart-souls (*pakaale*): of ancestors, 39–40, 236, 238; cures and healings for, 56–57, 59–60, 68–69, 71, 72, 83, 176, 290; and death, 180–81, 184–85, 351n4; Jaguar Bone as, 269; journeys of, 15–16, 56, 164; Kuwai and, 235–36, 252, 259, 284, 292–93, 339–41, 340, 351n4; maggots as, 265–66; of Nhiãperikuli, 23, 228, 238–39, 252, 259, 284; patrilineage and, 236, 238–39, 252, 284–85; sicknesses from, 272, 279, 340, *341*; of sorcerers, 124–25, 126, 127, 128; transformations of, 75. *See also* souls
Hehenewa, 223–25, 226
Hehenewa Metaphysics (Goldman), 148

Hekwapi. *See* universe

Hekwapi ienipe. *See* universe child

hekwapinai. *See* universe people

hierarchies: of cosmologies, 173, 331–32; and organization for ceremonies, 179, 223–24, 298, 343n1; of pajés, 12, 96–97; of specialists, 12–13; in This World and Other World, 86–87. *See also* levels

Hill, Jonathan, 93, 134, 148, 154, 179, 180–81, 226–27

Hipana: as birthplace and center of universe, 165, 177, 180–81, 209M, 210, 259; boulders and petroglyphs at, *211, 212, 213, 213*, 245; hole of emergence at, 152, 274–75; importance of, 3M, 3–4, 157–58; rapids of, 76, *211*; primordial tree of paxiúba, source of flutes at, 20, 274–75. *See also* Uapui

Hohodene: ancestors of, 178, 348n2; as guardians, 211; laws of society for, 270; religion and traditions of, 105–7, 139–40T, 181, 224–28, 299–300; regarding retribution and vengeance, 98–101, 120–21; sibs of, 3–4, 283, 348n2; regarding sorcery, 120, 128

holes: in bodies, 66, 122, 263; of emergence, 76, 152, 157–58, 178, 274–75, 283, 347–48n2; of

Kuwai, 24, 235, 243–44, 250, 339–41, 340; as orifices, 123, 190, 240–41, 260, 278

honey, 224, 290

House of Adorning, House of Adornment. *See* House of Adorning, (*Nakuliakarudapani*) 6, 303–4, 309–15, *313*

House of Shamans' Knowledge and Power. *See* Shamans' House of Power and Knowledge (*Malikai Dapana*)

House of the Souls of the Dead (*Iaradathi*), 16, 36, 82, 86, 243, 350n2

Hugh-Jones, Christine, 219

Hugh-Jones, Stephen, 219, 221

Humboldt, Alexander von, 222, 244, 334

ibacaba. See fruits

Içana River: communities of, 3M, 3–4, 13, 50, 134–35; development projects in, 302, 306–7, 318, 330; at Ehnípan, 209M, *214*, 249, 259; missionaries at, 21, 49, 299–301; petroglyphs and sacred sites of, 165–67, 182, 215–16; traditions of, 139–40T, 347–48n2; at Tunui Rapids, 3M, 4, 75–76, 209M

inauguration ceremonies, 319–24, *321*

industries, 48, 107, 108, 142, 224, 286–88

influenza (*hfetchi*), 287

inhalation, 45, 54, 64–66, 184, 200–201, 345n1

initiates (*itakenai*), 67, 81–83, 189–90, 212, *214*, 248–69, 253

initiation: baths during, 276, 278–79; for boys and first initiates, 212, *214*, 248–69, 277–79; centers for, 249, 257, 259; ceremonies for Kwaipan and, 34–35, 257, *313*; chants for, 102, 217–18; constellations during, 202, 204, 206, 211, 260, 261; fasting and seclusion during, 37–40, 66–70, 248–50, 253, 258–64, 278–79; for girls and women, 240, 248, 277–78, 281, 294; Kuwai mythscapes central to, 22, 217–18, 334; Kuwai stories about, 248–75; of Mandu da Silva, 37–40, 62–63; medicines during, 38–39; Nhiãperikuli stories about, 249, 251, 252, 256–59, 263, 264–68, 276–83; rites for, 165–66, 193, 204–6, 214, *214*, 217, 247–69, 313; rituals for, 189–90, 209M, 214, *214*, 240, 247–53, 256–69; time for, 204–6, 264; transformations regarding, 247–48; at Ukuki, 312–15, *313*. See also *kalidzamai*

Instituto SocioAmbiental (ISA), 301–4, 306–8, 310–11

instruments. See flutes; pets; trumpets

inyaime: as "Other Kuwai," 179, 243, 251, 260–63, 265; as spirit of the dead, 73, 125, 350n2

Jaguar Bones, 254–55, 269

jaguars, 98–99, 202, 203, 242–43

jaguar shamans: attacks and killings by, 75–76, 98–99, 327; attributes and functions of, 8–9T, 73–75, 150, 229, 327–28; communication through, 77–78, 81; cosmology of, 149–61; as guardians and warriors, 74–75, 150, 327, 328, 334; hierarchies of, 13, 86; journeys and voyages of, 16, 55, 60–61, 328; knowledge and understanding of, 13–15, 23, 124, 142, 159, 204; Macanilla as, 222, 329–30; maka and cloaks of, 75, 97; power of, 60–61, 327–28; and Shamans' House of Power and Knowledge, 315–24; spirits of, 78–79, 84–85, 86, 94, 203, 328; visions of, 60, 97–98, 159, 164–65, 175, 328. See also da Silva, Mandu

Jandú Rapids. See Ehnípan

Jawinaapi, Alexandre, 43, 45–46, 48, 62, 89–91, 93, 102

Jesus, Pedro de, 76

Journet, Nicolas, 348n4

journeys: of heart-souls and souls, 15–16, 56, 72, 82–87, 164, 350n2; of jaguar shamans, 16, 55, 60–61, 328; of pajés, 15–16,

Kudui: and conflicts about religion, 300; death and tomb of, 136–37, *138*; as pajé and prophet, 35–40, 42, 62, 63, 136–37, 140T

Kuripako. *See* Wakuenai

Kuwai: blood of, 64, 66, 175; body of, 155, 213, *213*, 240, 243–45, 273, 274–75, 339–41, *340*; bones of, 254–55, 269, 275, 339–41, *340*; as chief, 194; conception and birth of, 211–12, *212*, 237–43; cures from, 41, 70–71, 192, 224, 272; death and sacrifice of, 267–68, 271, 293, 350–51n4; disguises of, 249, 252; drawings of, 235, 334, *340*; flesh of, 259–60; flutes of, 92, *92*, 184, 213, *213*, 214, 268–69; foods of, 255, 257, 265; and heart-soul, 235–36, 252, 259, 284, 292–93, 339–41, *340*, 351n4; holes of, 24, 235, 243–44, 250, 339–41, *340*; as *inyaime* and "Other Kuwai," 179, 243, 251, 260–63, 265; Jaguar Bone and trumpets of, 184, 254–55, 268, 275; knowledge and power of, 291–93, 331, 334; Mandu da Silva experience of, 40–41, 82–84, 350n1; mouth of, 70, 166, 242–43, 251, 261; music and songs of, 244, 249, 254–56, 257–58, 282–83; mythscapes of, 22, 217–18, 334; as guardian of universe, 192; petroglyphs of, *211*, 211–13,

212, 213, 214, 244; religion and traditions of, 14–15, 21–24, 217, 219–27; as shadow-soul, 41, 71, 83, 155, 226, 351–52n4; sicknesses from, 192, 224, 272–73, 293, 340, 341; as sloth, 83, 155–56, 187–89, *188*, 272, 345n3, 348n5; as source for poisonings and sorcery, 130–31, 272, 331; stories about, 22–24, 130, 233–46, 248–75; tears of, 263, 264; transformations of, 83, 252, 260–61, 262, 266, 271–75, 333–34; and tricksters, 179, 227; umbilical cord of, 40, 82–83, 274, 350n1; vengeance of, 267–68, 272; village of, 84

Kuwaikaniri, 180–81, 187, 199–200, 225. *See also* Mawerikuli; universe people

Kuwaiwa, 224, 225, 226

Kwaipan. *See* initiation, ceremonies for Kwaipan and

laws, 220, 270, 325–26

layers. *See* hierarchies; levels

leadership, 2, 103, 142–43, 301–2, 308–9, 315, 329

leaves, 123, 343n2

legs, 57–59, *58*, 344–45nn5–6

levels: of Tree of Sustenance, 171–72, 201; of underworld, 196–97; of universe, 148–49, 162–64, *169*, 178. *See also* hierarchies

Lidzuna, 121–22

light, 153–54, 156–57, 162, 259

Likaime, 122–23
lizards, 154–55, 211, 290, 344n4
logs, 237, 242
longhouses, 6, 34–35, 104, 107,
    109–10, 309–15, *313*

Maaliawa, 213, *213*, 214, 244
Macanilla (jaguar shaman), 222,
    329–30
maggots, 264–66
maka, 97, 200. *See also* mantles
Malikai Dapana. *See* Shamans'
    House of Power and
    Knowledge
Manaus, 51, 116, 167
mandero, 309–10, 311, 312–14, *313*
manhene. See poisonings; poisons
maniocs. *See* bread; trees, maniocs
    as
mantles, 53–54, 75, 97. *See also*
    cloaks
Maroa, 18, 91, 132–33, 210, 222, 329
marriages: with birds, 39, 86, 97,
    191; of Mandu da Silva, 39, 48,
    110; in Northwest Amazon, 106;
    power and, 97, 280, 294, 326
masks (*hiwida ropathi*), 21, 85,
    155–56, 190, 215, 225
Maulieni, 105–8, *108*
Mavichikore, 224–25
Mawerikuli, 130, 180, 215, 225,
    351n4. *See also* Kuwaikaniri
medicines (*tápe*), 19–20, 38–39, 57,
    68–69, 91, 323
men, 277–80, 284, 332

menarche. *See* girls, menarche and
    menstruation of
menstruation (*kewiken,*
    kanupakan): blood from,
    65–66, 190, 191, 260–61, 278;
    initiation and *kalidzamai* for,
    240, 248, 281, 294; as trap, 262
metaphysics. *See* cosmologies, of
    Aiary River and Northwest
    Amazon; Goldman, Irving
mirrors, 73, 143
missionaries: depositions by,
    111, 112, 117; destruction of
    traditions by, 21, 24–25, 219;
    in Salesian Missionary Order,
    49, 50, 110, 113, 117, 136–37,
    220; Sophie Muller as, 14, 19,
    96, 140T, 226, 347n5. *See also*
    evangelicalism
monkeys, 155–56, 250, 253, 254, 272
Mothipana, 209M, 214, 276, 280
mouths, 70, 166, 242–43, 251, 261
Muller, Sophie, 14, 19, 96, 140T,
    226, 347n5
music: and songs of animals, 276,
    280, 339–41, *340*; and songs of
    Kuwai, 244, 249, 254–56, 257–58,
    282–83
myths. *See* stories
mythscapes: of Kuwai, 22, 217–18,
    334; in Northwest Amazon,
    20–21, 208–19, 209M, *211*, *212*,
    213, *214*, 349n1; petroglyphs in,
    21, 22–23, *211*, 211–14, *212*, *213*,
    214, 217. *See also* sacred sites

narratives (*iakuthi oopidali*). *See*
stories
necklaces. *See* collars
New Tribes Mission, 137
Nhiãperikuli: affine stories about,
174–75; anaconda stories about,
68, 209M, 213, 289; birds of,
215, 276, 280; body of, 173,
259, 263; as chief and warrior,
186, 194; City of, 209M, 215–16,
280; regarding conception
and birth of Kuwai, 237–39,
242–43; creation stories about,
168, 170; as Eternal Master
and father of all, 85, 157–58,
352n4; evangelicalism and,
347n6; heart-soul of, 23, 228,
238–39, 259, 284; initiation
stories about, 249, 251, 252,
256–59, 263, 264–68, 276–83;
pariká stories about, 63, 65,
177, 199–203; retribution and
vengeance by, 131, 175, 348n4;
as top of universe, *169*, 173;
transformations regarding, 75,
158–60, 174–75; trickster stories
about, 131, 226–27. *See also*
universe child
Night, 17, 158–60
Nimuendajú, Curt, 107, 346n1
nongovernmental organizations
NGOS, 19, 76, 301–11, 349n1
Northwest Amazon: Arawakan-
speaking people of, 1–6, 3M,
22, 139–40T, 343n1, 347–48n2;

cosmologies of, 20, 151, 227–28;
crimes against, 137; House
of Adorning in, 6, 303–4,
309–15, *313*; marriages in, 106;
mythscapes and sacred sites
in, 20–21, 208–19, 209M, *211*,
212, *213*, *214*, 349n1; Pamaale
complex in, 300, 301–7; seasons
of, 200, 204–6; Shamans' House
of Power and Knowledge in, 6,
25–26, 104, 315–24, *321*; sorcery
in, 121; traditions and religions
of, 21–23, 139–40T, 219–29;
Tree of Sustenance in, 20, 201;
Tukanoan-speaking people of,
1, 22, 139–40T, 343nn1–2, 348n2;
wise men and women of, 13–14
nuts, 250, 259–60, 350n1

oopi. See Before World
orations (*kalidzamai, iwapakethi*):
for births, 241; for cures and
treatments, 57, 59, 287, 288, 289,
291; for protection, 87, 88, 128,
291. *See also* chants
orifices. *See* holes, as orifices
"Other Kuwai," 179, 243, 251,
260–63, 265
Other World (*Apakwa Hekwapi*):
affines and phratries in, 178–79;
communication with, 77–81;
hierarchies and levels of, 86–87,
149–50, 164, 172, 173, 178–79;
jaguar shaman spirits in, 78–79,
84–85, 86, 94, 203, 328; journeys

97, 128–29; smoke for, 57, 59, 71, 87, 176, 291; of traditions, 325–26

Pukweipan, 155, 209M, 213, *213*, 244. *See also* Enukwa

purification, 83

Puwekaime, 123

rains, 204, 206, 260, 261–64

rattles (*kutheruda*), 43, 90, 91–95, *92*, 136–37

rebirths, 81–83, 86, 134, 183–84, 216

regeneration. *See* rebirths

Reichel-Dolmatoff, Gerardo, 219, 220, 347n1, 349nn1–2

religion: and traditions of Cubeo, 85–86, 140T, 223–26, 348n2; and traditions of Hehenewa, 223–25, 226; and traditions of Hohodene, 105–7, 139–40T, 181, 224–28, 299–300; and traditions of Kuwai, 14–15, 21–24, 217, 219–27; and traditions of Tukano, 22, 139–40T, 156, 219–21, 223–24, 343nn1–2, 348n2; and traditions of Yurupary, 21–22, 155–56, 219–20, 221, 343n2; of Walipere-dakenai, 299–300

reproduction: biological, 220, 238, 260–61; cultural, 236, 252, 282, 293

resentments. *See* envy

resources, 130, 131, 299, 307–8, 309, 346n2

restrictions: regarding celibacy and sexual relations, 66–67, 96–97, 261; for foods, 66–67, 68, 250, 253, 262, 269, 289; regarding girls and women, 38, 67, 72, 260–61; for initiates, 212, 250, 255, 261

retribution (*ikoada, ipwaminawa*): concerning Emí, 115, 118; killings for, 98–101, 126, 132, 327, 348n4. *See also* vengeance

revitalization movements: at House of Adorning, 6, 303–4, 309–15, *313*; at Pamaale, 300, 301–7; Shamans' House of Power and Knowledge in, 6, 25–26, 104, 315–24, *321*; usage of shaman knowledge in, 305–6, 347n1; and wealth as cause for sorcery, 18–19, 107–8, 110, 115, 117, 129

rites: for extractions, 58, 59; for healings, 60, 80–81; for initiation, 165–66, 193, 204–6, 214, *214*, 217, 247–69, 313; for initiation of boys, 277–79; for initiation of girls, 281, 294; for *kalidzamai*, 269–70, 281, 351n1. *See also* ceremonies; rituals

rituals: for cures and healings, 77, 92–93; for initiation and seclusion, 189–90, 209M, 214, *214*, 240, 247–53, 256–69. *See also* ceremonies; rites

rubber industry, 48, 107, 108, 142, 224

rubble, 212, 262

songs: for communication, 77–81, 345n2; and music of animals, 276, 280, 339–41, 340; and music of Kuwai, 244, 249, 254–56, 257–58, 282–83; usage of by pajés, 77–81, 84–85, 177

sorcerers: animal tribes of, 331; attacks and killings by, 88, 99–101; attributes and functions of, 81, 11, 12–13, 18, 326–27; bodies and heart-souls of, 124–25, 126, 127, 128; knowledge and power of, 11, 12–13, 18, 122, 124, 126, 326, 327; as owners of poisons, 120–27, 347n4. See also Emí (kin to Mandu da Silva)

sorcery (manhene, iupithatem): among affines, 106–8, 110, 127–28, 131, 132; from Amaru, 351n2; Baniwa and Hohodene regarding, 120–27, 128, 131–32; beginnings of, 17; causes for, 107–8, 110, 115, 117, 129–31, 331; methods for dealing with, 16, 19–20; by poisonings, 19–20, 106–7, 110–15, 120–24, 129–30; protection from, 97, 128–29; sicknesses from, 36, 61, 344n5

soul-flights, 16, 82, 86, 350n2

souls (ikaale): of animals, 141–42, 150, 172; bone-tubes and, 184–85; gourds as, 91–92, 94–95; journeys of, 72, 82–87, 350n2; payments for, 40, 83; songs

for, 78–79; usage of tobacco regarding, 47, 71. See also heart-souls

space-time, 149–51, 166–68, 170

specialists, 6–7, 7–11T, 11–14, 121, 196, 252, 326–29

specializations, 32, 45, 89–91, 121

spells, 76, 291, 344n5

spirit darts (walama). See darts

spirit of the dead. See inyaime, as spirit of the dead

spirits: attacks by, 73, 87; of jaguar shamans, 78–79, 84–85, 86, 94, 203, 328; knowledge and power of, 15, 192–96, 207; sicknesses from, 72, 290, 293; in underworld, 172, 197–98. See also yoopinai, sicknesses from

"stairways (shamanic)." See umbilical cords

stingrays, 212, 243

stones: in creation of universe, 152, 153; for initiation and seclusion, 38–39, 278; of pajés, 95–96; and pebbles in gourds, 91; as sacred sites, 21, 212, 213, 213–15. See also boulders

stories: about affines, 174–75; anacondas in, 68, 209M, 213; children in, 248–69, 350n3; about creation, 17, 130, 147, 152–61, 168, 170, 224, 227–28; about Dzuliferi, 65, 175–77; flutes in, 276–77, 279, 281–83, 285–86; about initiation, 249, 251,

149–50, 182, 217–18; warnings regarding, 2, 18, 133, 183, 222, 288, 329; of wise men and women, 13–14, 139–40T
trances, 64–65, 72, 81–82, 88, 185
transformations: cycles and seasons of, 74, 204, 206; from feathers, 199–200; into fish, 174–75; of heart-souls, 75; regarding initiation, 247–48; into jaguars, 98–99, 202, 203; of jaguar shamans, 204, 328; of Kuwai, 83, 252, 260–61, 262, 266, 271–75, 333–34; regarding Nhiãperikuli, 75, 158–60, 174–75; of pajés, 36, 74–75, 204; regarding pariká, 63–64, 65, 98–101, 202–3, 204; regarding poisons, 122–23, 124
translators. See communication
traps, 87–88, 251, 261–62, 277, 280, 350n2
treatments, 55, 57–59, 58, 68–69, 291. See also cures; healings
Tree of Sustenance, 20, 168, 170–72, 194–95, 201–2, 209M, 216
trees (as metaphor for the universe): regarding child labor and birth, 241, 242; darts from, 84, 203, 279; for fruit, 199–200; maniocs as, 194, 348n4; pariká from, 26, 64, 168, 170, 171, 195, 201–2; paxiuba palms as, 170, 184, 268–69, 274, 279; and time, 170–71, 201, 242

tribes, 124, 125, 182, 186, 331
tricksters, 131, 148, 179–80, 226–27
trumpets: adornments of, 277, 282; as ancestors, 170–71, 193, 257, 275, 282–83; birth and rebirth through, 184, 185, 283; cults of, 22, 222; exogamy and, 220; of Kuwai, 184, 193, 254–55, 268, 275
tubes, 151, 164–65, 169, 182–85, 274
Tukano: jaguar shamans of, 61, 75–76; religion and traditions of, 22, 139–40T, 156, 219–21, 223–24, 343nn1–2, 348n2; sorcery and vengeance killings by, 100–101, 121
Tunui, 3M, 4, 75–76, 209M
Turner, Victor, 23

Uapui: chiefs of, 31, 32, 48–50, 112, 117–18, 138; history of, 105–6, 108–19; rapids of, 5; religion of, 299; Shamans' House of Power and Knowledge in, 5–6, 25–26, 104, 315–24, 321; village of, 25, 31, 34–35, 47–48. See also Aiary River; Hipana
Uaracapory, 201, 209M, 216, 274
Uetsu mikuiri, 135–36, 139T
Ukuki: chiefs of, 135–36, 304, 307, 312, 313; elders of, xi, 234, 237–38, 261, 267–68, 309–10; House of Adorning at, 5–6, 303–4, 309–15, 313; religion of, 299–300; regarding sorcery, 128. See also Aiary River

Umawali. *See* anacondas

umbilical cords: of Kuwai, 40,
82–83, 274, 350n1; of the sky,
new life from, 158; as tubes, 151,
164–65, *169*, 184–85, 274

underworlds. *See* Place of Our
Bones

universe: beginnings and creation
of, 3–4, 147–54, 156–61, 173–74,
227–28; centers of, 20, 162–65,
169, 177, 274–75; knowledge and
power in, 186–87, 192–96, 207,
331; layers and levels of, 148–49,
161–64, *169*, 171–72, 178, 201;
ownership of, 192–96; sacred
sites in, 21, 165–66, 208–19,
209M, *211*, *212*, *214*; water as
bottom of and way to the sun,
164, 166, 167, *169*. *See also* world

universe child, 152–54, 156–57, 158,
225, 228. *See also* Nhiãperikuli

universe people, 62, 181–82, *183*

uephetti. See *walama-kaime*

Uwa, 43, 93–94

velho, José, 66, 98, 117, 250–51

vengeance: concerning Emí, 111,
115–16, 119; killings for, 99–101,
120–21, 131–32, 346n4; of Kuwai,
267–68, 272; of Nhiãperikuli,
131, 175, 348n4. *See also*
retribution

Vidal, Silvia, 220–21, 343n1, 347n2

villages: of Kuwai, 84; in Other
World, 171, 173, 175. *See also*

communities; Hipana; Uapui;
Ukuki

vines, 165, 190–91, 250

visions: and dreams of Mandu da
Silva, 36, 46–47, 61–62, 173; and
dreams of pajés, 56, 57, 72, 154–
55; feathers for, 174, 199–200; of
jaguar shamans, 60, 97–98, 159,
164–65, 175, 328; regarding This
World, 97–98, 198, 328

vomit, 38–39, 56, 58, 71, 83–84

voyages. *See* journeys

Waferinaipe Ianheke (Cornelio et
al.), 147, 152

Wakuenai, 2–3, 93, 139T, 148, 225,
270

walama-kaime, 67, 84, 123, 124, 279,
343n1

Waliadoa, 213, *213*, *214*, 244

Walipere-dakenai: ancestors of,
4, 85, 178, 209M, 210, 348n2;
history and location of, 3, 4,
105–7, 181; religion of, 299–300;
and vengeance killings, 100, 101

Waminali. *See* Kuwai

Wamundana. 'Black sloth shadow
soul', animal avatar name for
Kuwai. Said to have its own
'secretary', Tchitamali, a small,
white sloth with a tuft of red
fur onn its head.

Wanhiwa: killings by, 32, 98–101,
113–14, 115, 119, 121; as pajés, 89.
See also Piaroa

CPSIA information can be obtained
at www.ICGtesting.com
Printed in the USA
LVHW032049080319
610001LV00002B/195/P

9 780803 295230